A Violette History

David A. Violette
Rod Violette
Guy F. Dubay

CONTENTS

Table of Contents

ACKNOWLEDGMENTS

The Violette Family coat of arms as shown on the cover and on the first page of each chapter in this book was designed by Nancy Nolette, VFA #1702, of Boulder City NV. It was adopted by the Association membership at the Business Meeting in August 2011. The graphics were done by E. M. Szper of Flying Frog Illustration, Design & Typography.

The authors consulted many reference works and sources in the research and writing of this book, but several deserve special mention because they provided so much help and valuable information. Others are cited where used in the text.

Lippé, Rita Violette (1933-); *"Descendants of François Violet"*; Naiman Press, Lawrence, Massachusetts, 1984 is a primary source of information on history and genealogy for the Violette family. Major parts of this work are quoted here by permission of the author in Chapter 6.

Violette, Maurice (1921-2004); *"The Violette Family"*; first published by Letter Systems, Inc., 52 Water Street, Hallowell ME, 1990. This two-part work forms the majority of Chapters 7 and 8, and is used with permission of the author.

Pelletier, Martine A, and Monica Dionne Ferretti; *"Van Buren, Maine History"*; St John Valley Publishing Co, Inc, Madawaska, Maine, 1979. The maps by Michaud showing the property owners in the Deane & Kavanagh survey of 1831 proved useful.

Albert, Thomas; *"The History of Madawaska"*, English translation by Sister Therese Doucette and Dr Francis Doucette; Madawaska Historical Society, Madawaska, Maine, 1989.

Paradis, Roger; *"Papers of Prudent L. Mercure"*; Madawaska Historical Society, Madawaska, Maine, 1998. These papers are a very important source of information. They are a compilation of some 2200 pages of manuscripts copied by hand by Prudent Mercure and later transcribed into book form by Roger Paradis. Many of these papers were the source of information for Fr. Thomas Albert when writing *"The History of Madawaska"*.

Craig, Béatrice, and Maxime Dagenais, with Lisa Ornstein and Guy Dubay; *"The Land In Between: The Upper St John Valley, Prehistory to World War I"*; Tilbury House, Publishers, Gardiner, Maine, 2009. This work provides a good understanding of the region, though not from the point of view of the Violette family.

Both Rod and Guy rely heavily on compilations by Jean-Guy Poitras, of Edmundstion NB. He was the winner of the Percy W. Foy award, an honor received from the Société Généalogique Canadienne-Française for 1995 for the category of the best publication (inventory, census, dictionnary, etc,) for his book entitled *"Répertoire généalogique des descendants et descendantes d'André Levesque et d'Angelique Ouellette"*. This is one of about 20 Répertoires he has written and published in recent years. But his works used with the author's permission in the preparation of this book include:

Poitras, Jean-Guy; *"Répertoire des naissances et des décès, Saint-Basile, comté de Madawaska, Nouveau-Brunswick, 1792-2005"*, Jean-Guy Poitras publisher, Edmundston NB, April 2010

ibid; *"Répertoire des mariages au Nord-Ouest du Nouveau-Brunswick, 1792-2012; Saint-Bruno Van Buren, Maine 1838-1870; Sainte-Luce Frenchville, Maine 1843-1860"*; Jean-Guy Poitras publisher, trimester 2013.

McLennan, J. S.; *"Louisbourg from its Foundation to its Fall 1713-1758"*; MacMillan & Co, Ltd, publisher. London 1918. Third Edition by Fortress Press 1969. Fourth Edition by The Book Room Limited, Halifax, NS 1978. Used extensively to research the history of Fortress Louisbourg and the battles fought there.

Johnston, A. J. B.; *"Endgame 1758"*; University of Nebraska, 2007. Considered the definitive study of the 1758 Battle of Louisbourg.

Lang, Ernest, Monseigneur (priest); *"Dictionnnaire Genealogique Du Madawaska: Répertoire des mariages"*; St. John Valley Times publisher, 1971. Guy Dubay assisted Msgr Lang in his research by driving him to various parishes around the region.

-; *"The Upper St. John River Valley, Northern Aroostook County, Maine and Madawaska & Victoria Counties, New Brunswick. A history of the communities and people"*; web site at www.upperstjohn.com. This site contains, among other information, censuses, church records, land grants, and region maps and history. Most especially the Deane & Kavanagh survey of 1831 is reported here and presented at length and in detail.

ABOUT THE COAT OF ARMS

There is no historic coat of arms for the Violette family, probably because members of the family in historic times did not participate in battles as primary combatants and did not need the identification. Those Violettes we know of were of lesser rank. While various vendors have offered to the public a purported coat of arms or crest for the Violette family, those had no basis in history and were likely created in modern times for commercial purposes.

But over the years many Violettes wanted a symbol to identify their family history, and the Violette Family Association decided at the Violette Family Reunion in 2008 to undertake development of a family coat of arms. Nancy Nolette, VFA# 1702, has an interest in things heraldic and was appointed to create such a device for the membership to approve. Her design was presented at the Violette Family Reunion in 2011 and the membership approved the design with a few minor modifications. The coat of arms used in this book is the finally-adopted version.

Coats of arms traditionally consisted of a shield with emblems denoting important accomplishments in the history of the family. The coat of arms adopted by the Violette Family Assocation notes important times and places in the life of François Violet, our ancestor whose life and path is described in this book.

The four emblems on the shield represent the nations under which François lived. He was born in France (represented by the fleur-de-lis, or lily), moved to what is now Cape Breton Island/Nova Scotia but was then called Acadia (represented by the golden star), moved later to southern New Brunswick which was then under British rule but later became part of Canada (represented by the red maple leaf), and finally pioneered the Upper St John River Valley and part of his holdings became part of the United States (represented by the eagle). The fleur-de-lis was not only a symbol of France, but is also on the flag of Quebec. The gold star is associated with the Virgin Mary, the patron saint of the Acadians, and is included on the Acadian flag. Though the red maple leaf was only adopted by Canada in 1965, it is widely recognized as the modern emblem of that country. And the eagle has long represented the United States as its national bird and symbol used on currency and national emblems.

The fifth emblem, at the bottom of the shield, is a water wheel used to power not only grist mills such as that François built in the early days in the upper St John, but many other factories and systems where mechanical power was needed. And the stalks represent the grains that he milled in his grist mill. Such mills were an important feature in early pioneer settlements and were vital to the community. Having such a business also made François an important and valued member of the community and helped to build the standing of the family.

The blue background in the shield represents water, and water played an important role in François' life. He crossed the Atlantic Ocean with his parents to settle at Fortress Louisbourg, on a bay on Cape Breton Island, he later settled on the Hammond River where he farmed for twenty years, and then he moved up the St John River to settle on both banks in the Madawaska Territory. And what became known as Violette Brook ran through part of his lands and was the source of power for turning the grist mill grinding stones.

The purple or violet background in the bottom section of the shield represents the basis of the name Violet/Violette, for it is the name for the violet flower.

At the top, the name is ensconced in the banner above the shield and emblems and the violet flower is included to denote the meaning of the name. The phrase "We Are One" is the motto of the Violette Family Association.

FOREWORD

All who have had an interest in their Violette family history owe a debt of gratitude to Rita Violette Lippé, VFA #1. It was she who did the original research that led to the discovery of the Violette family roots.

Her quest began when she was still in high school when her curiosity was aroused by her teachers, the Sisters of the Immaculate Heart of Mary, many of whom had previously taught Violettes in the Van Buren, Maine area. She wondered whether perchance she was related to those Violettes. A correspondence then began with Sister Dorothy Violette SCIM, of Van Buren. Four years later, in 1952, Rita boarded a bus in Lawrence, Massachusetts headed for the all-important town of Van Buren, Maine. During this two week visit, she became fairly well acquainted with the St. John Valley area and fell in love with it. She was introduced to many elderly Violettes and had several lengthy conversations with them. However, being young and inexperienced in genealogy her interest soon subsided.

In 1973, Rita's interest in genealogy was rekindled. She realized that her father remembered a great deal about his childhood, although he had not once returned to New Brunswick since his departure some fifty-five years prior. It was in the month of August that Rita, her husband Bob, her daughter Celeste, and mother and dad, returned to the land of her father's birth. They visited Drummond, St. Basile, and St. Quentin, New Brunswick, as well as the entire St. John Valley.

This vacation proved to be a turning point, her curiosity and fascination with the past was to remain with her throughout her lifetime. Immediately upon returning home, serious research began. Letters were written, books read, and maps carefully examined. Her research led her to the source of the Violette family in North America. She soon discovered that all trails led her back to Van Buren and François Violet. One year later, in 1974, another trip took place. This time Louisbourg, Nova Scotia was the destination. This is where Charles and his son François had landed back in 1749. The Fortress of Louisbourg fascinated her. She visited the Archives and met Steven White, the foremost Acadian genealogist with whom she later corresponded. There Rita learned that Charles Violet was not a military man but a "couvreur de toits", a roofer. From here on her interest in genealogy in general, and the Violette family in particular, took on a whole new dimension leading in 1984 to the publishing of the Violette genealogy and history- *The Descendants of François Violet*.

By this time Rita had been joined in her search by Maurice Violette, VFA #14, of Augusta, Maine. Their research for their roots had come to a dead end at Louisbourg. Rita and Maurice wrote time and again to officials in France, vainly trying to establish the missing link. Their only clues came from the old documents unearthed in Louisbourg. Those documents gave "Paroisse de Jesus" as the birthplace of Charles Violet and "Sainx" as the birthplace of Charles' wife Marie David. Their letters were returned. Neither place was known. No map carried those place names. Playing a desperate hunch, Maurice wrote a letter to the city in southwest France called "Saintes", a city that dates back to the Roman days. Amazingly he got a reply. Yes, wrote an archivist, "Saintes" had once been called "Sainx" back during the 14th century. And, yes a Marie David had been born there on 10 May 1705.

In 1978 by pure serendipitous circumstances, Maurice met Claude Meche, a Frenchman visiting Maurice's home down of Augusta, Maine. Maurice told him of his genealogical pursuit. Meche it turns out was a roofer by trade, just as Charles Violet had been when he came to the New World. Meche was commissioned to do on the spot genealogical research upon his return to France. Meche did a tremendous job unearthing all Violet family records despite the fact that the French revolution had caused the destruction or hiding of so many. He found that the elusive "Paroisse of Jesus" had become the tiny hamlet of Villejésus. He found the birth and marriage records of Charles Violet and Marie David, and christening records of François, the grand Violette patriarch of the New World. Charles' baptismal records also revealed the names of his parents, Louis Violet and Marie Doux. Unfortunately, the 7 Jan 1715 marriage record for Louis and Marie Doux does not enumerate the names of their parents, thus we are again at a dead end. Although there are several Violet families in the area, because of the lack of Louis' parents' names, we may never make a formal family connection, but we know that we are all cousins.

Thus it was that on 22 September 1982 that 47 Acadians from North America, having embarked on a voyage of discovery and reunion, descended on the tiny village of Villejésus to find the roots from which they had all sprung. Within a moment the Violettes of North America were embracing the Violets of Villejésus, cousins all.

But, that is a whole other story to be told in chapters of this book.

When Rita published her book in 1984 it contained approximately 9,600 names of François' descendants and their spouses. That data base now (July 2014) contains over 26,200 direct descendants of François and over 75,000 entries when their spouses and the extension of the spouse's families are included.

By no means is research complete on the descendants of François. Genealogy is a living and vibrant study. Many important details remain hidden in the past. Hence, this is an on-going project. It is hoped that this publication will encourage many of you to share the information you have, and that errors might be corrected and the listing of Violettes made more complete.

Because of her efforts on behalf of all Violettes, we dedicate this book to Rita.

David A. Violette, VFA #621
Guy Dubay, VFA #892
Rod Violette, VFA #12

July 2014

INTRODUCTION

Rod Violette, VFA #12

At the conclusion of the Violette Family Reunion at Windsor Locks CT in August of 2008, the last volume of Rita Violette Lippé's book *The Descendants of François Violet* was auctioned off. We continue to get requests for copies as new generations become aware of their Violette roots and heritage, but there are no more to buy.

The original volume, published in 1984, contained about 9,600 names of descendants (and their spouses) of François. I took on the Genealogist role for the Association in 2002 and computerized the genealogical info and greatly expanded it. The Violette genealogy now (July 2014) contains over 26,200 direct descendants of François and over 75,000 entries, when their spouses and the extension of the spouse's families are included. There was some talk of having the book reprinted as is, but that would exclude thousands of Violettes who have come since or whose names have been added. There was also talk about expanding the publication to add more of the genealogy that had been accumulated since it was originally published in 1984.

We concluded that simply attempting to reprint the entire genealogy of the Violette family was not practical or useful. The study of genealogy is better pursued with the use of computers, especially since there is always new information coming to light, and there is always more research to be done. I have always made available to whomever is interested a copy of their direct line all the way back to Louis, the grandfather of François, and I plan to continue to do so.

After I had done the research for a talk I gave at the 2002 Violette Family Reunion in Edmundston NB, *"The Life and Times of François Violet"*, it came to me that a more formal and complete history of the Violette family should be written. My lack of knowledge of the history beyond the time François settled in Van Buren in about 1791 made that impossible, so I approached Guy Dubay for a collaborative effort. I discussed with Guy, a local historian and genealogist in Madawaska ME and a Violette descendant, the possibility of writing the history of the Violette family instead. He has written many articles for the local newspapers about every subject imaginable concerning the history of the area and its people. He had accumulated a rather thick file containing all these articles and related research. He was very interested, so I started to investigate further. Since neither Guy nor I have the computer skills to facilitate such an endeavor, I approached David Violette, our Association Webmaster, who has the necessary skills, and he was very enthusiastic. David is a civil engineer by profession and was very creative with charts and maps. He also turned out to be a very good writer. So the three of us agreed to take on this project and originally planned a completion date in time for the Violette Family Reunion in August of 2011. While the first twelve chapters were done in draft by that time, there remained three major chapters to complete the book, so work has continued since that time.

David suggested that we ask the entire membership for their input. As we completed a chapter in draft, David posted it at the Association's web site and emailed it for their comments to the members whose email addresses we had on file. We valued very much any input in the way of suggestions and corrections from our members, and we provided a means for members (and others) to submit comments or questions at the web site.

This work in Volume 1 has been a major research effort to get details not yet uncovered by others and to expand upon what was known about our Violette ancestors. We feel we have added to the body of Violette knowledge and welcomed the opportunity to set it out for others to read and for others to build on.

As we progressed and made decisions about what to include in this volume, we found many stories about individual Violettes that we felt needed to be told but that did not seem to fit in the context of this book. We also wanted to include material submitted to us by the membership, such as stories and photos about their relatives of note. We decided these stories are best handled in a second volume to this work. As we receive feedback from others we will add new stories or update previous stories as appropriate in Volume 2. Our newsletters will keep members current with the state of the project.

ABOUT THE AUTHORS

The authors are all descendants of François Violet and Marie-Luce Thibodeau, the progenitors of many of the readers of this book, and thus are related in some distant way. Other readers are descended from François' second wife, Marie-Rose Cormier, or his third wife, Genevieve Tardif. The authors come from far different backgrounds and life experiences, but were brought together to produce this work because of their interest in the genealogy and history of their ancestral family and because of a desire to pass along to others the fascinating story of this pioneer family.

David A. Violette, VFA #621, was born in Concord NH in August 1939 and lived in that state until 1959. He is the son of Alderic Violette and Alice Bartlett, à Cyr Regis Violette and Adeline Soucie, à Bruno Violette and Elodie Cyr, à Laurent Violette and Elise Cyr, à Charles Violet and Theotiste Tardif, à François Violet and Marie-Luce Thibodeau. He graduated with a degree in Civil Engineering from The University of Connecticut and practiced as a Professional Civil Engineer throughout his career. During that career he was the prime author of many studies and other technical documents, and was an early adopter of the use of computers and software in the production of documents of many types. He was also an early web developer, starting in 1993. He first converted the Violette Family Association membership records from file cards to a computer database around 1987 and served as Secretary of the Association from 1990 through 1996. He developed the Association's web site in 2001 and continues as Webmaster. He also served as President from 2011-14. Dave brings a love of history and a focus on details, structure, and organization to this project. He served as synthesizer, editor, researcher, and writer and produced the content documents from material and ideas supplied by Rod and Guy. Dave sees himself as a story teller. Dave and his wife Elaine live full-time in a 40-foot motorhome and explore the US and Canada. He writes a daily blog about their travels, found at www.Violette.com. He can be reached by email at David@Violette.com.

"I agreed to participate in this project because I knew my skills would help Rod and Guy get the story across that they wanted to tell, and because I want to share with others the fascinating story of François and Marie Luce Violet, my great-great-great-great grandparents. I love to tell their story. It has been a challenging project."

Guy F. Dubay, VFA #892, was born in Van Buren ME in December 1942 and has lived in Van Buren and Madawaska ME all his life. He is the son of Edward G. Dubay and Eveline Violette, à Abel Violette and Marcelline Deschenes, à Jean Benoni (Belonie) Violette and Suzanne Theriault, à François Violet and Marguerite Fournier, à François Violet and Marie-Luce Thibodeau. Guy was yet a child when he first heard his Uncle John Violette speak of "Les Premiers Temps" (The Pioneer Days) and describe his own father in the generational lineage format given above. He graduated from Van Buren Boys' High School, taught by the Marist Fathers and lay teachers and then enrolled in Fort Kent Normal School. By the time he graduated with a Bachelor's Degree in Education in 1964 that institution had become Fort Kent State Teachers' College and later the University of Maine at Fort Kent, one of five campuses of the University of Maine System.

Guy went on to teach in the public schools of Madawaska until 1971, when he became the Principal of Evangeline and St Thomas Schools in that system. Summers not spent at the University of Maine were spent researching family and local history at the Northern Aroostook Registry of Deeds. Since his paternal grandfather had been an attorney, Guy describes that part of his research as *"Following up on my Grandfather's paper trail."* This research took him not only through family history, but also the history of mills and their development in the St John Valley. In September 1973 he published an historical feature on the Violette Grist Mill.

Guy is also the author of several genealogical and historical works; the quickest access to those title is by doing a search at URSUS, the University of Maine Systems Library (ursus.maine.edu) and doing a search for author "Dubay, Guy F."

Guy summarizes his life course this way: *"Education was my profession, but local and family history became my avocation".* Guy married Ernestine Soucy, whose mother was Winifred Violette Soucy, à Joseph Violette and Catherine Cyr, à Frederick Violette and Suzanne Parent, à Jean Benoni (Belonie) Violette and Suzanne Theriault, à François Violet and Marguerite Fournier, à François Violet and Marie-Luce Thibodeau. They have two adult children and continue to live in Madawaska. He can be reached by email at info@clubfrancais.org.

Rodrigue (Rod) R Violette, VFA #12, was born in St Leonard NB in May 1932. He is the son of Edgar Violette and Ida Marie Doucet, à Come Violette and Flavie Cyr, à François Violette and Sarah Mercure, à Theodore Violette and Louise Parent, à Charles Violet and Theotiste Tardif, à François Violet and Marie-Luce Thibodeau. He graduated from St. Thomas University in Chatham, NB in 1955. He was a fighter pilot in the Royal Canadian Air Force from

1955 to 1965. He left the Air Force and became an airline pilot with United Airlines until retirement in 1994. He became interested in genealogy through the efforts of his father. He had memorized the names of his grandfathers all the way up to Francois. When Rita Violette Lippé was doing her initial genealogical research and reaching out to Violettes, Rod used his travels as an airline pilot to find Violettes listed in telephone directories all over the country. He would write to them and forwarded the information he received to Rita.

Rod was the one who came up with the idea for this book, and helped form the structure for this project. He contributed many historical topics to the chapters, but was most valuable in providing the genealogical information used in the book. He has also done extensive reviews of each chapter as they were written and rewritten.

Rod has been a member of the Violette Family Association since its inception in 1978, holds membership number 12, and has been on the Board since 2002 when he was elected Secretary, and continued the work of Rita Violette Lippé as Genealogist.

Genealogy evolved from a hobby to an avocation for Rod. He spends many hours each week providing family information to members and logging the information he gets in return. He is constantly searching for new information in Ancestry.com, census reports and numerous genealogical dictionaries. And in the course of his genealogical work he has amassed a library of genealogical references more than twelve feet long.

Rod and his wife, Helene, live in Lincoln CA. Rod can be reached by email at rviolette@att.net.

"Genealogy is not a burden, but a labor of love"

CHAPTER 1 - CHARLES VIOLET BORN IN VILLEJÉSUS
Time Span: 1715-1741

Thursday, February 13, 1716, was an exciting day for a young couple in Villejésus, France named Louis and Marie Violet. Married thirteen months before, on January 7th, 1715, now at ages 26 and 23 they were expecting their first child.

Father and mother were both from Villejésus, and their families probably had been there for many generations before. Information found in recent times may indicate that the home in Villejésus may have been in the Violet family since 1640, or about 50 years before Louis was born. Though we don't have family records for Louis, we do know that Marie's father – Louis Doux – was born around 1649 and would die three years after his grandson was born. We don't have information about Marie's mother – Jeanne Rivet.

Yes, the baby born that February day was a boy - named Charles Francois Violet. He was the first of four children for Louis and Marie. Catherine would be born on July 24, 1718; Jeanne on May 23, 1719 and would die two years later; and Francois on April 1, 1725 only to die two weeks later on April 15th. We don't have a record of when either Louis or Marie died.

Where is Villejésus? What was the town like?

Let's see where in the world Charles was born. Map 1-1 shows where the town is located. It is in the present-day Administrative Region of Poitou-Charentes, as shown in the closer look in Map 1-2. That Region was divided into the four Departments Charente, Charente-Maritime, Deux-Sevres, and Vienne after the French Revolution in 1789. Villejésus' population in 2008 was 568 and it occupies 6.65 square miles (4256 acres, 1722 hectares). The elevation in the area ranges from 200 to 495 feet (61 to 151 m) above sea level. Map 1-3 shows an aerial view of Villejésus today.

It was from this area that most of the Acadian and Cajun populations of North America (settlements founded in New Brunswick, Louisiana, Nova Scotia, Prince Edward Island, the Gaspe Peninsula of Quebec, Maine and Newfoundland) came. Their ancestors emigrated from the region during the 17th and 18th centuries, as we will see happen later in Charles' life.

Map 1-1: Villejésus, France

Map 1-2: Villejésus in the Poitou-Charentes Region of France

Map 1-3: Aerial view of Villejésus

Villejésus has several picturesque buildings such as the Town Hall shown in Photo 1-1. Villejésus also has a culinary specialty called Cagouilles – these are snails, but they call them by the special name instead of the traditional French escargot. They even have a statue of the cagouille at Villejésus!

Photo 1-1: Villejésus Town Hall

Photo 1-2: Statue of Cagouille in Villejésus

Learning about our ancestors and their origins

The quest to learn about our ancestors was a long and difficult one. It started around 1974 when Rita Violette Lippé from Methuen MA wanted to learn more about her Violette heritage and culminated with 47 Violettes traveling to France to see the places and talk with people in those places where the Violette family traces its roots. That trip in 1982 was chronicled by Bill Caldwell, journalist with the *Maine Sunday Telegram*, in his article from October 3, 1982. Let's hear how Mr. Caldwell tells the story:

Maine Sunday Telegram, October 3, 1982
The American cousins go home and discover the love of family

Columnist Bill Caldwell accompanied members of the Violette family, many of whom are from Maine, to France last month as they went in search of their family's past. Struck by the emotion generated by the unusual trip, Caldwell filed this personal report.

VILLEJÉSUS, France — Hesitantly, one by one, the Violettes from North America, 47 of them, stepped from their bus to meet the Violets from Villejésus, France.

Villejésus is a tiny and ancient hamlet in southwestern France containing 540 souls. The town, not much more than a bend in the road, is a cluster of tile red roofs, chipped stone barns and homes, an old gray church, a cafe with a decrepit billiard table and an oldtime U.S. one-armed bandit converted to francs, and a few winding, cobblestone, narrow streets.

It is tranquil, imperturbable, geared to the slow process of raising grapes in hillside vineyards century after century.

This is Villejésus — the village of Jesus — into which the Violettes of Maine and North America step out of their bus: a bald, barrel-chested trash collector from Augusta, a potato farmer from Van Buren, a nun from California, a bookkeeper from Methuen, Mass., a coach from Winslow, a backhoe operator from Oakland, an auto dealer from Grand Falls, an old pilot from Hallowell, a school teacher from Cony High.

Within a moment, the Violettes from North America are embracing the Violets of Villejésus, cousins all — families separated for more than two centuries by 3,000 miles of ocean, wars of independence and revolution, unknown fen by name to each other until this moment.

Never has there been so much happiness and joy or so many tears and so many smiles, or so much unbridled love of family in the tiny town of Villejésus as there was all day and all night on Thursday, Sept. 22, 1982.

That was the unforgettable day when the Violette family of Van Buren, Maine, came to this hamlet in the Cognac country of France to find the roots from which they had sprung more than 200 years ago. It was the first time a Franco American family had come home to its ancestral roots since the fall of Acadia in 1759.

The bells from the ancient church rang out in celebration. It is the same church where Louis Violet and Marie Doux of this parish exchanged marriage vows in January 1715.

Louis was the farmer who fathered Charles. Charles is the Violet who sailed from La Rochelle in 1749 to help colonize French North America, failed and abandoned his 6-year-old son Francois in Louisbourg. **(Ed note: Charles actually went to French North America to work on the military fortifications at Louisbourg. It was his roofing business that failed, and he had to assign care of his two children to friends as part of his bankruptcy settlement. See later chapters for "the rest of the story".)**

And Francois grew up to become first Frenchman to raise a pioneering family in Maine and to father 23 children alongside Violet Stream, now the site of the town of Van Buren.

The creaking doors of the ancient church, seldom used these days, swung open and the Violettes of Maine walked down the aisle arm-in-arm with the Violets of Villejésus.

In this church the Violets and Violettes celebrated a special communion Mass of family reunion. The vested priest delivered his short sermon in mellifluous French, praising the gift of families rejoined by heaven after so many generations of separation, worshipping together in the church where their mutual forefathers were baptized and married.

The voices from Waterville, from Van Buren and Augusta and South Portland mingled loudly and well with the voices of the French villagers.

Mass was over- As Violettes and Violets came out into the sunshine and met together under the ancient trees on the village green, the church bells pealed out again in joyous sound.

On the outskirts of Villejésus, farmers tending their grapes in the vineyards looked up, startled at the ringing of the bells on a Thursday morning.

On the cobblestone village streets, old French grandmothers, dressed in long shiny black dresses and white beribboned caps, opened their tiny houses to cousins from far away.

This was the scene that melted the minds and hearts of the travelers from North America. From small Yankee villages, from the coast of California, from the potato fields of Maine and the border towns, they had traveled far to discover their roots.

They had flown to Paris, traveled by bus eight hours to the port of La Rochelle from which their ancestors sailed, stayed in Rochefort and Saintes and Angouleme, digging into their pasts, so long forgotten.

Now they stood at the watershed, the simple village whence the Violettes had sprung. They felt they were home.

They grasped the vineyard-worn hand of the man from Villejésus standing by them. Flesh pressed to flesh. Eyes looked into eyes- And no man nor woman showed shame at the tears that filled their eyes or the strange joy that surged in their hearts.

Photo 1-3: Hillside Vineyards Surround Villejésus

The villagers and the visitors walked through the narrow streets to a house on a hillside bend in the road. It was a house of chinked stone and red tiled roof, boarded up because the present owner, a long-retired school teacher, was sick in a distant hospital

This was the old Violet homestead, traced back to deeds of the 1640s. It was no beauty. Windows and doors were boarded up now- There were holes where plaster had fallen away, scars where bullets once hit. And the barns stood silent and empty.

But to the travelers it seemed a sacred place. And suddenly the mayor of Villejésus felt their unspoken message.

In a happy shout, the mayor announced, "We of Villejésus will place a plaque on these walls commemorating this as the Violet ancestral home. And it shall stay there in memory of your homecoming today."

And then we moved on to the Salon de Fetes, a town meeting room, for a "vin d'honnuer," and speeches and toasts. The hosts uncorked endless bottles of Pineau, the fine regional drink made through a delicious, fruity combination of unfermented grapes and aged local cognac.

But soon the hallowed hour of noon arrived, and the bus and cars carried the throng to ancient farmhouses nearby where a splendid country feast had been prepared to welcome the cousins from America.

Horseshoe tables for 25 were set up in low ceilinged rooms with dazzling white cloths and a myriad of country flowers. Great crusty loaves of fresh bread the size and shape of life rings and steaming bowls of golden turnip soup awaited us. Then came platters of cold jellied rabbit and vegetables. Then huge tureens of country chicken stew and scores of bottles of wine from the vineyards.

Violets and Violettes began singing the old country folk songs together, songs that had crossed the Atlantic two centuries and more before and had stayed alive.

Then came delicious tarts from every fruit and cakes overflowing with homemade butter and home-grown eggs. And enormous trays of cheeses — Brie and Camembert and mysterious tasting cheeses made from the milk of local goats, goats that are bigger than Maine deer and just as brown in fur. Then trays of fresh fruit, just picked from trees in the wall garden, still warm and pouring with juice from the French sun.

Finally, platters of fresh pears, grapes and apples, sliced into a nectar concoction, were served with strong, bitter coffee and the crowning glory of double distilled, fiery strong cognac, made here in the finest of France's cognac country.

Newly found cousinship was in full flood. The decibels of excited, passionate, affectionate, joyous sound peaked by 4 p.m.

There was no language barrier at all. In an extraordinary discovery, we found that the French spoken by the Violette families from Maine, New Brunswick and Quebec was almost precisely the same as the French spoken by the farming families of Villejésus and Fontenille.

The peculiarities of pronunciation and accent — and even the patois and local idioms that mark the French spoken in Maine — are almost precisely the same ones that mark the accent in these villages in the Charentes district of France.

This local dialect came across the ocean in sailing ships 233 years ago and persists today, almost unchanged on both sides of the ocean.

For the last two or three hours of the afternoon, the Franco-Americans were whisked off to visit the famed vineyards and wine and cognac distilleries of the region. But the day was just a curtain-raiser to what Villejésus had planned for the evening reunion with the Violettes.

By 7 p.m., the Hotel de Ville, the tiny town hall of Villejésus, was thronged. Farmers, back from their vineyards, came dressed in Sunday black, with beaming wives and wide-eyed children. Mayors from surrounding villages came in tricolor ribbons, sashes and medallions of office.

Pineau flowed again. Again, speeches, toasts across the sea, exchanges of gifts. Before long the French formalities were swamped in a torrent of bonhommie.

The happy mob moved into the assembly room of the village school next door. There the women of Villejésus had staged a "fete au campagne" — a mammoth, endless country supper.

Photo 1-4: Rita Violette Lippe toasting with Mayor of Villejésus

Hundreds were there, downing local pate de foie gras, cold chicken, cold pork, cheeses, magnificent pastries and uncounted liters of wine.

Children ran happily through the mob; parents danced. The Americans handed out violet baseball caps emblazoned with the name "Violette" and staid French mayors wore them as badges of happy cousinship.

Women swapped photos of children, homes, grandchildren, ancestors; exchanged addresses; arranged for pen pals. The singing and dancing and music enveloped them all in unity.

Suddenly it was past 10 p.m. The Violettes from America climbed aboard their bus. The Violets from France stood on the village common, beside the church where we had jointly celebrated mass that morning, and waved to us in the moonlight.

Children, up way past bedtime, stood on the town walls and waved "au revoir." And all shared in the same tears and simple human joy in finding each other.

Hunger for roots inspires search

This hunger to find out has grown widespread in America since the publication of Alex Haley's book "Roots" and its television serial. This same hunger began haunting Rita Violette Lippe eight years ago in her hometown of Methuen, Mass.

She was a bookkeeper and wife and mother, hungry to know more about her Violette roots. She began digging intensely into the genealogical records, the church and state and parochial records of Violettes in the United States and Canada.

In Augusta, Maurice Violette, a Navy veteran of 20 years and now a market analyst for Central Maine Power Co., was making a similar search. They joined forces.

They traced the Violette ancestry back to the city of Louisbourg, Isle Royale, Acadia; to Charles Violet, the first of the line who emigrated from France in 1749. There the trail went cold and at first seemed to end without any documentary links back into France.

Nevertheless, Rita Violette Lippe set her sights on a family reunion at her home in Methuen in 1978, expecting 75 "cousins" might show up. But more than 310 came!

They came because Rita had written letters to more than 200 Violette families across the nation. Their names largely had been gathered by Roderick Violette, an airline pilot from San Mateo, Calif, who copied Violette names from phone books in airports across the country.

"I got 20 friends to make 1,500 meatballs and 48 bowls of chop suey in my kitchen, and we fed well over 300 Violettes at our first family gathering in 1978. Two days after it was over, I felt an awful letdown and found that we had $119 profit," says Rita, "so I used the money to send out the first Violette Family newsletter.

"Replies and donations for more research came pouring in. Soon I was up to 1,200 newsletters. Then we had the next family reunion in Augusta in 1980, and over 500 Violettes came. Last year, we had the third reunion in Van Buren, where the first Violette, Francois, settled in Maine. This time over 800 came from 23 states and Canada. Maine Supreme Court Justice Elmer Violette was chairman."

At that meeting, it was decided to send a delegation of Violettes to France to retrace the roots of the family, based on research already done. This Sept. 16, the delegation gathered at Logan Airport, Boston, to fly to Paris. I went along for the Telegram,

Departure stirs emotion

The travel agent in charge wept. "Dammit! The sight of all those Violettes makes me cry! I've seen a thousand departures and never shed a tear before," said travel agent Kathy Kearney of Crimson Travel, as she and I watched Rita Violette Lippe marshal her huge family toward the night flight to France.

"Families in America are splitting up today, disintegrating. But here are the Violettes all coming together to find their roots in a French village!"

She watched Rita call out a dozen names or so at a time. "Come forward together. Until tonight some of you may never have seen each other before. But each of you is a close relative. Each in this group is descended from the same great-great-grandfather."

Rita, the genealogist, handed each group of eight to 10 people, a single sheet tracing their common ancestry over 200 years.

The Violettes aboard the TWA flight to Paris were all descended from Francois Violet, probably the first Frenchman to pioneer and raise a family at what is now Van Buren. Rita and others had fairly easily documented that fact. But where did Francois come from?

Abandoned boy provides link

The search was hard. The writing in the records in the basements of Louisbourg, Nova Scotia, was in ancient script, old French sometimes, often yellow-stained and brittle.

But finally, with the help of Eric Krause, supervisor of old documents at the Fortress of Louisbourg, court records dated June 1751 were discovered.

One document showed that Charles Violet, who had shipped from La Rochelle to the New World as a would-be colonist aboard the vessel "L'Intrepide" in 1749, had given up his only living son, Francois, age 6, to five friends, due to the death of his wife, Marie David.

In the same proceedings, Charles Violet, who listed his occupation as roofer, pleaded bankruptcy.

More documents revealed that Charles married again and by 1759 had negotiated passage back to France with his new wife, a Marie Anne Sudois of La Rochelle, France. **(Ed Note: Actually, Charles and Marie were deported with the French as the French forces were leaving Louisbourg.)** *However, he failed to mention that he had left behind in Acadia his young son, Francois, the boy destined to become the patriarch of all American Violettes, who number 30,000 today.*

It took painstaking research in France, Canada and the United States to trace Charles' and Marie David's origins, to positively link Francois to Charles and to trace Charles back into France.

Help came from a wholly unexpected quarter in 1978. A group of Paris businessmen, with roots to the ancient Provence de Maine in France, came to the United States on a visit. They decided to end their tour in Augusta, capital of the American State of Maine.

That meeting in Augusta brought Maurice Violette into contact with Claude Meche of Paris. By trade, Claude Meche was a roofer (at Versailles), just as Charles Violet had been a roofer in 1749 when he sailed to the New World.

Meche agreed to work as the legman and on-the-spot researcher into the origins of the Violet family in France.

Meche broke the ground so well and made so many discoveries that in 1979 Maurice Violette and his friend Ray Fecteau, a barber in Augusta, flew to France on their vacations and spent a month with Meche, bird-dogging the trail of Charles Violet through the villages and musty records of southwestern France.

They returned to Maine with documentary proof Charles Violet and wife and son set sail to Louisbourg in 1749; that Charles and his second wife had returned to France and settled at Rochefort; and that Charles had, upon her death, married a third time.

They tracked Charles back to his birthplace and to his first marriage in Villejésus, and found there the birth records of his abandoned son Francois. **(Ed Note: Francois was born in Saintes, not Villejésus, and he was not abandoned. See Ed Note on page 5.)**

Discovery of these early links to North America — and the fact that descendants of the Violets were living and flourishing — caused waves of news in French papers and television.

Among the American Violette family, gathered over 800 strong in Van Buren last summer, the documents caused even greater waves.

These Violettes had been proud of their ancestor Francois, who had rafted down **(Ed Note: Francois went upriver; the St John River is really placid in most reaches.)** *the turbulent St. John River to where Van Buren stands now, who had married three times, fathered 23 children and began the Violette clan. Not bad for an abandoned boy!*

Now the clan was eager to get their own feet on French soil, to see whence they had sprung, to meet long-lost cousins in Villejésus.

Thus on the night of Sept. 16, 47 of them boarded the plane for France. The sight of this conjunction of family and history in Logan Airport made the travel agent cry.

Trip fulfills shared dream

They came from all over America and Canada and from the hard working class. More than half of the 47 came from Maine, where the Violettes had started.

All 47 had roots going back to Van Buren and the abandoned boy who became patriarch of the clan, Francois. Their faces, their laughter and tears, their characters and jokes and emotions will be imprinted always in my memory.

They were not well-to-do retirees or college kids traveling on Daddy. Each Violette had scrimped, drained savings or borrowed money—to make this homecoming pilgrimage, price $1,250.

Each told me they had secretly nursed a dream, a yearning to somehow get to France, to discover their roots. But until each set foot on French soil, none believed the dream would come true.

I see each of them now as I write this account of their trip. But there are too many stories, too many backgrounds to recite here.

The quietest man on the bus was Vinal Violette. His name was misspelled Final Violette, and he was indeed often late.

Photo 1-5: (L - R) Vinal Violette, Maurice Violette, Mayor's wife, Mayor of Fontenille

He favored a black coat, always wore a tie, then bought himself a black beret, and the result was that Final Violette from Van Buren looked more French than any Frenchman in Paris. Not until the last moments of our homeward flight did this quiet man tell me the moving gist of his story.

"I have some of the last land from the original Violette holdings. Farmed it mostly in potatoes. The market was bad. Had to sell all but 400 acres **(Ed Note: 162 ha)** *outside of Van Buren. Gave up the old homestead and took an apartment in Van Buren. Now I work as a steel rigger down in Hinckley and go home on weekends.*

"But," he said leaning close to my plane seat, "1 am a bachelor. I've turned 61. And I've got the last 400 acres **(Ed Note: 162 ha)** *of the original Violette land in Violette hands: And I've got no kids. No sons. Just two nieces, one in Las Vegas, the other in Florida.*

"After being on this trip to our roots, after seeing the people in Villejésus, it bothers me to think I may be the last of the Violettes on the last of the original Violette land. What shall I do, at 61?"

I advised him to get married. Maybe to a woman from Villejésus.

Many of the Violettes came as strangers to each other. But after 10 days they parted as the closest friends, linked by roots they had found together, families and cousins they had never known.

It was a joy to witness how quickly the French too, in the small towns, took these unknown cousins from America to their hearts. When they met and talked together, it was clear they were cut from the same basic cloth, be it hundreds of years ago.

It was clear they were deeply moved, everlastingly changed by the people they met, the cousins they found, the roots they discovered.

"I have seen a new world with my eyes, and my head is swimming with new sounds and new sights I never thought to see," said Jeanette Betit as we parted Boston.

"I'm filled with those things I saw and those people I met. But what will last forever from this trip is what I now carry in my heart.

We will learn more about Charles and his travels and his family in subsequent chapters, as we follow his movements and introduce other members of our ancestral family.

(End of Caldwell story)

But now let's hear about that trip to France from one of our members: Diane Violette Pruett VFA #64 wrote about it in the Violette Family Association Newsletter for November 1982. Here's her story:

VOL 6 No. 4 November 1982

Enfin! The Violette clan finally met at Logan Int. Airport on Thursday, Sept. 16 for the very much anticipated ancestral trip to France. There were Violettes from Maine, Mass., Conn., Calif., Washington & Canada. (**Ed Note: U.S. states Maine, Massachusetts, Connecticut, California, and Washington**) *Thanks to Rita Violette Lippé, we were able to discover to what degree we were all related. Each person was given a "family tree sheet" which provided us with the information that traced us all back to Louis Violet. We discovered to whom we were more closely related and chatted amongst ourselves before the flight. Needless to say, we were all excited and looking forward to the next eleven days.*

On Friday, we arrived in Paris at 9:30 PM (with a loss of 6 hrs). We were all exhausted but simply dazzled with Charles de Gaulle Airport. We were greeted by our guide and bus driver and immediately boarded. Our first stop was Vallet where we were graciously met by our cousins, Renée Viollet Sanarens, Francoise Viollet Marche' and Andre Viollet. Francoise presented each of us with a key to the city (in the form of a corkscrew) with a Violette inscription. The Mayor André Barre formally greeted us and entertained us with wine and pastries. We left Vallet and arrived in beautiful LaRochelle where we got our first glimpse of the outdoor cafés, the narrow streets, and the boutique shops.

On Saturday, we were greeted at the Hôtel de Ville by representatives of the city. We were graciously welcomed and invited to "dégust" some Pineau Noir and Cognac. The rest of the day was spent touring the city. All of us were impressed by this lovely harbor city. We sadly left LaRochelle and headed to Rochefort where we were to spend the next three nights.

On Sunday, we met with the Mayor of Rochefort, Jean Louis Frot, and again had a wonderful wine reception. Our highlight of the day was a visit to St. Louis Church where Charles Violet was buried. We also visited the Corderie from which Charles departed for Acadia in 1749. We toured the Pierre Lote' Museum and other sites.

On Monday we were warmly received in Saintes by the Assistant Mayor, Bernard Thiebaud. Saintes is one of the oldest cities in France which dates back to 100 B.C. We visited the roman amphitheater, arch, abbey, and the Church of St. Vivien, where Francois Violette was baptized in 1744. This is also where Charles was married to Marie David in 1741. As we were entering the church, the bells were ringing - just for us! Very moving!

On Sunday we arrived in Angou1ème and we were met at the Hôtel de Ville for another wine reception. Along the route to Angoulème we saw vineyards galore! We visited St. Peter's Cathedral and the Hôtel de Ville. That evening a few of us went to a concert in St. Peter's Cathedral.

Wednesday was the highlight of our trip! We departed from Angoulème to Villejésus and had Mass in the Church of Villejésus where Louis and Marie Doux were married in 1715. Again, we were received by the beautiful church bells. After Mass we were taken by bus to Fontenille and warmly received by Mayor Fernand Videau and his wife. There we met many of our cousins from France. We had lunch in a restaurant owned and operated by a charming young French couple. Our meal was fantastic! In the afternoon we toured two distilleries. The first one was a small family-owned one and the other was the famous Ricard Distillery in Ligneres. We returned to Villejésus where another wine reception awaited us. Mayor J. P. Montussac greeted us and invited us to have a buffet dinner in the community hall. All the people of Villejésus were invited thus having another opportunity to speak with our cousins. This was a very emotional, heartwarming day for all!

Thursday was a very much needed "catch-up" day. Most of us shopped in Angoulème, rested or toured the city on our own.

Friday we left for Paris at 900 AM. We stopped in Amboise for lunch and had a chance to see the castle there. In a chapel in the castle is where Leonardo da Vinci is buried. We rode along the well-known Loire River Valley and caught glimpses of other castles along the way. After settling into our hotels, most of us went on an illumination tour of Paris. Beautiful!

On Saturday we had a guided tour of the famous Castle of Versailles. The gardens, flowers, and fountains were absolutely breath-taking. In the afternoon, we had free time to shop or tour.

Map 1-4: Places visited during France trip

Sunday, our last full day, was an extremely busy one. First, we had Mass at Notre Dame de Paris, then we toured the city and stopped for lunch near the Louvre. We were given 1 hr. to visit this famous art museum. Later we saw the famous Eiffel Tower, the Arc of Triumph, the left bank, Champs Elysees, and many other important historical sites. We rode up the hill to Montmartre where we saw a spectacular view of Paris. Some people went to the Moulin Rouge that evening, others ventured on the metro to visit other parts of Paris.

Monday morning we were taken to Charles de Gaulle Airport for our return flight to Boston. Aside from all the guided tours, visits to cities, wine receptions, etc., the most touching part of the trip to me was actually meeting our Violette cousins in Vallet, Fontenille and Villejésus. Our French cousins are truly sincere and beautiful people. We were deeply moved by their warmth, their hospitality and their genuine interest in our familial ties. Needless to say, the trip was a most gratifying and emotional one, and one which we shall never forget.

Finally, and most importantly, the Violettes and friends of the Violettes who (bravely) took the trip are the people who made the voyage a success. Without their enthusiasm, encouragement, stamina and love for each other, this trip could not possibly have been as worthwhile as it was.

The friendships formed among us shall never be forgotten. We are all anxiously awaiting to see each other at the next reunion (if not before!).

Diane Violette Pruett #64

(End of Pruett story)

The Research Challenge: Another Language, Another Time

So just what did Maurice, Rita, and their helpers Claude Meche and Ray Fecteau have to deal with in tracking our ancestors? When the Villejésus origin finally came into focus they were fortunate to locate old records from the parish of Villejésus: the records of centuries of marriages, births, deaths, burials for the village. Those of us who are used to today's documents would be dismayed to see and try to work with the documents of that era – the mid-18th century. To start with, all records were, of course, in the French language and in the vernacular of that region. Then, to make it worse, all records had to be handwritten and by many different hands, with many different handwriting styles. In the section that follows we can see some of those source documents that pertain to the Villejésus era in our history.

Louis Violet and Marie Doux marry (documents)

The first item shows the extract of the record of this marriage.

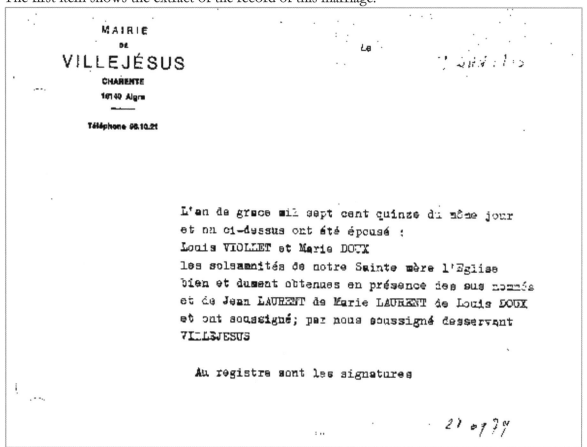

Document 1-1: "The year of our Lord seventeen hundred and fifteen on the same day indicated below were married Louis VIOLLET and Marie DOUX. The blessing of our Holy Mother the Church being duly received in the presence of the below enumerated Jean LAURENT and Marie LAURENT and Louis DOUX and they have signed below. By our signature, serving VILLEJÉSUS. The signatures are on the register."

Following is a copy of the actual page.

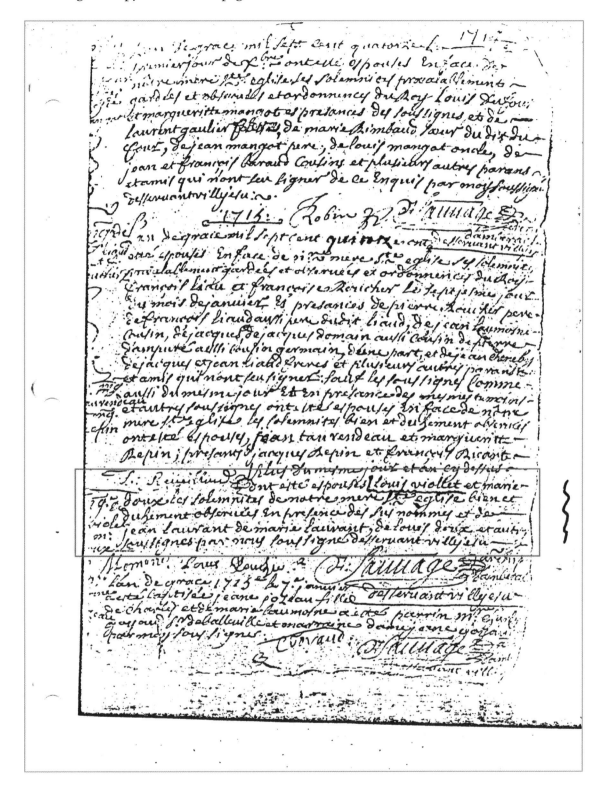

Charles Violet baptized (documents)

The first item shows the extract of the record of this baptism.

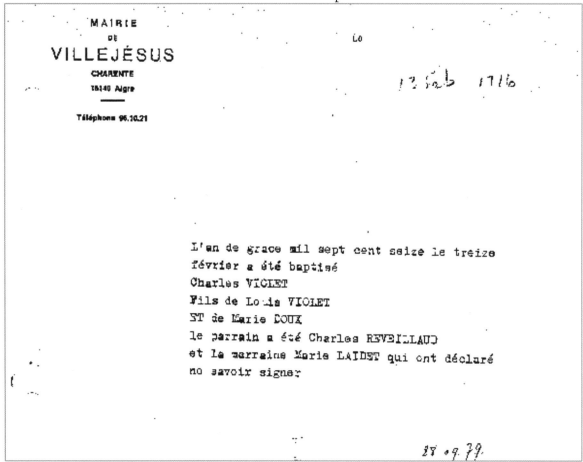

Document 1-2: "The year of our Lord seventeen hundred and sixteen the thirteenth of February was baptized Charles Violet son of Louis VIOLET and Marie DOUX, the godfather was Charles REVEILLAUD and the godmother Marie LAIDET, who declared they did not know how to sign."

Following is a copy of the actual page.

What was happening in the world at that time

France had a new king – five-year-old Louis XV – was crowned the September before following the death of Louis XIV, who had reigned for 72 years.

The Gulf Coast of North America was being settled and developed. Natchez, one of the oldest towns on the Mississippi River, was founded in 1716. Natchitoches was founded as the first permanent European settlement in the Louisiana Territory, after Biloxi (1699) and Mobile (Alabama) in 1702.

Meanwhile, in the northeastern part of North America, Britain and France were laying claims and creating settlements. Map 1-5 shows how that area was divided by those two powers after 1713. Prior to that time the whole area had been claimed by France, but they had to give up to the British the lands shown in red in Map 1-5 at the end of that most recent conflict. Louisbourg, established in 1713 on Cape Breton Island (Île Royale), will play a big role in Charles' future!

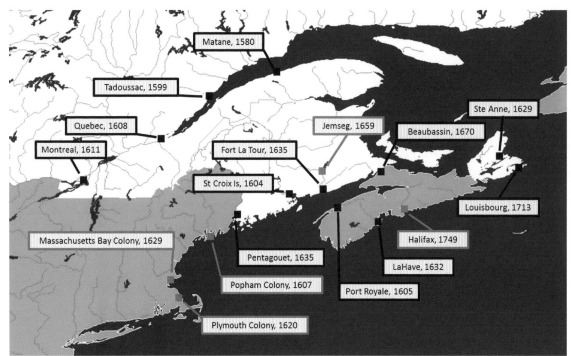

Map 1-5: British and French claims in North America

CHAPTER 2 - CHARLES MARRIES, FRANCOIS VIOLET BORN IN SAINTES

Time Span: 1741-1744

In the chapter about Villejésus we saw that Louis Violet and Marie Doux were married and gave birth to three children, among them our ancestor, Charles. We next find Charles 25 years later in Saintes, France. Since we don't have any other records from his childhood and young adulthood, and we don't know where his parents – Louis and Marie Violet – died, we might assume that he moved as an adult from Villejésus to Saintes to find work. Villejésus was (and is still) a small town, with probably not much building construction and probably only subsistence farming, so opportunities for employment were likely few. At some point Charles became trained as a roofer ("couvreur de toits"), since we know that it was in that capacity he was employed later in his life. Did he learn the roofing trade in Villejésus, or did he learn it in Saintes? We don't know. We also don't know how he received his training, though the more common route was apprenticeship. Perhaps he served as an apprentice to a roofer in Villejésus but when he was ready to go out on his own he had to move somewhere else because there was no opportunity in Villejésus. We know from his later life that he was an enterprising young man and was willing to take chances and try new things.

Saintes is the "big city" to Villejésus' "small town", and would be a natural place for young Charles to migrate to in search of more to do and in search of employment. The population of Saintes (2008) was 27,934 compared with (2008) 568 for Villejésus. Saintes was also an important city along the Charente River and had been an important crossing point for the main Roman road through Gaul, having been established by the Romans about 20 BC. Saintes was the center for the Gallic tribe, the Santones, and was later the center for a district known as Saintonge. Many buildings still in use today date back to the 12th century – 600 years before Charles arrived there to seek his fortune. This move for Charles was about 60 miles from his birthplace.

And because Saintes had so many older buildings the need to reroof them was great, thus providing more opportunities for a young roofer setting out on his own.

Charles Marries

So, on a typical fall market day in 1741 in Saintes we find a couple standing with friends in St Vivien parish just outside Saintes and pledging themselves to each other. On Friday, November 6th, Charles married Marie David, a widowed woman from Saintes. Marie was older than Charles – 36 to his 25 – and had already been married and widowed and had a young son, Alexis Hilaret. Our "Grandmère" Marie had been married to Jean Isaac Hilaret and Alexis was born sometime in 1733; we don't have any records of Jean's death or Alexis' birth, though. Charles adopted Alexis at some point. Marie's parents were Jean David and Marie Gaindet, but we do not have any more information about them other than their names. We will see more about Alexis in later chapters.

How did a young man of 25 come to marry a widow of 36? Age 36 in those times, especially for women, was approaching her middle years and might not have been considered a candidate for marriage with a younger man. Looking through our genealogical records from that time we see a typical age for marrying for females is 18-20 while that for males is 24-28. Charles own father, Louis, married when he was 25. And although it was not uncommon for a man to marry a widow with children this most usually occurred with his second or later marriage and after he already had children with his first wife (life was difficult for women in those times and they usually died before their husbands).

The family is expanded

A year and a half later Charles and Marie's first child was born – a son, Helie, on July 22, 1743. Sadly Helie was to only live for three years.

Then another year and a half later a son, François, was born on December 16, 1744. We will, of course, hear much, much more about our ancestor François!

Where is Saintes? What was the town like?

Charles did not leave the region when he moved to Saintes, for it is in the same present-day region as Villejésus, Poitou-Charentes. Located 60 miles (97 km) to the west and closer to the coast, its location is shown in Map 2-1. Map 2-2 shows Saintes in Poitou-Charentes, along with Villejésus.

Map 2-1: Saintes, France

Map 2-2: Saintes and Villejésus, Poitou-Charentes, France

Map 2-3 shows an aerial view of the Saintes area today, while Map 2-4 shows the outline of the medieval era fortifications superimposed over the area. The parish/village of St Vivien lies to the north, outside the Roman walls

Map 2-3: Aerial View of Saintes Today

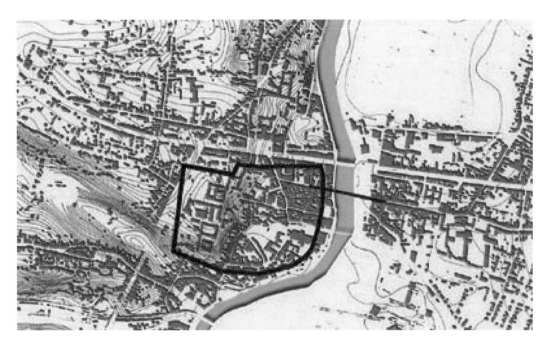

Map 2-4: Medieval Fortification Walls in Saintes (circa 1700). Walls and bridge shown in black.

The black line crossing the Charente River in Map 2-4 shows the location of the Roman river bridge. Map 2-5 shows the location of the church where Charles and Marie were married.

Map 2-5: St Vivien Church in Saintes

The fortified area within the walls shown in Map 2-4 is approximately 46 acres (18.5 hectares) and was mostly filled with houses and churches. Only a few gardens offered the possibility of fresh food within the fortifications.

Obviously Saintes was well-established when Charles arrived; it had been in existence for almost 1800 years at that time! The Romans established the place and called it Mediolanum Saintonium, and it played a significant role as the capitol of their Aquitaine Province. Many artifacts from the Roman era can still be seen today such as an amphitheater (Photo 2-1) and the wonderful Arc de Germanicus (Photo 2-2). The Arc de Germanicus was originally built at the entrance on the Saintes side to the Roman bridge over the Charente River but was later disassembled in 1843 when the old bridge was demolished and the Arc was reassembled at its present location on the right bank.

Photo 2-1: Roman Amphitheater at Saintes

Photo 2-2: Roman Arc de Germanicus at Saintes

Photos 2-1 and 2-2 by Myrabella (Own work), via Wikimedia Commons

Years of Research Finally Pay Off

How did Rita Violette Lippé and Maurice Violette trace our family to Saintes and Villejésus, France? It wasn't easy! As you will see from this story written by Bill Caldwell in the Maine Sunday Telegram they got only so far tracing back from present time and ran into a dead end with François Violet in Fort Louisbourg in Acadia (Nova Scotia).

Time went by and then another breakthrough – the discovery of the link between François and his father, Charles. Those documents pointed to France and the "paroisse de Jesus" and "Sainx". But no place by either name could be found in France! Another dead end!

But Maurice and Rita did not quit, and finally Maurice got another breakthrough. Let's let Bill Caldwell tell us how this story unfolds:

Maine Sunday Telegram, November, 1982
How one family unlocked its past
Columnist Bill Caldwell accompanied members of the Violette family, many of whom are from Maine, to France last month as they went in search of their family's past.

THEY DON'T LOOK like detectives, with worn shopping bags at their weary feet, spectacles on their noses and ledger-like volumes spread before them.

But they are bloodhounds, sniffing out trails, picking up clues, getting an intoxicating whiff just as they are about to shut down the case as "unsolved".

And then they are off again, in full cry, baying at the trail.

They are the ancestor-hunters.

You find them by the score almost every day in the Maine State Archives in Augusta, in the Maine Historical Society in Portland, in the musty old shelves of town halls and village libraries across Maine.

They are searching for their half- lost families, for the roots from which they grew, for knowledge of whose blood runs in their veins.

Once, in foolish ignorance, I was apt to smile at their patient labor. I used to whiz by them when I was hot on the trail of a specific juicy morsel of Maine history to flesh out a column for tomorrow's newspaper.

But at last I am learning better. These moles are unearthing the sinews and old bones which make us all alive today.

Across Maine, and in every state, tens of thousands of people are doing this kind of detective work, unsung and unthanked.

This column is a small shout of praise and thanks to that unthanked army of detectives who seldom make the news and never get into runaway bestsellers, the men and women who are on the quiet hunt for ancestors and for family and village history throughout Maine.

BECAUSE THE VIOLETTES from Van Buren broke through a genealogical iron curtain, I have been on a 10-day trip through France, retracing the steps of their ancestors who came to the New World in 1749. Thanks to one 4- year-old boy, François Violet, who made that cross-Atlantic trip, there are now 30,000 Violettes here in North America.

But finding the missing links was quite a detective story.

If you are trying to trace your own family roots across the centuries and oceans, the way the Violettes did it may give you courage.

You need persistence, patience, time; and most of all you need a streak of unexpected luck.

The persistence and patience came mostly from Rita Violette Lippe of Methuen, Mass., and Maurice Violette of Augusta. They started their hunt in earnest some seven years ago. It began with letters to hundreds of Violette families in New England, Canada and across most of America. The names came largely from a Violette in California. He **(Ed note: Rod Violette, now Secretary/Genealogist for the Violette Family Association)** *was an airline pilot. And wherever he landed, he'd copy the names and addresses of Violettes from local phone books and send these to Rita. Then she would write hundreds of letters.*

"I'd send 30 or 40 to Violettes in one town or region, and ask about grandparents and great-grandparents and promise to send them information. I'd get back maybe five replies from a region. That was enough. Because most of the Violettes would have talked with each other about my inquiry."

AS THE INFORMATION poured in, and as Rita and Maurice Violette carried on their own joint research into state and local archives, all trails led back to Van Buren. Violettes still live there.

And all finally traced their roots back to François Violet who had rafted down the St. John River and settled there some 200 years ago. He married three times and left a brood of 23 children, which was a good start, and a tradition carried on by eight generations of Violettes until there are today an estimated 30,000 of the clan spread across North America.

They were able to trace François back to Louisbourg, Isle Royale, Acadia and the 1750s. But there the trail seemed to end without a clue as to what went before.

Detective work is donkey work, dull, often fruitless, eye-straining work that seems to get you nowhere. All good detectives and genealogists and even journalists know this. But finally ancient documents in the Royal Court of Isle Royale, dated 1751, revealed that in June 1751, Charles Violet, a roofer from southwest France, had pleaded bankruptcy before the court. And with this document, the hot pursuit was on.

Another court document of the same month of June 1751, showed the same Charles Violet petitioning the court to allow him to give custody of his son, François, and his step-brother, Alexis Hilaret, to "five friends and neighbors."

THE ARCHIVISTS in Louisbourg had hit upon what was an unexpected treasure trove of documents for the Violettes of Van Buren. Next they found a document showing Charles Violet's first wife, Marie David, had died in Louisbourg in 1750, and that Charles was remarrying, this time to a Marie Sudois, who had come to Louisbourg from France. A third document in 1759 showed Charles Violet and his new wife, Marie Sudois, had taken ship from Louisbourg for La Rochelle in France.

But here again the Violettes came to a dead end. Rita and Maurice and others wrote time and again to officials in France, vainly trying to establish the missing link. Their only clues came from the old documents unearthed in Louisbourg and those gave "Paroisse de Jesus" as the birthplace of Charles Violet and "Sainx" as the birthplace of Marie David. Their letters were returned. Neither place was known. No map carried those place names. No cartographic record revealed any such places in France.

Enter luck again. Playing a desperate hunch, Maurice Violette wrote a letter one night to the city in southwest France called "Saintes," a city which dates back to the Roman days.

Amazingly he got a reply. Yes, wrote an archivist, "Saintes" had once been called "Sainx" back during the 14th century. And yes, a Marie David had been born on May 10, 1705.

MORE LUCK hit the persistent Violettes. By pure chance, Maurice met Claude Meche, a Frenchman visiting Augusta, and told him of the genealogical hunt. Meche, it turned out, was a roofer by trade, just as Charles Violet had been when he came to the New World and went broke in the 1750s. Meche was commissioned to do on-the-spot legwork on his return to France. Meche did an enormous and immaculate job, unearthing all family records, despite the fact that the French Revolution had caused the destruction or hiding of so many. He found that the elusive "Paroisse (Parish) of Jesus" had become the tiny hamlet of Villejésus. He found birth and marriage records of Charles and Marie, and christening records of François, the grand patriarch of New World Violettes.

But evidence that Charles and Marie had sailed to the New World with their infant son was almost impossible to uncover. Nowhere in France were there any such records. The reason was their departure was part of a wartime state secret.

In 1749 a secret convoy of 13 French ships sailed with troops and colonizers for Louisbourg to help seize the New World from the English settlers. **(Ed Note: Actually, Île Royale and Louisbourg were still in French hands after 1713 and the French in 1749 wanted to strengthen their defenses to guard against British expansion of territory.)** *The only copy of the manifest was sent with the ships. It was finally unearthed in Louisbourg. On it were the names of Charles and Marie and François Violet.*

The detective work was done. The whole puzzle came together and fit. Last month I flew with 47 Violettes to France as town-by-town they retraced their ancestors and embraced their cousins lost to each other centuries ago.

And so this toast to the unsung detectives we see looking unglamorous in the back rooms of libraries, tracing their families, piecing together the immortal story of how America began, answering the questions: "Who are we? Where did we come from?

(End of Caldwell text)

Some mysteries solved

So now we have our ancestor, François, in place and living in Saintes, France, with his father, mother, and sister. The final steps in the research had been completed and our origins were established. But as Bill Caldwell reported, much more is known going forward in time and our next chapters will follow this family as they go on further adventures.

CHAPTER 3 - CHARLES AND MARIE MOVE FAMILY TO ROCHEFORT

Time Span: 1744-1749

Charles and Marie and their two young children – Helie and François – and the older child – Alexis Hilaret - moved to Rochefort a couple of years after François was born. While we don't know the exact date of the move, it must have been prior to September 2, 1746, for on that date Helie died in Rochefort (see Document 3-1). François had been born on December 16, 1744 and Helie on July 22, 1743. Helie was only a little over three years old when he died. Alexis was born around 1733, so he was 13-14 years old at this time.

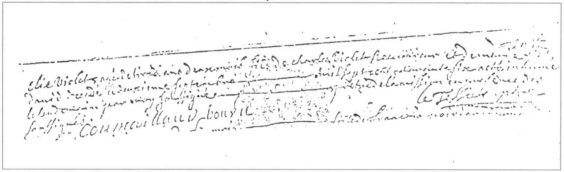

Document 3-1: Translation: "Helie Violet, 3 months old this month, son of Charles Violet, roofer, and of the lady Marie David, died 2 September 1746, and was buried the next day by me, the undersigned, priest of the mission in the presence of the undersigned."

We also do not know why the family moved. Rochefort is only about 25 miles north and west of Saintes, where Charles and Marie were married and where Helie and François were born.

Rochefort has about the same population as Saintes. The population of Saintes (2008) was 27,934 compared with (2008) 26,455 for Rochefort. Though we don't have earlier population estimates for Saintes, we know that in 1806 Rochefort's population was 14,615. Saintes is an important city along the Charente River but Rochefort is a port on the Charente estuary near the French coast.

The family is expanded again, temporarily

The third child born to Marie and Charles was Marie, born January 31, 1747 (see Document 3-2). Poor Marie did not live long, however, for she died on October 14, 1747 (See Document 3-3) at age 8½ months, only just over a year after her older brother Helie.

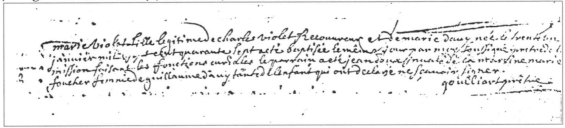

Document 3-2: Translation: "Marie Violet, legitimate daughter of Charles Violet, roofer, and of Marie Davy, was born 31 January 1747 and was baptized the same day by me, undersigned priest of the mission doing pastoral duties, sponsor was Jean Doux, disabled Marine, Marie Foucher, wife of Guillaume Davy, aunt of the infant, who claim they do not know how to sign. Signatures follow."

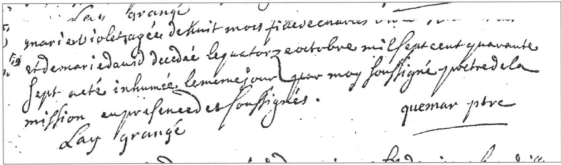

Document 3-3: Translation: "Marie Violet, 8 months old, daughter of Charles Violet, roofer, and of Marie David, died on 4 October 1747, and was buried the same day by me undersigned, priest of the mission in the presence of the undersigned. Signatures follow."

In praise of our genealogists, notice how difficult it is to try to read and follow old records. Not only are they difficult to read due to the old script and a wide range of handwriting skills but names are not always properly recorded. Note in Documents 3-1 and 3-3 Marie's last (maiden name) was recorded as David, while in Document 3-2 it was recorded as Davy! This probably came about because the French pronunciation of "David" sounds like "Dayveed", which could easily be mistaken for Davy.

Notice also in Document 3-2 that we learn that Marie David (Davy) Violet had a brother, Guillaume Davy, whose wife's maiden name was Marie Foucher. We have no other record of Guillaume and his wife, Marie, but we can suppose that they also lived in Rochefort since they attended the burial. Were Guillaume and Marie Davy living in Rochefort when Charles and Marie Violet moved there, and was that what drew Charles and Marie to Rochefort?

Notice also in all three record excerpts that Charles was identified as a roofer; this means he was probably working in that trade throughout that time.

Where is Rochefort? What was the town like?

Charles did not leave the region when he moved to Rochefort, for it is in the same present-day Administrative Region as Saintes and Villejésus - Poitou-Charente – and in the Charente-Maritime Department. Located close to the coast and on the Charente River estuary, about 20 miles (32 km) northwest of Saintes, its location is shown in Map 3-1. Map 3-2 shows Rochefort in Poitou-Charentes along with Saintes and Villejésus. Map 3-3 shows an aerial view of the Rochefort area today.

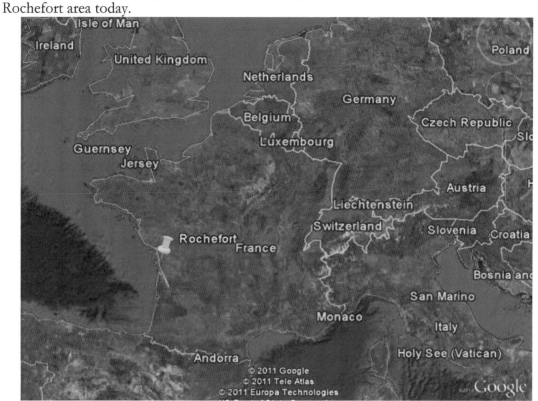

Map 3-1: Rochefort, France

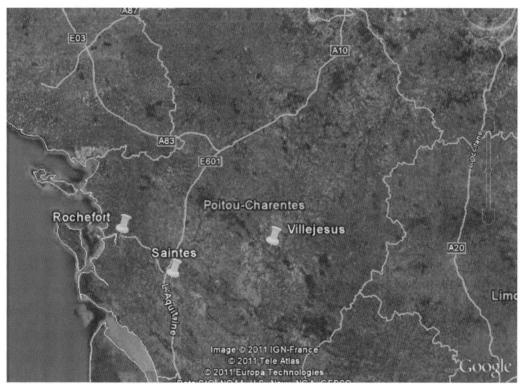

Map 3-2: Rochefort, Saintes, and Villejésus, Poitou-Charentes, France

Map 3-3: Aerial View of Rochefort Today

Rochefort was built as a "new city" starting around 1665, and was perhaps one of the first planned cities in history. It was designed to be a place of refuge, defense, and supply for the French Navy. The reason for building Rochefort was to a large extent because royal power could hardly depend on rebellious Protestant (Huguenot) La Rochelle, also a port city nearby, which Cardinal Richelieu had to besiege a few decades earlier. Rochefort's location on the Charente River made it a valid port for naval operations but being a distance from the coast provided considerable protection for the naval base (see Map 3-3). During 1666-1669 the Corderie Royale was built; this was the longest building in Europe at the time and was where cordage (ropes) for French ships of war was made. Its closeness to the Atlantic Ocean gave rise to the formal name for the community - Rochefort-sur-Mer – but the last part of the name is often omitted. However, the record excerpts we have on file and shown in Documents 3-1 through 3-3 were generated in 1980 and were attested to as true copies on letterhead from the Mairie de Rochefort-Sur-Mer (Rochefort-Sur-Mer City Hall).

Photo 3-1: Corderie Royale is the long, skinny building in the foreground

Rochefort not only had access to a deep channel of the Charente River that allowed ocean-going ships to reach it, but marshes surrounding it to the north and west effectively protected the city from land attack from those directions.

While Rochefort had great growth about 75 years before Charles and Marie brought their family there and an even greater growth spurt due to construction of a major prison a few years after they left for La Rochelle, we think that there was nothing new going on to draw the family to Rochefort. We know that Charles was working as a roofer (according to the records shown in Documents 3-1 through 3-3), and the age of the early buildings probably required reroofing to keep him employed. Rochefort had to be a busy place because the base for naval operations was there as well as the rope manufacturing plant.

Photo 3-2: Large rope of type made in Rochefort at the Corderie Royale in Charles and Marie's time

Photo 3-3: Maritime Museum at Rochefort was part of military operations when Charles and Marie lived there

Photo 3-4: More cordage from the Corderie Royale

Photo 3-5: View of part of Corderie Royale

But living in Rochefort at that time must have been exciting due to the ships coming and going to all parts of the world. The sailors from those ships would bring with them stories of where they had been and what they had seen and perhaps these stories sparked an adventurous fire in young Charles, for they did not stay long in Rochefort but would soon cross the Atlantic to Louisbourg. We will cover those travels in other chapters.

So here we have a young man, Charles, born in a small village (Villejesus), moving to a larger town, Saintes, and marrying an older woman with a son and then moving to the bustling city of Rochefort. He was obviously not satisfied with a quiet country life and sought to do and see more. Charles was about 29 when they moved to Rochefort. His wife, Marie, was about 40 years old and had given birth to three children by that time. The life expectancy for women in those years was probably less than 45 years, so she was fairly far along in life. It had to have been hard for Marie to make this move, but as we will see she had even harder circumstances to come.

CHAPTER 4: CHARLES AND MARIE SET SAIL FROM LA ROCHELLE

Time Span: 1749-1749

Once again we find Charles and Marie and their children – Alexis (age 16) and François (age 5) – on the move, this time from La Rochelle. Son Helie had been born in Saintes in 1743 but died in 1746 while the family lived in Rochefort. Daughter Marie was born and died in Rochefort in 1747. We don't think they actually moved to La Rochelle, but it was the port from which they left France in June 1749. Charles was taking his family to settle and work in Louisbourg on Cape Breton Island in what is now Nova Scotia, and we know that the convoy going to Louisbourg embarked from La Rochelle.

What gave rise for the move from France to the New World?

Here was a young family, married eight years, with two young boys (Helie had recently died), taking the big step to leave the country of their birth and cross the ocean to a new world. True, they would not be pioneering because Louisbourg had been developed for 36 years but it was still an outpost and did not have the history of commerce and development in their home area of Poitou-Charente. Poitou-Charente had had much agriculture and viticulture for many years and life there had already established its own rhythm. The paths were worn and the patterns known. Was Charles having trouble finding work as a roofer and needed to move? Certainly there was going to be a lot of roofing and other construction employment in Louisbourg because Louisbourg had just undergone a military siege and bombardment and much needed to be rebuilt. Or did Charles have an itch to travel somewhere he had never been? He had already moved from Villejésus to Saintes and then to Rochefort, and we don't know why he made those moves. But those moves were very small compared with crossing the Atlantic to a new world! Did he want to establish his own roofing business (which we know he would do in Louisbourg) but could not break into the competition in France? Or was it just the lure of the financial reward the King was offering for people to move to Louisbourg? No records have been found to give us clues to why the move, but the move was to be pivotal for those of us who came after!

We think that it was events transpiring in North America that gave an opportunity for Charles and his family to come to the New World and an impetus to do so, rather than any situation in France.

Hostilities between France and England had been on and off in North America since 1689 with alternating periods of peace and war, and some of this played itself out in La Rochelle as well as in the New World. The city had changed hands between the French and English several times during the French Wars of Religion. During the Reformation, in 1568, La Rochelle became a center for the Huguenots and the city declared itself an Independent Reformed Republic. This led to numerous conflicts with the Catholic central government of France. After several Huguenot revolts Louis XIV in 1685 revoked the Edict of Nantes which had given the Huguenots some religious freedom. Many Huguenots immigrated, mostly to England.

Meanwhile across the ocean France had controlled the northern coast of North America since the days of Jacques Cartier in 1534. In 1710 France lost most of the territory from Newfoundland to present-day Maine in a war against England. The Treaty of Utrecht in 1713 gave to France all of British North America plus all the islands in the Gulf of St. Lawrence, which included Cape Breton Island (Île Royale). Cape Breton Island and Fort Louisbourg became a sentinel in the gateway of the St. Lawrence, through which passed much traffic for the interior of northern North America. Map 4-1 shows the relationship of Louisbourg to the whole Gulf of St. Lawrence.

Map 4-1: Louisbourg Guards the Entry to the St. Lawrence River

All commerce for the interior of the continent passed through this opening and to protect its holdings (Québec City, for example) it was important for France to protect this entry. *(Ref; Louisbourg by J.S. McLennan P.2)* So, in 1713 France decided to build a significant fortress at Louisbourg.

In 1744 war again resumed between England and France and in 1745, Louisbourg fell to the English. In 1748 the Treaty of Aix-la-Chapelle gave Cape Breton and Louisbourg back to the French, and France then decided once again to strengthen the garrison and improve fortifications at Louisbourg.

This new construction is what gave Charles the opportunity to come to the New World. He and his wife Marie David and sons Alexis and François set sail from La Rochelle with the new governor, in a flotilla that included the man-of-war ships *Tigre* and *Intrepide* and the frigate

Anemone. These protected a convoy of transports carrying 500 troops and civilian inhabitants that set sail on June 29, 1749 and landed at Louisbourg on July 23, 1749, a relatively quick crossing. The French king, Louis XV, encouraged people who had lived in Louisbourg before to return and he offered the sum of 150 pounds to French citizens who would emigrate to settle in Louisbourg to establish a stronger French presence. Most likely he also wanted people to raise crops and livestock locally to help support the garrison, for it was long and costly to haul provisions from France.

How much was that 150-pound grant worth?

The French pound, or livre, varied in size and value over the years but we can estimate its value during the period when Charles and Marie lived by doing some comparisons. No direct calculation is possible but we can take maybe three approaches to arriving at an estimate.

1. Since the livre had a gold basis we might use the value of gold for comparison purposes. In 1726, under Louis XV's minister Cardinal Fleury, a system of monetary stability was put in place that established, among other things, that the French Louis D'Or gold coin was worth 24 French livres (pounds). ***(Ref: French livre, From Wikipedia, the free encyclopedia)*** During the reigns of Louis XIII and Louis XIV the weight of the Louis D'Or was set at 6.75 grams, though under Louis XVI it was increased to a weight of 7.6490 g, a fineness of 0.917, and gold content of 0.2255 troy oz. ***(Ref: Louis d'or, From Wikipedia, the free encyclopedia)*** The percentage of gold in the d'or of Louis XIII and Louis XIV was not established, so we don't really know its gold content. But if we assume it was the same as for the d'or of Louis XVI then one Louis d'or in Charles and Marie's time probably had 0.199 troy oz. of gold. So, 150 pounds (livres) was probably worth about 6.25 Louis d'ors, with a weight of approximately 42.2 grams, or 1.24 troy ounces. At today's prices (Feb 2011) a troy ounce of gold is worth roughly $1,400 so Charles and Marie would have been given a grant of approximately $1,750 to move to Louisbourg.

2. Another approach is to compare the sum with what people were paid at the time. From the records of A. & S. Dufour in Madawaska from 1848 we can see that day laborer wages were 2 shillings, 6 pence per day and that river drivers (workers who moved logs downriver) made the same. For eight days work that would be 1 pound. By that measure, the 100 pounds would be equivalent to 800 days' labor. Recognize, of course, that the monetary units for that merchant were British pounds. In an account about some New Englanders captured and sold to the French in Quebec in 1752 the price of £200 was said to be equivalent to about $1,540 today, so £150 would be approximately $1,155.

3. Another comparison can be made by considering the value of Charles' property in Louisbourg a few years later. Briefly, Charles was forced to file bankruptcy in 1751 and the total value of his furniture and effects was appraised at approximately £328.84. So the £150 grant to relocate was equivalent to about one-half of the cost of setting up a household in the new country! We might assume that they were able to bring at least some of their personal belongings (but not furniture and household items) with them, though. *(More about Charles' bankruptcy in later chapters.)*

Where is La Rochelle? What was the town like?

La Rochelle is in the same present-day Region as Rochefort, Saintes, and Villejésus - Poitou-Charente – and in the Charente-Maritime Department. Located on the coast and about 20 miles northwest of Rochefort, its location is shown in Map 4-2. Map 4-3 shows La Rochelle in Poitou-Charentes along with Rochefort, Saintes, and Villejésus. Map 4-4 shows an aerial view of the La Rochelle area today.

Map 4-2: La Rochelle, France

Map 4-3: La Rochelle, Rochefort, Saintes, and Villejésus, Poitou-Charentes, France

Map 4-4: Aerial View of La Rochelle Today

The area of La Rochelle was occupied in antiquity by Gaul tribes, then by the Romans. The Romans developed salt production at La Rochelle through evaporation of sea water and exported wine production from the region throughout the Roman Empire.

La Rochelle is a seaport on the Bay of Biscay, part of the Atlantic Ocean, and the port has existed since at least the sixth century. Because La Rochelle is located more to the west than other ports it saved several days sailing for the western Atlantic and its important fishing grounds, so La Rochelle was a popular port during the 16th century. As a result, La Rochelle was an important port connecting the east Atlantic with the west Atlantic both under British rule (1154 to 1224, 1360 to 1372, 1560s to 1685) and French rule thereafter. Until the 15th century, La Rochelle was to be the largest French harbor on the Atlantic coast, dealing mainly in wine, salt, and cheese. La Rochelle became very active in triangular trade with the New World, dealing in the slave trade with Africa, sugar trade with plantations of the Antilles, and fur trade with Canada (French or British North America). **(Ref: La Rochelle, From Wikipedia, the free encyclopedia)**

So it was from La Rochelle that the fleet assembled and embarked for the Gulf of St Lawrence in 1749, for La Rochelle had had a continued connection with the New World. See Map 4-5. Map 4-5 shows the relationship between La Rochelle and Louisbourg.

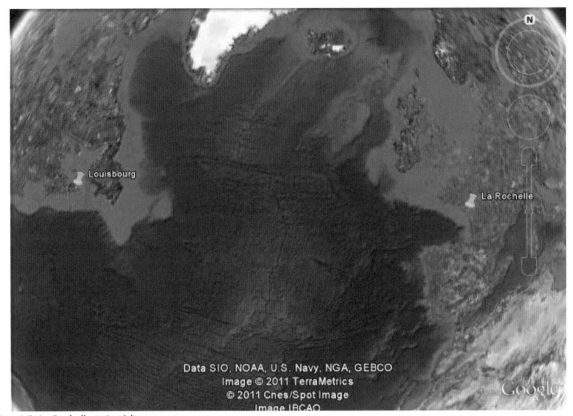

Map 4-5: La Rochelle to Louisbourg

CHAPTER 5 - IN THE NEW WORLD, AT LOUIS-BOURG

Time Span: 1749-1758

Our last chapter found Charles, Marie, and their children Alexis, and François leaving France from the port of La Rochelle and setting sail for a place called Louisbourg. Although we don't know the exact reason why they moved, we suspect that the prospect of a grant of £150 from the King of France played a large role in their decision. But why would the King offer this money to his subjects and what was so important about this place called Louisbourg?

Louisbourg

Louisbourg's location on an island at the entrance to the important St Lawrence River gave it a strategic role in the New World, and it passed back and forth between France and England. But we have to go back and review some history to find our answers, for that whole region was in a state of flux for a century or more as it developed.

Prior to 1497, the whole area from Massachusetts Bay to the mouth of the St Lawrence River was inhabited by native peoples who had gradually moved into the area from other parts of the continent. 1497 marked the landfall by John Cabot, who then claimed the area for England. Within a short time the area had been visited by fishing and whaling expeditions by the French, the Portuguese, the English, and the Basques, but no group established any communities in this new land at that time. Those seasonal visits continued for another century or so, but by the end of the sixteenth century permanent settlements were being formed by Europeans. The French, for example, opened a trading post at Tadoussac in 1599 and Pierre Dugua tried one on St. Croix Island in 1604. The latter was moved to Port Royal the next year. Samuel de Champlain founded Quebec in 1608. The English tried a settlement at Popham ME around 1607 but this, too, failed. The English then had a settlement at Plymouth MA in 1620, followed by the Massachusetts Bay Colony in 1629. From these various starts settlements soon sprung up along the Gulf of Maine and up the St Lawrence River, for these were locations readily accessible from the sea. Map 5-1 shows the locations of some of the key pre-1700 settlements. The locations marked with a red box were founded by British interests, those in black by the French.

Louisbourg was located in a region called Acadia, and we will hear more about Acadia in later chapters. The term "Acadia" refers to the region settled by the French that included much of present-day Nova Scotia, Prince Edward Island, New Brunswick, and Maine. The original settlement was at

Port Royal (see Map 1) but they soon spread to other areas as well. The French who settled Acadia came from many parts of France, so they were not a homogenous group.

Map 5-1: Settlements prior to 1700

Laying Claim to the Land

Though explorers and fishing crews from several nationalities often visited the area, it was Britain and France who claimed lands for their own. Map 5-2 shows how those two nations roughly divided up the land between them. Remember, though, that there were no formal borders at this time and their claims often overlapped. Again, the red areas show British claims and the white the French claims. The year 1713 marked the end of (the then-current) war between Britain and France; France lost and ceded the portion of Acadia that included the Nova Scotia peninsula to Britain in the Treaty of Utrecht. France kept Île Royale (Cape Breton Island) and Île Saint-Jean (Prince Edward Island), so the French interests did not totally disappear from the North Atlantic community. France also maintained a strong hold in the St Lawrence region.

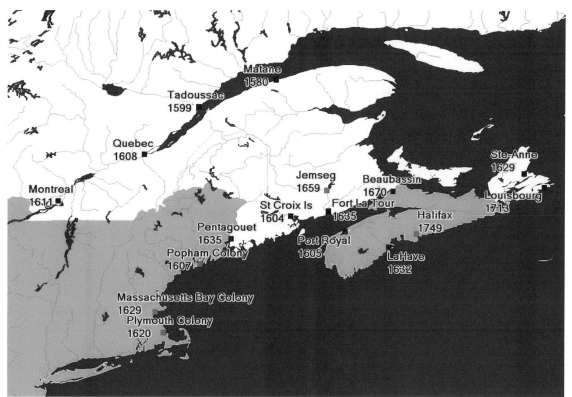

Map 5-2: Rough Division of National Interests after 1713

However war between the two resumed in 1744 and lasted until 1763 with a truce between 1748 and 1754. The Treaty of Paris in 1763 gave all the holdings in the region to Britain. In fact, Britain gained possession of all lands east of the Appalachian Mountains as shown in Map 5-3, except for the Madeleine Islands east of the Nova Scotia peninsula.

Compare this with our family's timeline:

1. *Charles Violet was born in 1716, Marie David was born in 1705; they were married in 1741*
2. *Alexis Hilaret was born in 1733*
3. *Helie Violet was born in 1743, died in 1746; François Violet was born in 1744*
4. *The family moved to Louisbourg in 1749*
5. *Marie David died in Louisbourg in 1751*
6. *Charles and his new wife, Marie Sudois, returned to France in 1759*

Map 5-3: Britain Holds All Lands by the Treaty of 1763

Development of Louisbourg

The French wanted to fortify to protect their holdings in Nova Scotia and on Cape Breton Island (Île Royale). They had constructed a fort at Fort Ste-Anne (see Map 5-4) around 1629 but had abandoned it around 1641. After the 1713 treaty, 72 years later, they started building a port and naval support facilities at the site of the old Fort Ste-Anne, but icy winter conditions made them rethink this plan and they moved instead to another harbor in the southeastern part of the island. This harbor was well protected and largely ice-free, and they made it the winter port for French naval forces in the North Atlantic. This new place was named Louisbourg, after King Louis XIV.

Construction of a fort at Louisbourg began in 1719 and continued into 1745. This was an important port and facility for the French and they spent large sums to develop the fortifications and the supporting community. The first lighthouse in the area was built in 1734 to help show sailors the coast during foggy conditions. The community of Louisbourg developed into an important port for the French, with a bustling economy based on fishing on the Grand Banks.

The British intended to extend their hold on the continent and began battling with the French over the French holdings in the area. The British made a siege of Louisbourg in 1745 and again in 1758. The first siege was actually done by New Englander forces supported by the British Navy, and the New Englander forces won their battle when the fort capitulated in June. Fortress Louisbourg was designed to defend against attacks from the sea, but the New Englanders made their approach by land behind the fortifications and were able to defeat them. The French tried to retake the fort the next year, but were not successful.

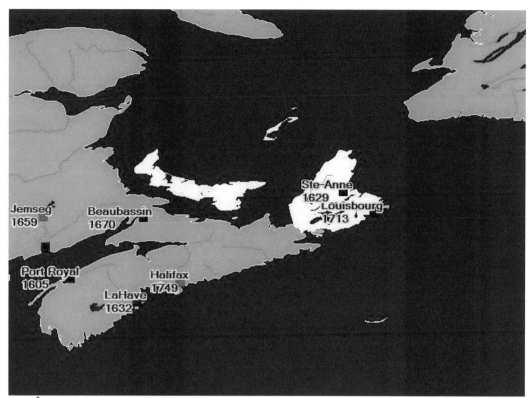

Map 5-4: Île Royale and Fort Louisbourg

But three years later, much to the disgust of the New Englanders who had taken it in 1745, Louisbourg was returned to France under terms of the Treaty of Aix-la-Chapelle. The British then developed their own fortifications at what became Halifax (1749), and this became the largest British Navy base in North America.

The New Englanders were upset because France wanted to cut off their access to lands to the west on the continent that the New Englanders had come to think of as their own. Military action started locally with the French-and-Indian War in 1755 but soon expanded into European conflicts two years later with the Seven Years War. A second siege of Louisbourg was undertaken by the British in 1758, which resulted in the French surrender. The British destroyed the fort and town at Louisbourg to try to prevent the French from gaining a hold in the area again. Map 5-5 shows the location of Fortress Louisbourg, now a Canadian National Historic Site.

Map 5-5: Location of Fortress Louisbourg on Cape Breton Island

Back to the family

But the last got ahead of our story, for Charles, Marie, and family arrived in 1749. Charles was 33 years of age, Marie 44, Alexis 16, and François 5. They sailed to Louisbourg on a ship that was part of a large convoy sent from France by the King to improve and strengthen fortifications and the French presence in Louisbourg. The large convoy transported the new Governor, Charles Desherbiers de la Raliere, along with 500 military personnel and a civil population of just under two thousand men, women, and children to Louisbourg. Once traces of the previous inhabitants were removed, French authorities planned to move even more families to Louisbourg. Most of the people in the convoy were familiar with the town because they had lived there prior to its capture in 1745, and had been given the opportunity to return. This was not the case for Charles and his family though, as this was their first voyage to the New World.

When this convoy arrived at Louisbourg on June 29th the fort was still occupied by the British. They had to wait until the next day, June 30th, to enter the harbor. The actual transfer of possession did not happen until July 23rd, and the British troops did not sail away until July 30th.

The Louisbourg of July 1749 was not exactly the place the French had sailed from in 1745. The effects of the siege and of the subsequent occupation by Anglo-American and then British troops had brought many changes. Some houses and storehouses remained unrepaired from the British bombardment of 1745.

(Ed Note: For more complete information and history of Louisbourg we strongly recommend "Louisbourg from its foundation to its fall 1713-1758" by J.S. McLennan, and "Endgame 1758" by A. J. B. Johnston. Approximately one-fourth of the site has been reconstructed and is operated as Fortress of Louisbourg National Historic Site of Canada.)

Charles' years in Louisbourg were filled with difficulties

Charles only stayed in Louisbourg from 1749-1759, and his decade there was fraught with many misfortunes. First, the death of his spouse Marie David in May 1751, then barely one month later, he is involved in bankruptcy proceedings wherein he was obliged to assign his stepson Alexis Hilaret (child of Marie David) and his own son François to subrogate guardians. After marrying Marianne Sudois in June of 1751, they lost their first child Therese, born in April 1752, who died in January 1753.

Charles' name appears many more times after 1751 in court proceedings dealing with his now successful roofing business.

In addition to the above Charles' family had to sustain themselves through several medical epidemics, a seven week siege which brought on food scarcity and fear of death from bombardment, and finally deportation back to France.

Several people played a significant role in helping us reach our current understanding of how the Violettes came to be on this continent, but two took the work a step further in writing up their research for the rest of us to follow. One of these was Maurice Violette, VFA #14, of Augusta ME (1921-2004). We read in the chapter on Villejésus how his work helped bridge the Atlantic Ocean gap. Research by Maurice and by Rita Violette Lippé had traced our ancestor François from northern Maine back to Louisbourg on Cape Breton Island (part of what is now Nova Scotia). But there the trail stopped, until a fortuitous visit by some French to Augusta allowed Maurice to make the leap back to Saintes and Villejésus.

Maurice presented his initial work at the Violette Family Association Reunion in Augusta ME in 1978 and later printed his talk in a pamphlet titled ***"The Life and Times of Charles Violet 1751 Louisbourg Isle Royale, Acadia"***. We decided to republish that work here in total rather than include parts in the various chapters into which we are organizing this work. His monumental work deserves to be told in his own voice. We will insert *"Ed notes"* in the text that follows to tell you about information that became available after Maurice published the work from which we are quoting. Maurice continued in his research and made two or more trips to France in this effort; he was part of the group trip of Association members in 1982 that we reported on in Chapters 1 and 2. Then, in 1984, Maurice published a booklet titled ***"The Violette Family"*** which expanded on his earlier work included here. Because of the detail Maurice included in his 1984 work we will publish it in its entirety in Chapter 7 of this book.

(Begin Maurice's text. Maurice's text is shown here as indented text in the font as below)

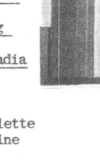

The Life and Times

of Charles Violet

1751 Louisbourg

Isle Royale, Acadia

by:
   Maurice Violette
   Augusta, Maine

A great awakening of interest in genealogy has taken place in recent years; especially since the celebration of our American Bi-Centennial. It seems that everyone is searching for his or her roots. There is to be no stone unturned by over-zealous, almost fanatic exponents of the past. In some manner, we all have become victim of the compelling need to know and the compulsive dedication, scratching for every available lead to uncover our antecedents. However, we who are deeply committed to this search should go into the past with an open mind, with a broad sense of evaluation, ever ready to be surprised as to what we may find. It can be shocking as well as gratifying.

It is noteworthy to add that the more things change - the more they remain the same. As we pour over old script, yellowed, mutilated and un-decipherable parchment and fuzzy microfilm records, we find that they who preceded us were faced with the same everyday concerns that make our lives so hectic. They as well were faced with legal problems, with sociological and economic advantages and disadvantages, and political upheavals which would be considered insurmountable in our day and age. As we contemplate the hardship and the trials and tribulations of the ancients, we become thankful that conditions in our modern era provide us with a greater sense of security and comfort as compared with the unsettled and uncertain living conditions of colonial days.

Can you imagine moving your entire family today in a wilderness for two or three hundred miles? Can you imagine scratching for food on foot, by river, or through hostile settlements, looked upon as enemies, constantly hounding you and providing massive opposition and barriers to your customs and beliefs? Can you imagine the denial of having the benefit of clergy for routine ceremonies such as baptisms, marriages, and even funerals for the departed? Can you imagine having to settle in remote areas of the countryside, in the wilds of the Kennebecasis

River in New Brunswick in order to avoid repressive and tyrannical dictates of oppressors? Such was a way of life. Customs and traditions were in a constant state of flux and they were quite different from what we accept today. We gain a semblance of the attitudes of the ancients by the manner in which events were recorded. This is a most important aspect for us to retain and remember.

The Violette genealogy provides the same as well as many other mysteries for us to solve that others have faced in their quest for knowledge about the past. In searching for information, from time to time, most of us have come up against a blank wall from which there seems to be no available information as to what occurred before. Prior to 1751 the Violette genealogy search is replete with unanswered questions and we can only conjecture as to what happened from the scant records and scribblings of ancient scholars and scribes recording information with a quill pen. Such archaic writings as we can find, with shortcomings as confusing "s' s" and "f's" as well as the open-ended "a's" and "o's" with consonants shaped like "u' s" all entered contiguously word on word, do not provide us with a clear and concise picture of events as they occurred. The archaic language in use is a constant obstacle to the amateur historian. There were so few who could or would make the necessary records. Le Grand Dérangement itself bears evidence to the cruel and hard days in which the recording of information not only became impossible but in many areas, if not destroyed, were put in writing years later based on the memory of those concerned.

When viewing little bits of information here and there however, we are able to arrive at an interestingly intriguing and fascinating journey through time. We participate in a historical meal and an almost credible inventory of the life of the first Violet in the New World.

Charles VIOLET, the first of the line and I might add, the only one which can be found, is responsible for our dilemma. He left confusing information. It is recorded that he was married to Marie David, the widow of Jean Plairet, of Louisbourg, Isle Royale, Acadia. This marriage brought forth a son, François. It is also recorded that Marie David had an eighteen year old son named Alexis Plairet, issue of her first marriage. *(Ed note: We have used the name Hilaret in previous chapters instead of Plairet.)* No record can be found of the union of Charles Violet and Marie David. *(Ed note: those records have been found and are reported in earlier chapters of this book.)* The problems become compounded with Charles' second marriage to Marie Anne Sudois in which his father is listed as Louis VIOLET of Belle-Eglise, Vigneron, County of Angouleme, in France. It is assumed that this information was furnished by Charles Violet himself to this extent and complicates our search today inasmuch as there is no existing information concerning a "Louis Violet" anywhere. Another journal reveals that Marie Anne Sudois originated from LaRochelle in France in the immediate area of Vigneron. This is cognac country. *(Ed note: Maurice and others found more records concerning Charles Violet, Marie David, and their parents after Maurice published the work we quote from here. That later information was included in the earlier chapters of the current work.)*

Furnishing further aggravation in the matter is the fact in Jan-Feb 1759, a notation is found in a register in LaRochelle, France, that Charles Violet is now residing in that city and later in March of 1759, has joined his wife in Rochefort, France. No mention of his children is made. Was he deported? Did he return on his own? Were there family or community problems? Were there financial or sociological pitfalls? So much is left unanswered.

Once more the records become quite unsettling when documents are found in the Fortress of Louisbourg in which all of Charles' effects and general articles of life with Marie David are inventoried and assigned to "friends and neighbors" in Louisbourg. There is no disputing this area as these are records of court rulings dated June 28, 1751, in which Charles is pleading with the Royal Court in Louisbourg for a ruling on bankruptcy. Another document of the same date is found and reveals that his only son, François, and stepson Alexis Plairet, are also awarded to the same "friends and neighbors" who are to become their substitute guardians. On this date, Charles Violet divested himself of everything that tied him to his first wife, Marie David, our maternal, original grandmother in the land. Analysing *(sic)* the various date of events in this period provided an interesting bit of information which adds color to the possible moral values of Charles Violet. In one register we find that Marie David died on May 26, 1751, and another entry indicates his marriage to Marie Anne Sudois approximately one month later, June 29, 1751, after publication of a single ban. *(Ed note: In the Roman Catholic Church the parish priest reads from the pulpit on three successive Sundays a notice that the couple intends to be married by the Church so that anyone who may have a protest or reason against the marriage can make their thoughts known. These are called the "bans of marriage".)* Marie David is interred in the parish cemetery of Louisbourg.

From the meager records available, we can reconstruct the important events in the life of Charles Violet, circa 1751 and following, but how do we explain the fact there is a void of information on the other side of that line--even in France, there is no information to be found, neither in LaRochelle nor in Rochefort before or after 1759. Another approach is evidently required to find the answer. *(Ed note: This publication by Maurice was done in 1978, but subsequent research by Maurice and others have found the records of Charles' French origins that we reported in previous chapters in this work and his life after Louisbourg that will be reported in later chapters.)*

The early days of the Violet line in Acadia provide prime examples of surprises which await all of us in the past. The most traumatic of these is the document which was uncovered in the Genealogy Center of the University of Moncton. It concerns the origin of the Violettes du Madawaska. It is entitled L'Origine des Jaillet, de Bouctouche et des Violettes du Madawaska.

I quote as translated from original French of 1890: "From December 1889 through the commencement of July, 1890, M. Le Grand Vicar Michaud, Curé de Bouctouche, under the pen name of Sylvain published in the columns of the Monitor a long series of articles entitled Some Notes on Bouctouche." I have taken what he said of the Violettes of Madawaska and the Jaillets of Bouctouche as follows: "The origin of the Violettes is absolutely the same as those of the Jaillets. The first Violette, so says the tradition, was a little cabin boy who originated from Switzerland, and of a huguenot family. *(Ed note: The Huguenots were French Protestants most of whom eventually came to follow the teachings of John Calvin, and who, due to religious persecution, were forced to flee France to other countries in the sixteenth and seventeenth centuries. Ref www.huguenot.netnation.com)* He deserted his ship upon which he had signed somewhere in St. John (Kennebequachie). He found his way to Fredericton (St. Anne - Ekopahog) where he met some French people and lived among them. He became Catholic and wed an Acadienne. It is said that he had a truly angelic voice and the missionaries who instructed him in the dogma of the religion also taught him at the same time in the plain chant for which he had a great esteem and aptitude. His descendants have become very numerous in the Madawaska area. It is also said that the name of Swiss is often given to the Jaillets of Bouctouche. As well, in Madawaska, we call the Violettes Swiss and that portends their origin.

This was a strange development indeed. For over two hundred years we have expounded on the fact that we are of a "purist" French strain and this tarnished, frayed, yellow piece of paper refutes all. Swiss no less! And Protestant to boot!

The following is not designed to be a pronouncement as the true manifest concerning the origin and life of Charles Violet of Louisbourg but when taking into consideration the events which occurred, the non-availability of information where there should be information, such items as were recorded, and the correlation of events of Le Grand Dérangement with the factual accounts of the settling of the Territory of Madawaska, we can add credence to the following ties with the past and of Charles Violet of 1751 of Louisbourg, Isle Royale, Acadia. It is your option to make up your own conclusions. *(Emphasis in original)*

(Ed note: From his earlier research Maurice went on at length in this publication about the possibility of a Swiss origin, but this has been discounted with later research by him and by others, so the reader should not place much validity to the conjectures offered by Maurice in this earlier work.)

First. In the origin of the Violette of Madawaska by Michaud, it is noted that the first Violette was a Swiss sailor, a cabin or deck boy, who married an acadienne. The evidence points dramatically that this was François, son of Charles Violet of Louisbourg, who sought to find a better life at sea away from his guardians and also because Charles, his father, had gone to France in 1759. The acadienne appears to have been Marie Luce Thibodeau. A record of this union is found in the Genealogical Library of the University of Moncton, in reference to the register of

the Reverend Abbe Charles-François Bailly de Messein, Missionary from Caraquet which states this marriage occurred on May 6, 1770. François would have
been twenty-five years of age and would have been between fourteen and sixteen years of age as a cabin boy. In this period, François would have had ample
time to meet Marie Luce Thibodeau and receive instructions to become a Catholic. Like his father Charles, he too had married after publication of but a single
ban. From this episode, we gain further insight of life in this harsh period. It is
noted that a daughter, Marguerite, was born July 25, 1770, less than three
months after the Nuptial Blessing. Was this an accident? Not necessarily so. An
obscure entry is discovered that François and Marie Thibodeau were married in a
civil ceremony in 1769. It is also interesting to note that on the occasion of the
Nuptial Benediction of this marriage the record shows that François' mother's
name, Marie David, was omitted and a blank dotted line appears where her
name should have been recorded as the legitimate wife of Charles Violet. This
verifies the cruel and emotional treatment afforded François when at the age of
six and a half he was awarded to "friends and neighbors" in Louisbourg by his father. He could not remember his mother's name for the record although his father Charles is noted. Another custom comes to light when entries in the official
records state that the first three children of François and Marie Luce Thibodeau
were baptized in 1774, four years after the Nuptial Blessing by an Acadian Reverend Joseph M. Bourg, when he visited Kennebequachie. This tells us and explains
the discrepancy between the dates of marriages and the birth of the first born
resulting from unions when Acadians did not have the benefit of clergy to perform church rites and records were made years later when the occasion presented itself. It became a simple matter when a couple decided to marry, they
would obtain the permission of their parents and either lived together by mutual
consent or would obtain a civil marriage in lieu of a church service.

Second. Are we Jaillets or are we Violets? How can we account for the change of
name from Jaillet to Violet if this were the actual evolution? Name corruption
does not seem to be the answer. However, when studying the court rulings assigning all the worldly goods of Charles Violet to "friends and neighbors" in Louisbourg, as well as of his only son François and his stepson Alexis Plairet also of the
same city, a connection can be made which might be the answer to the change
of name. It is noted that in those days in writing with a quill pen, all words were
of the ancient flourish which was the custom and of a type to be found in monas-
teries where monks record histories and reproduce other works by hand. It is
noted that all capital "V's" and "J's" are made in the same fashion! They look
alike! Either can pass for either! Further, the custom of leaving "o's" and "a's"
open-ended shaped like "u's" complete the change. "VIOLLET" looks exactly like
"JAILLET" when written in ancient script. It can be surmised that this would have
been acceptable to Charles Violet as a means of achieving acceptance in a
French-Catholic community like Louisbourg using a French name instead of the

foreign "Jaillet". *(Ed note: We think that subsequent records found in France and described in earlier chapters of this book refute the idea that either Charles or François were Swiss, since we have records that both were born in France and baptized and married in the Catholic Church as was Charles' father, Louis.)*

WHO WHAT and WHY then is Charles Violet of 1751 Louisbourg, Isle Royale, Acadia? Some of these questions may never be resolved. A look at the inventory of his worldly possessions in 1751 reveals that his household contained the barest of necessities. A couple of beds, a couple of chests, a sparse if not the minimum of dishes and utensils for daily necessity. Very few clothes and likewise a few blankets and towels. Most everything well worn and in bad condition. An iron stove for heating. An open hearth with its stew pots and hooks. It is recorded that he was a successful businessman in the town and that his occupation was that of a roofer. Success did not come to Charles Violet before 1755 as he apparently had married into a well-to-do- family and was able to circumvent his early problem of bankruptcy. Few tools were noted to provide the proof as to his exact vocation but we must accept the Royal Court's identification as a roofer. Two small hammers and a pair of pliers, small tools, were inventoried. A roofer in 1751 meant that he was proficient in the installation of thatched and slate roofs which were in vogue during the period. Other items were a table and three straw-filled chairs. Strange when there were four members in the family. This portends there might have been some family problems involving the older son of Marie David Plairet and that he might not have been living with them and, in the end, could have precipitated the guardianship case by "friends and neighbors."
In the attic, two flour barrels were found to contain 667 books worth sixty-six Pounds. This was quite a revelation by the fact that Charles was illiterate and no where can we find his signature on the many documents available whereas we do find his mark. It can be surmised that Marie David was well-educated and the books were hers. At the time of divestiture, Charles Violet was worth 458 Pounds and 19 Sols. A Pound then was the equivalent value of one Pound of Silver. Twenty Sols, an ancient French coin, made up one Pound. This was apparently below the normal standard for the time when living conditions were primitive at best. The unfriendly community atmosphere of a catholic society undoubtedly caused bankruptcy in 1751 for Charles Violet. *(Ed note: The current editors discount Maurice's proposition that Charles was not part of the "catholic" community. Charles, his father, Louis, and his son François were all baptized and married in the Catholic Church as the records found later prove.)* He could not prevail against these odds. It is natural to assume that he could not gain community support possibly due to his background as a Swiss and a Protestant. It is quite feasible that the Sudois arrangement required that Charles disown his children before he could remarry and François, age six and a half, became the victim by the fact that he could not remember his own true mother's name nineteen years later. It must be concluded that Charles Violet's journey to France in 1759 alludes to us in the modern era that we accept François as the first Violette in our line. But the fact still remains that Charles was the first and through him we must seek further.

What happened to Charles Violet following the court proceedings? He cultivated a new set of friends and acquaintances as evidenced by the godparents of the children of his new family with the Sudois line. He sired four as we know. Thérèse, died after eight months of life on April 22, 1752; Hiérome, born June 17, 1753; Marie Anne LeViolet, born August 21, 1755 and Charlotte born October 10, 1756. It is seen that in the birth of Marie Anne, Charles has now added the "Le" with its connotation of aristocracy. After all, it was at this point that he became a respected merchant in town.

It is possible that Charles had a speech impediment or habit. His illiteracy provides us with this assumption. He might have pronounced his "J's" like "H's" as the birth records show his second born of the Sudois marriage as "Hiérome" and later it is found to be written as "Jérome". As he could not read, he was incapable of correcting the record. We do not find any other children in this new line of Charles Violet after 1756. *(Ed note: We now have records of another child, Marianne Violet, born Dec 9, 1759 in Rochefort, France. We also have records that Charles married yet a third time on Apr 13, 1761 in Rochefort and that this marriage produced another child, Jean-Nicolas, born Jan 18, 1766 in Rochefort.)*

With the fall of the French of Acadia, it can also be said that Charles did participate in the siege of Louisbourg in 1758 by the fact that he was there and many of his friends were in the military. Whether he actually fired a shot is not known as he is not listed as a member of their defending forces in any capacity but we must assume that all inhabitants took part as they became beneficiary to its outcome.

The record of Charles Violet of Louisbourg, 1751 through 1759, arrives at the point of extinction. This was possibly due to the policies of the English who systematically began exporting, expelling all to the lower colonies, to the hinterlands, and to Europe. *(Ed note: Louisbourg and Île Royale came under British control again in 1759 and Charles and family were deported along with the French fleet and returned to France.)*

The last recorded information to be filed is a short two sentences filed at the University of Moncton which reads: "Charles Violet, Roofer. Charles Violet--has taken location in La Rochelle (France) through the 31st of January and moved out on 14 February. Marie Anne Sudois his wife IDEM, is in Rochefort with her husband since the 1st of March. Noted in La Rochelle on April 28, 1759."

It is now a fact that Charles has emigrated to France with his family although no children are mentioned and has taken residence with the Sudois' in the Bordeaux wine producing valley. *(Ed note: We now know that Charles did not emigrate but was deported to France in 1759 when the British took over Louisbourg again. Also, we can ignore Maurice's discussion that follows about being Swiss.)* How did he accomplish this trip to France? It could be that politics came into play and perhaps using his neutral Swiss background and his status as a successful merchant obtained authority from the English to sail for France. He certainly did not follow the path of the Acadians who were deported to Belle-Isle en Mer during this period from Louisbourg. It is noted that the word Négociant appears at the beginning of the last notation concerning his location in France implying that possibly he had applied, negotiated with the authorities, and was granted permission to leave Acadia, late in 1758.

We have all faced challenges which appear to be insurmountable. No less challenging is the Violette heritage prior to 1751. In France, there can be found almost negligible information. According to M. F. Rene Perron of Sevre, France, who sought to assist me in a possible lead, an exhaustive search produced little success. The only valid information is indeed the arrival of Charles Violet in LaRochelle in 1759. Mr. Perron compliments his findings with the fact that during the French Revolution of 1789, a tremendous amount of records were destroyed by the "Sans Culottes" and forever lost. *(Ed note: Again, we refer the reader to those earlier records reported in earlier chapters.)*

Although we have reached an impasse to seek out Charles Violet in Europe this is not important to us as this line took another course and became half-cousins in Europe. We must not be discouraged because our true heritage lies with the Violet-David union and that is where we may still find our deeper roots and the real truth. If indeed our true name is Jaillet can you not be convinced that we may yet be able to tie in the missing link to our genealogical puzzle, that elusive tie to what happened prior to l75l? As for the development and growth of the Violettes in North America, it is a matter of record. We can begin with Charles Violet of Louisbourg, Isle Royale, Acadia, followed by François who married three times -- fourteen children from his first marriage - five from his second - and four from his third. The first wife was Marie Luce Thibodeau in a civil ceremony in Kennebequachie in 1769; the second wife Rose Cormier in St. Basile, Madawaska, July 4, 1803; and finally Genevieve Tardif in St. Basile, Madawaska on January 17, 1814. Records reveal that the last child was born when François was seventy-nine years of age! The records also show that "he died suddenly at the age of eighty-five". I don't wonder. François in his life had performed many tasks. As the patriarch of the clan he was at one time or other a blacksmith, a laborer, and a farmer.

The Violette traces have been well documented from the Kennebecasis River in New Brunswick through Ekopahog (Frederickton) to St. Basile on the shore of the upper reaches of the St. John River and the settlement at Van Buren, Maine, in the year 1790. The descendants of Charles, which include you, if all were living today would number over 140,000. This proves the old adage that "there are

More Violettes than People". So when we meet someone with the name of Violette in North America we can be very sincere in our greeting to each other. Just say "Hello Cousin" because that's what we are!

(End of Maurice's text)

The Fortress Louisbourg Historical Site

Fortress Louisbourg has had a long history and has been attacked and placed under siege many times over the centuries. It was built by the French for two reasons: to protect Quebec City, a major French holding in North America, and to support a significant fishing industry. Louisbourg's site was protected by a reef to the south and batteries on a large island in the harbor, so British ships were required to negotiate a narrow 500-foot wide channel and could be easily attacked. Though relatively secure from sea attack, Fortress Louisbourg was not so secure from land attack.

Construction started around 1716 and by 1719 the population was 823; by 1726 it was 1296; in 1734, 1616; in 1752 (while Charles, Marie, and their family lived there) it was 4174. The fortifications at Louisbourg took over 28 years to complete.

Louisbourg maintained a large economy. As a port it was the third largest in North America – only Boston and Philadelphia were larger. The North American fishing trade employed over 10,000 people and much of it was shipped out of Louisbourg.

Louisbourg was far more than a fort. It was a large enough city to have a commercial district, a residential district, military arenas, marketplaces, inns, taverns and suburbs, and so needed a population of people to operate those businesses.

Photo 5-1: An aerial view of Fortress Louisbourg today, showing the partial restorations

Photo 5-2: A view of houses and commercial buildings in restored Fortress Louisbourg

Photo 5-3: Barracks that housed military staff

Photo 5-4: Reenactment of dancing and costumes in Louisbourg

The photos above are from Wikipedia Commons and show conditions today in Louisbourg. Louisbourg has been reconstructed by the Canadian Government starting in 1961. It is now a national park by Parks Canada as a National Historical Site. The reconstruction used stones from the original fort to the extent possible, and other construction materials were selected to be as true to original construction as possible. Unemployed coal miners from the industrial Cape Breton area were trained in French masonry techniques from the 18th century so that the replicas would be accurate. The current reconstruction includes about one-fourth of the original town and fort.

APPENDIX 5-A

A Personal Story by Dave Violette, VFA #621

I took the opportunity during our travels following the Violette Family Reunion 2011 to visit the Louisbourg area to learn more about where my ancestors had lived. I wanted to walk the streets and get the feel for the place where Charles, Marie David, and François had lived during the period 1749-1758. My visit was during late August so the place was open for visits and there were a moderate number of visitors during my visits. The National Park also has a few dozen people dressed in period costumes that engage in programmed activities to illustrate aspects of life in Louisbourg in 1745. The portrayed timeframe is just before the British and New Englanders laid siege to Louisbourg in 1745, as described in this chapter, and at the peak of a long phase of French development of the port and city that had started around 1713. The French community in Louisbourg was well developed and the society and community there had had many years to mature.

The reconstruction of the fortified town of Louisbourg by the government of Canada was started in 1961 and has resulted in approximately 25% of the town being rebuilt. The buildings are authentic and even have original materials used where they could be found. But all reconstruction has been faithful to the methods and materials of construction in use at the time.

Our ancestors arrived in Louisbourg in 1749, however, after the siege of 1745 resulted in the British taking over Louisbourg and subsequently letting go of it three years later. So the Louisbourg we see today in reconstruction shows what it would have looked like prior to the siege and bombardments in 1745 and prior to any changes made by the British during their occupation of 1745-48. Remember that the reason Charles went to Louisbourg was to work on reconstruction of Louisbourg when the French took it back.

So the Louisbourg we see today is different from what Charles and François saw when they lived there and we have no idea what "their" Louisbourg looked like. However, we can suppose that the French did not change their styles of construction during this period and they probably resurrected the layout of the town following the scheme they had used during 1719-1745.

François was five years old when he came to Louisbourg and was fourteen when his father returned to France; he was assigned to (and probably moved in with) a surrogate guardian when he was seven. During my visits to Louisbourg I tried to look at Louisbourg from two different points of view: as it might have been for a child of those ages, and as an adult of today trying to understand the history.

Part of trying to see Louisbourg through those eyes required trying to determine where Charles and Francois lived, to see if it was in one of the structures that have been reconstructed. We have no specific address or property description to help us in this search, but there is some information that might be helpful. Maurice Violette found records that in 1753 Charles contracted for a house on Rue D'Orleans (see Chapter 7 and Chapter 8) about one block away from the Citadel (see Chapter 8). Charles apparently wanted not only a residence but also a place to have a boutique. Maurice also describes Charles' house to be near the hospital and the Convent of Notre Dame.

The lease contract does not give the location of the property but does give the name of the owner, Allain Le Gras. After some searching I was able to find that M. Le Gras owned some property on Lots G and H in Block 19, on Rue D'Orleans. The map below (Map 5A-1) shows where that property was located and indicates where the hospital and convent were. The map was taken from the document published by Yvon Leblanc, former restoration architect for the Louisbourg restoration project. See http://fortress.uccb.ns.ca/**yvon**leblanc/ for more information.

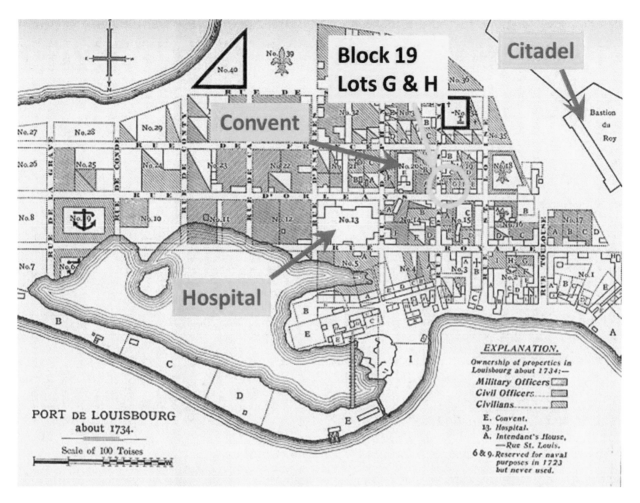

Map 5A-1: Map showing location of hospital, convent, citadel, and Block 19

The description contained in the contract language included in Maurice's text (see Chapter 8) seems to describe an arrangement of buildings that agrees with what is portrayed in Figure 5A-2 below; this figure was taken from the research documents prepared by Yvon Leblanc to determine what had been in Louisbourg and how it should be restored. Figure 5A-2 shows an enlargement of the Block 19 area.

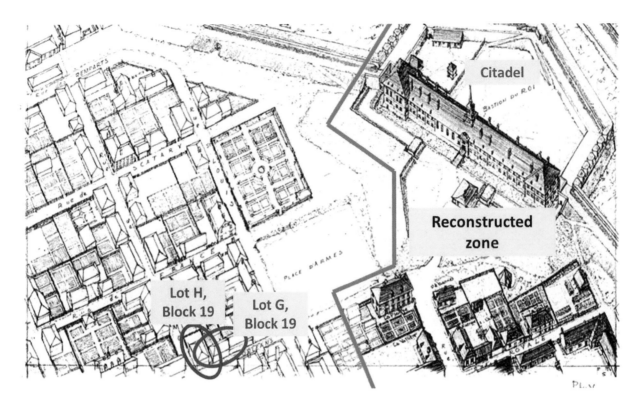

Figure 5A-1: Map showing buildings on Block 19 and surrounding area

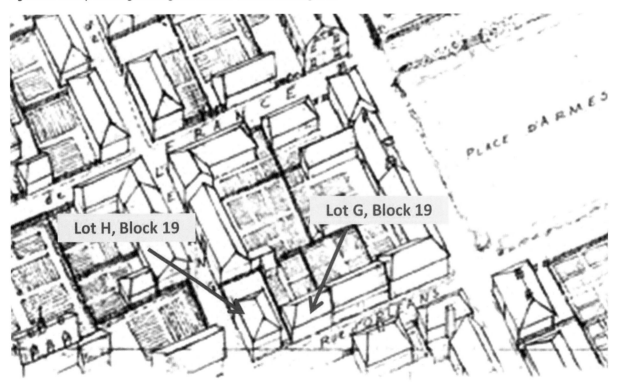

Figure 5A-2: Probable shape of buildings on Block 19

Unfortunately, the current reconstruction did not include Block 19; as can be seen in Figure 5A-1 reconstruction stopped a block and a half short (see blue line). The site of the hospital and convent are marked in the field, but none of the other buildings on Rue D'Orleans outside the reconstruction area are identified.

But the Block 19 residence came after Charles's bankruptcy in 1751, and we do not know where Charles and his family lived prior to that. We can assume that it was further away from the center of town, however, since the homes nearer the center were occupied by military officers, merchants, and governmental officials. The most likely area is somewhere in the area near the top in Photo 5-1.

After Charles's bankruptcy François and Alexis were sent to live with their surrogate parents so they would not have lived in the Block 19 residence.

We know from the court proceedings reported by Maurice Violette (see Chapter 7) that François became the ward of Jacques Bognais de la Boissiere and Alexis the ward of Pierre Jauvin. (Both surrogates' names are spelled differently in different sections of the Petition and Judgment, so we are not exactly sure how to spell them.) We have tried to track down more info about Bognais and where his family might have lived, but without success so far. We think it likely that Bognais was a military officer but have not yet found any record of him in that capacity. We have found some baptismal records for two Bognais children that show military officers or people related to the military being godparents for the Bognais children, and that is a basis for suggesting that Bognais was military himself.

In trying to see Louisbourg through François' eyes I have tried to imagine what he might have been doing during those years. He was young – seven years old – when he was assigned to the Bognais family so prior to that he probably did not have much in the way of duties. Assuming Charles's family lived in the outskirts of the town François probably spent most of his time in the area around their residence. It is not likely that he wandered the 8-12 blocks from where he lived into the center of town. We also do not know where the Bognais family lived, though we have tried to find references for this. Since Bognais had his family in Louisbourg he must have been an officer and as an officer he must have had a French title. His name as given in the records seems to indicate this: the "de la Boissiere" part tells us the reference for his title but we have not yet found more details about that holding. But as an officer he most likely lived closer into town, such as in the general area where Block 19 was located.

We also don't know how and when François left Louisbourg. It is likely that Bognais, if he survived the bombardment of 1758, returned to France with the military after Louisbourg was lost to the British. Did François leave with the Bognais family? He would have been fourteen at that time and not likely to have been emancipated. Then too, we do not know where the Bognais family went to when they left.

So, Francois might have been with the Bognais family from around age seven to age fourteen. We don't know what life as a surrogate child was like; were they treated as children of the family or were they treated more like servants who had to work to repay the debt of their natural parents?

In any case, as I walked the streets of Louisbourg I could imagine François running along the street, perhaps on an errand to pick up an item or two at a store, or bakery, or tavern. When I stood in the former Engineer's back yard and saw the gardens there I could imagine François working at tending the vegetables growing there. When I saw the goats in the pen at the residence near the King's Bastion I could imagine François perhaps feeding the animals that would provide milk and cheese for his family. When I walked along the quay I could imagine François standing on the street watching in amazement and wonder at all the activity in the harbor filled with ships as load after load came ashore with materials to support the Louisbourg community.

The photos on the next pages show scenes in the reconstructed Louisbourg and were taken during my visit in August 2011. The period portrayed in Reconstructed Louisbourg is 1745; though this is just before the siege and capture by the British and New Englanders in 1748 Louisbourg as reconstructed by the French starting in 1749 probably looked very similar to what is portrayed here.

In selecting the photos to show here I tried to find images of scenes that François might have seen in his time.

Photo 5-5: Soldiers at King's Bastion

Photo 5-6: Inside church

Photo 5-7: Soldiers marching

Photo 5-8: Soldiers firing along quay

Photo 5-9: Kitchen hearth

Photo 5-10: Making lace

Photo 5-11:Garden in back yard

Photo 5-12: Another garden

Photo 5-13: Geese in yard

Photo 5-14: Girls and soldier looking at sheep

Photo 5-15: A typical back yard

Photo 5-16: Shops along quay

Photo 5-17: Looking down Rue Toulouse

Photo 5-18: The King's Gate

Photo 5-19: Shops and stores

Photo 5-20: Piper in tavern

Photo 5-21: Maids in training

Photo 5-22: The stores building

CHAPTER 6 - HISTORY OF THE VIOLETTE FAMILY, RITA VIOLETTE-LIPPÉ

(Note to the Reader: This work was written by Rita Violette-Lippé and is excerpted from "The Descendants of François Violet", published by Naiman Press, Lawrence MA, 1984. It is republished here by permission; the book is now out of print. The original publication contained genealogical tables consisting of some 9,600 Violette descendants of François. The content included here is from the front matter of the book. The editors have added some comments to help in understanding, as well as to update the text with more recent information. The editors also added the maps.)

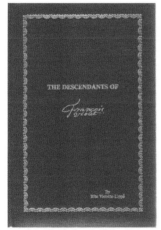

Figure 6-1: Rita's book, "The Descendants of Francois Violet", was published in 1984

Figure 6-2: The last copy of Rita's book was raffled off at Reunion 2008. Richard Violette (VFA #7, Rita's brother); Rita (VFA #1); raffle winner Peter Girard (VFA #1330) of Rocky Hill CT

Rita's Foreword

As a Violette, I have always been somewhat interested in the Violette name and in the origin of the Violette Family. In 1947 and 1948, while in high school, my curiosity was aroused by my religious teachers, the Sisters of the Immaculate Heart of Mary, many of whom had previously taught Violettes in the Van Buren, Maine, area. Was I, perchance, related to the Violettes of the St. John Valley, they wondered? I knew very little of my heritage and ancestry then, but was aware that Van Buren had played a significant part in them. A correspondence then began with Dorothy Violette of Van Buren, presently Sister Dorothy Violette SCIM. Four years later, I boarded a bus in Lawrence, Massachusetts, headed for what I considered the all-important town of Van Buren, Maine. During this two-week long visit, I became fairly well acquainted with the St. John Valley area and simply fell in love with it. I was introduced to many elderly Violettes and had several lengthy conversations with them. However, I was young and inexperienced in genealogy and my interest subsided.

In 1973, my interest in genealogy was rekindled. At this time, I realized that my father remembered a great deal about his childhood, although he had not once returned to New Brunswick since his departure some fifty-five years prior. It was in the month of August when my husband, daughter, Mom, Dad and I returned to the land of Dad's birth and childhood. We visited Drummond, St. Basile and St. Quentin, New Brunswick, as well as the entire St. John Valley.

This vacation proved to be a turning point: my curiosity and fascination with the past was to remain with me throughout my lifetime. Immediately upon our return home, serious research began. Letters were written, books read and maps carefully examined. A year later, another trip took place. This time Louisbourg, Nova Scotia, was the destination, the soil where our ancestors had landed back in 1749. The Fortress of Louisbourg fascinated us. We visited the archives and questioned the Chief Historian, Gilles Proulx, rather extensively. We learned that Charles Violet was not a military person but a "couvreur de toits", a roofer. Other information pertaining to the death of Charles Violet's wife, Marie David, his re-marriage and his other children was made available to us.

Shortly after returning home, I wrote to Louisbourg for additional information. It is then that I received two documents concerning Charles, Francois and Charles' step-son, Alexis Hilaret. These documents will be discussed later. From here on, my interest in genealogy in general, and in the Violette Family in particular, took on a whole new dimension leading eventually to the publishing of the Violette Genealogy *"The Descendants of Francois Violet"*.

By no means is research complete on the descendants of Francois. Genealogy is a living and vibrant study. Many important details remain hidden in the past. Hence, this is an ongoing project. This book is merely a compilation of my personal research on the Violettes to date *(Ed note: 1984)*. It is hoped that this publication will encourage many of you to share the information you have with me, that errors might be corrected and the listing of Violettes made more complete. *(Ed note: Rod Violette, VFA#12, has continued and expanded on Rita's work. Rod moved the genealogical info into a database format and has expanded it from Rita's 9,600 Violettes to more than 24,000 Violettes plus another 40,000 associated persons.)*

When possible, the children of female Violettes are also listed in this study along with all available information. In the interest of clarity, the organization of the genealogical sections is such that the Violette surname appears in the first section exclusively. Other surnames, the offspring of the female Violettes, are listed in the second section. The third section concerns those Violettes whom I have been unable to tie into the Francois lineage at this time.

Information relating to the Violette Genealogy was gathered from State Archives and Vital Statistics Records, micro-films from the Church of Latter-Day Saints in Salt Lake City, Catholic Church Records, newspaper obituaries, Marriage Repertoires, personal contacts and verbal and written communications. Since the Catholic Church Records deal with baptisms, many birth dates and places of birth listed in this study are actually baptism dates and places of baptism. Occasionally, this situation leads to certain discrepancies. Should the reader be aware of such, he or she is encouraged to forward all additions and corrections to the author at *(Ed note: Rita's prior address is removed from this text. For questions, additions, and corrections please contact Rod Violette, VFA #12, 1775 Barn Valley Lane, Lincoln, CA 95648, Tel: 916-434-8136, Fax: 916-434-8136, Email: rviolette@att.net.)*

(End of Rita's section "Foreword")

Rita's History of the Violette Family

(Ed note: The material quoted here contains much that is repetitive of material in the earlier chapters of this book. Rita's work was done earlier and formed the basis for much work that came after. Where later research has shed new light on the topics covered by Rita we have inserted editor notes with the most current information.) The very first mention of our ancestors on this continent coincides with the arrival of the ship L'INTREPIDE in Louisbourg, Nova Scotia, in 1749. Listed as passengers on the INTREPIDE are

Charles Violet, his wife Marie David and their son, Francois. The records in Louis-bourg show that Charles was not a military person but a "couvreur de toits", a roofer.

The image above shows a naval battle between the L'Intrepide (left background) rushing to the aid of the French ship "The Thunderer" (right foreground) attacked by several British ships at the height of Cape Finisterre in Brittany, October 17, 1747. This was two years before L'Intrepide was the ship in a convoy to Louisbourg on which Charles, Marie, Alexis, and François traveled. The painting was done by Pierre Julien Gilbert and is available for purchase at art.com.

(Ed note: The French ship L'Intrepide was of a type called a xebec. These were small, fast ships primarily used for trading in the Mediterranean Sea. Xebecs were similar to the galleys used by Berber corsairs and Barbary pirates and had both lateen sails and oars for propulsion. The early xebecs had two masts, the later ones three. Xebecs had displacements in the range of 150-200 tons burden and they were armed with from 18-24 guns. In the eighteenth and early nineteenth centuries, a large polacre-xebec carried a square rig on the foremast, lateen sails on the other masts, a bowsprit, and two headsails. L'Intrepide appears to be of this type of xebec. These types of ships were often used as "corsairs", another term for the privateers commissioned by the French King to conduct raids on ships of the French enemies. They were well suited to this use because they were small and built for fast maneuvering, and by having oars they could approach quietly from any direction regardless of wind conditions.)

Exactly who was this Violet family and where did they come from? Charles Violet and Marie David (also spelled Davy on some documents) were married on December 6, 1741 in the Church of St. Vivien in Saintes, France. Charles was born on February 13, 1716 in Villejesus, France, the son of Louis Violet and Marie Doux. Marie David was born on May 10, 1705 in Saintes, France, the daughter of Jean David and Marie Gaindet. Three children were born to this couple:

1. Elie b. July 22, 1743 Saintes, France; d. September 2, 1746 Rochefort, France
(Ed note: More recent research show the his name was probably Helie.)

2. Francois b. October 16, 1744 Saintes, France; d. April 10, 1824 St. Basile, New Brunswick *(Ed note: More recent records show François' birthdate as December 16, 1744.)*

3. Marie b. January 31, 1747 Rochefort, France; d. October 14, 1747 Rochefort, France

These births and deaths show us that all descendants of Charles Violet and Marie David come from one child, Francois, our ancestor. It is very likely that Charles has other descendants in France from his second wife, Marie Sudois, and from his third wife, Catherine Estie. Research has not come up with the marriages of any of the children from the second and third wives. *(Ed note: Chapter 14 will provide more information about Marie Sudois and her children and Catherine Estie and her children. Catherine's last name is shown as Ytier in current genealogical records.)* Surely we must be distantly related to the Violets in Saintes, Villejesus and the entire Charente Maritime area. Just where the tie comes in is unknown due to the lack of marriage documentation of Charles' other children. *(Ed note: Actually, this is due to a lack of information about Louis's parents.)*

It was not long after Charles Violet and Marie David's arrival in Louisbourg that tragedy struck this adventurous family. On May 26, 1751, in Louisbourg, Marie David Violet passed away. *(Ed note: We have since found Louisbourg Parish death records and know she died on May 28, 1751.)* Her death record shows that she was the wife of Charles Violet and the widow of Jean Hilaret. Very shortly thereafter legal papers dealing with the Violet Family were filed in Louisbourg. Two separate documents were filed: Court of Request #486 dated June 26, 1751 concerning the guardianship of Alexis Hilaret, the stepson of Charles Violet; and Court of Request #487, also dated June 26, 1751 concerning the guardianship of Francois Violette. Apparently Charles deemed it necessary or desirable, in view of his imminent second marriage, to take certain precautions to safeguard and differentiate between the legal rights of his stepson, Alexis, and those of his son, Francois. It would serve little purpose to include these lengthy documents as they are in French and copies of these old documents are hardly legible. *(Ed note: Maurice Violette provided much more detail about these proceedings and we include his work in Chapters 7 and 8 of this book.)* These documents reveal that Pierre Jauvin was named Alexis' principal guardian with several friends and neighbors as subrogate guardians. Alexis at this time was only 18 years of age and the legal age for parental responsibility was 25. However, Charles remained the principal guardian of Francois with Jacques Labossiere as subrogate guardian. The responsibility for Francois remained totally with his father, Charles. Francois was neither put up for adoption nor abandoned, as some have held, at this tender age of six. The fact that Charles remained the legal guardian is proof of such a statement.

The following day, a very interesting event took place. On June 27, 1751 in Louisbourg, Charles married Marie Sudois, the daughter of Pierre Paul Sudois and Anne Deniot. Five children were born of this marriage:

1. Therese b. April 22, 1751 Louisbourg, Nova Scotia; d. January 31, 1753 Louisbourg, Nova Scotia (Ed note: Louisbourg Parish records show her birthdate as April 22, 1752.)

2. Jerome b. June 31, 1753 Louisbourg, Nova Scotia (Ed note: Louisbourg Parish records show her birthdate as June 17, 1753)

3. Marie Anne Francoise b. August 21, l755 Louisbourg, Nova Scotia (Ed note: Louisbourg Parish birth records show her last name as Le Violet)

4. Charlotte b. October 10, 1756 Louisbourg, Nova Scotia (Ed note: Louisbourg Parish birth records show her last name as Viollet)

5. Marianne b. December 9, 1759 Rochefort, France

These births reveal two very interesting facets in the life of Charles Violet. The baptism record of Marie Anne Francoise in Louisbourg shows her godfather to be none other than Alexis Hilaret, the stepson of Charles. This baptism occurred four years after the Court of Request #486 concerning the guardianship of Alexis Hilaret. Although Charles gave up all responsibility for Alexis, he certainly must have remained close to him. Otherwise, why would Alexis be granted the honor of being the godfather of one of Charles' children? Since Charles kept in such close contact with his stepson, Alexis Hilaret, how much closer must he have remained to Francois, his only son from his first marriage, for whom he remained the principal guardian?

Although Alexis Hilaret is not a Violette descendant, he is a David descendant just as all of us are. So we must view him as at least a distant relative. Were we to be doing the genealogy of Marie David, Alexis, as well as all of us, would be a part of this genealogy. What happened to Alexis? This much we know: on July 2, 1765 in Cayenne, West Indies, Alexis married Cecile Caissie.

Returning now to the children of the second marriage, how is it that Marianne was born in Rochefort, France? The LaRochelle, France, records of April 28, 1759 list Charles and his wife, Marie Sudois, as arrivals along with officers, magistrates and various other inhabitants of the "Colonie de l'Isle Royale", inhabitants which, as it is stated, "had left the said location with permission". They disembarked in LaRochelle but soon thereafter moved on to Rochefort where Marianne was born of December 9, 1759. This list makes no mention of children with the parents. Was Francois with them? We do not know. All we do know is that we have absolutely no information on Francois from 1751 to 1770 when he married Marie Luce Thibodeau in the New World. Francois would have been 14 years of age when his father and stepmother returned to France. It is entirely possible that he remained in Nova Scotia and it is just as possible that he returned to France temporarily. A fourteen-year-old could have gone reluctantly with the determination of returning some day to the land of his childhood. To say he remained, as well as to say he returned to France, would be mere conjecture. This is certainly an interesting subject worthy of future research, a project in itself.

Why did Charles return to France? How did he manage to avoid the "deportement" from Louisbourg in 1758, the very fortress he inhabited at that time? The circumstances which surround Charles' departure from the New World, as well as the reasons for his leaving France originally, remain unknowns. *(Ed note: Actually, Charles and Marie were deported from Louisbourg, along with all the other French civilians and the French military. However, we have no record of Francois in these matters so we do not know if he returned to France with his family and then came back to North America or whether he remained on Île Royale.)*

Charles was not in Rochefort long before he again was left with several small children. Marie Sudois Violet died on November 16, 1760 in Rochefort. Less than five months later, on April 13, 1761 in Rochefort, Charles married Catherine Estie, the widow of Jean Poinsot. A son, Jean Nicolas, was born to Charles and Catherine on January 8, 1766 in Rochefort.

However Charles died on November 13, 1765 in Rochefort before the birth of Jean Nicolas.

There are those who ask: Are we Acadian or are we not Acadian? We certainly are, although the Violet name is not listed among the groups of Acadians who were dispersed from Annapolis and Port Royal, Nova Scotia, in 1755. In that year Charles and his family were residents of Louisbourg. We are Acadian by virtue of the fact that over the period of 1749 to 1758, Charles and his family, as stated earlier, inhabited Louisbourg. Additionally, we are Acadian by virtue of his (Ed note: François) marriage to Marie Luce Thibodeau, the Thibodeaus being one of the well known Acadian families. Since Francois was the only Violette in Acadia and since we can account for his presence from the time of his marriage (1770) to the time of his death (1824) there is no basis for assuming that any Violette was deported to the United States, to Quebec or to the Islands of St. Pierre and Miquelon.

All the marriages and baptisms referred to in this bit of history, including the marriage of Louis Violet and Marie Doux on January 7, 1715 in Villejesus, France, took place in the Roman Catholic Church. This appears to be in contradiction to that which we have heard in the past, specifically that we may have been Huguenots. A plausible explanation for this earlier inaccuracy is that we once associated Charles with the City of LaRochelle, France, a city reportedly 95% Huguenot. But, Charles never lived in LaRochelle. He lived in Rochefort, Saintes and Villejesus, all cities and towns primarily of Catholic populations. The marriage of Louis Violet and Marie Doux does not list the names of their parents. For this reason we are unable to extend our lineage beyond 1715. *(Ed note: later research has provided info about the parents of Marie)* Nevertheless, it is possible that prior to 1715 some Violets may have been Huguenots. For the same reason, we cannot claim a connection to any Violet or Violette Coat of Arms. Violette Coats of Arms do exist. However, there is no documentation that any one of these is ours or that we even have one.

Recorded in the Ecoupag, New Brunswick records by Rev. Charles Bailly is the marriage of Francois Violette to Marie Luce Thibodeau on May 5, 1770. A notation on this document states that this marriage was "rehabilite" which means "blessed". New Brunswick in those days was missionary territory. Priests came from miles away to minister to the spiritual needs of the people. It is also found in the Ecoupag records that Francois' three oldest children, Marguerite, born July 25, l770; Augustin, born September 15, 1771; and Marie Genevieve, born March 15, 1774 were all baptized on September 15,1774. Francois and his family were residents of the Kennebeccasis, an area serviced by the Missionaries of Ecoupag. Parenthetically, Ecoupag, also spelled Ecoupahag and Aukpague' was an Indian village at Springhill, six miles north of the center of the city of Fredericton and within the city limits.

Those familiar with the history of the Acadians are aware that these unfortunate and courageous colonists were stripped of their lands and possessions, not only as a result of the expulsion from Nova Scotia during the period of 1755 to 1758, but again and again. Some of the Acadians who had settled in the Kennebeccasis region lost their homes and lands to the immigrants of New England and to the Loyalist Americans in the 1780's. Lacking formal and legal titles to their lands they simply were put out, causing some of them to migrate to Madawaska, a county situated at that time on both sides of the St. John River in northwestern New Brunswick. *(Ed note: This will be covered in more detail in Chapter 13.)*

Fortunately, two Loyalists, Edward Winslow and Ward Chipman, saw to it that some of these Acadians were made restitution by granting them the land bordering the Kennebeccasis or Hammond River, in King's County. New Brunswick. The land grant in question was registered in Fredericton, New Brunswick, on the twelfth day of April 1787. The lengthy, ten page document is entitled "Widow Sarah Hunt and Others" and describes the granting of approximately 6,888 acres divided into 42 lots. Given therein are the names of the recipients and their respective lots: Francois being granted Lot 14, a parcel of land amounting to 210 acres of the Eastern Division. The exact wording follows: "unto the said John

Thompson the lot Number Thirteen containing one hundred and eighty five acres, unto the said Francis Violet the lot Number Fourteen containing two hundred and ten acres, unto the said Andrew Sherwood the lot Number Sixteen containing one hundred and seventy acres"

Noteworthy is the fact that all lots in the region were awarded by this document with the exception of one lot, Lot number l5 adjacent to Francois' land on the south side. Why this exception? More about Lot 15 a bit later. Also noteworthy is the fact that grants were awarded such that the Acadians were dispersed among the Loyalists. In Francois' case, his neighbors were John Thompson and Andrew Sherwood.

The document also specifies the conditions of the grant in terms of acreage to be cleared (i.e. three acres per year for each 50 granted), in terms of cattle, in terms of dwelling to be erected within three years (i.e. one good dwelling house to be at least 20 feet in length and l6 feet in breath), etc. Additionally, payment was to be made at a rate of two shillings per year per hundred acres for a period of ten years, payable at the feast of St. Michael. Annexed to the Land Grant is a plan of the subdivision of the land.

It is difficult for us who have never had to clear land to appreciate the full significance of these terms. Ponder if you will, the toil, the labor involved in clearing 12 acres - for that was indeed Francois' task - of virgin forest a year, and this with essentially nothing more than hand implements! In addition there was a dwelling to build, food to grow, animals to tend, a few shillings to be earned, etc... Such a task calls for a strong will, determination, physical and emotional strength, and a dedication to and a tremendous capacity for....work.

Undoubtedly, there was much displeasure among the Acadians inhabiting lots intertwined with those of the Loyalists in the Kennebeccasis area, as petitions for land in the Madawaska region were soon submitted by Francois and others. One petition for land grants submitted by "Francis Violet and other inhabitants of the French Village on the Little Kennebeccasis" is dated August 28, 1789. A second petition submitted by the same people is dated December 21, 1789 and asks for land "below the settlement Madoueska". These petitions intimate that the petitioners were displeased with their conditions in the Kennebeccasis region - that is interspersed among the Loyalists on land deemed insufficient for their large families. At the time of the petitions Francois had seven sons and five daughters.

Seemingly, Francois had doubts of ever being granted the lands in Madoueska for within three to four weeks he entered into a contract agreeing to purchase "Lot Fifteen". The contract dated January 15, 1790 bound "Francis Vilette", as it is written in the original, to pay Henry Darling the sum of one hundred pounds of lawful money for Lot Fifteen, the land adjacent his own as we have seen earlier.

Among the signatures appearing at the end of the contract we find that of Francois himself, proof that he was literate at least to the extent of being capable of signing his name. This is the first document on which Francois' signature appears.

The January 15, 1790 contract is somewhat puzzling. It would seem that while the Francis Vilette - Henry Darling contract was being drawn up, Francois was not yet aware of the fact that his December 21, 1789 petition for lands in Madoueska had already been granted on December 24, 1789. Exactly when Francois left the Kennebeccasis region is not known. *(Ed note: More information about François' activities in the Kennebecasis region will be provided in Chapter 12 –François at Hammond River.)*

However, Francois and his family were settled in the Madoueska region by 1791 since his son, Alexandre, born September 29, 1789 at Kennebeccasis, was baptized on June 23, 1791 in St. Basile. This early St. Basile baptism was found in documents in Rimouski, Quebec. Francois' land was situated in St. Basile Parish on both sides of the St. John River in what is known today as St. Leonard, New Brunswick, and Van Buren, Maine. It was the Violettes and the Cyrs who first settled these lands. Francois built and operated the first grist mill in the area. It was located on the brook known as Violette Brook.

This brief history of the Acadians and these few biographical details concerning Francois are a prelude to his most important contribution, that which is the "raison d'etre" of this publication, namely, Francois Violet's descendants. Violettes have since settled throughout Canada and the United States. The New England States are the home of the majority of the Violettes today, with Maine boasting their greatest concentration.

Note: When referring to Francois, the author has used the surname Violet, remaining faithful to Francois' own signature. The spelling of the surname soon became Violette and has remained thus with all of his descendants.

(End of Rita's section "History of the Violette Family")

Rita's The Birth and Growth of the Violette Family Association

After having written to literally hundreds of Violettes over a period of three years, in 1977 I began to entertain the thought of having a Violette Family Reunion. Since there were only a dozen or so Violettes in the Greater Lawrence-Greater Lowell area, I was understandably a bit hesitant. Somehow I did not feel that geographically speaking, Methuen, Massachusetts, was a likely place for a successful Violette reunion. Seemingly, Maine would be a more appropriate area for such a function. However, I decided to attempt it.

Ten months prior to the reunion, a letter was sent to all Violettes with whom I had had previous contact. The announcement of the reunion was made specifying that it would be geared to the entire family. A few preliminary details as to date and location were given. A follow-up letter to be mailed approximately three months prior to the reunion was also announced. The main concern at this point was to make Violettes aware of that which was to take place. Then came the final letter with all the details as to the cost, the tentative agenda and the availability of motels in the Methuen, Massachusetts, area. Also included was a registration form to be returned by those who wished to attend. I hadn't the vaguest idea as to the kind of response such an invitation would elicit. Since this was the first time such an endeavor was attempted, I decided that if 50 people attended, the reunion would be considered a great success. July 16, 1978, finally arrived and with it, a gathering of 375 people at St. Theresa's Parish Hall in Methuen, Massachusetts. They came from Rome, the Provinces of Quebec, New Brunswick and Ontario and from the States of Maine, Massachusetts, New Hampshire, Connecticut, Rhode Island, New York, Arizona, California, Illinois, West Virginia, Florida and Indiana. The hall swelled with excitement and warmth. An invisible, but nonetheless real, bond unified all attendees: a vivid interest in one's heritage. All were descendants of Francois Violet. Each Violette, who had pre-registered, found displayed on the wall his or her direct lineage back to France. This made it possible for each and everyone to know his or her relationship to any other Violette in attendance.

The reunion was a tremendous success and too quickly came to an end. However, this was but the beginning. This moment was indeed an opportune one to pursue my search for Violettes and hence was born the idea of a family association. Since all the groundwork had been done for the reunion, the birth of the Association was fairly simple and proceeded very smoothly. Within one month, the first newsletter was sent to all adults who had attended the reunion. Their attendance automatically granted them membership into the Association. The Association at this time numbered 281 members representing 175 families.

The $119 profit realized at the Methuen Reunion provided the funds necessary to organize the Violette Family Association. A Constitution and By-Laws were drafted and officers were named. As Founder of the Association, I became its President-Secretary, Richard Violette of Lowell, Massachusetts, became Vice-President, and Joseph Violette of Methuen, Massachusetts, Treasurer. The motto chosen was the one used at the first reunion: **We Are One**. Our logo consists of a violet flower centered in a white circle and beneath the flower, the words "We Are One". Within six months the Violette Family Association was a registered non-profit organization. During the first year of existence, membership grew to 361.

In 1979 in Augusta, Maine, a second reunion was held. The success of this reunion, organized by Maurice Violette of Augusta, is attested to by the size of the attendance: no less than 550 Violettes gathered at the Calumet Club in Augusta, Maine, on Saturday, August 4, 1979. That very day, the Association membership grew to 620.

Van Buren, Maine, Violette Country! In August of 1981, 800 people traveled up to the St. John Valley, more specifically, to the town of Van Buren, Maine, to attend the third Violette Reunion. Superior Court Judge Elmer Violette of Van Buren served as Chairman. For some this was a return to the homeland they had left many years prior; for others, it was a visit to the homeland of their parents, grandparents or great-grandparents. For all, it was an emotion filled experience. During this two day reunion, the Association erected a monument in memory of our ancestor, Francois. This monument stands on land adjacent to the Violette Brook, the area presently called Violette Brook Park.

In September of 1982, 49 members of the Association traveled to France. At departure time each traveler was given his or her ancestry back to France, enabling each person to establish his or her relationship to each other on the tour. The result was a closely-knit family who would share emotions, experiences and memories to be cherished forever. Over a twelve day period, we visited in depth the Charente Maritime area, namely, Angouleme, Saintes, Rochefort, Villejesus and LaRochelle, all towns and cities of our ancestors. Thanks to the foresight of Maurice Violette of Augusta, Maine, in each city we were greeted by the local dignitaries. We were honored with a reception by these dignitaries and townspeople. Words cannot adequately describe the pride and emotion experienced by each and every one of us.

Five and one half years have passed since the inception of the Association *(Ed note: Rita's text was written in 1983)*. We now have 1218 members, representative of four Provinces of Canada: Alberta, Ontario, Quebec and New Brunswick; thirty-two States: Massachusetts, Rhode Island, New Hampshire, Maine, Vermont, Connecticut, New Jersey, New York, Pennsylvania, Ohio, Indiana, Michigan, Wisconsin, Minnesota, Illinois, Delaware, Virginia, West Virginia, North Carolina, Georgia, Florida, Tennessee, Texas, Colorado, Wyoming, Arizona, Nevada, California, Oregon, Washington and Alaska; and from the countries of Spain, Sweden, France, Italy and Japan. Our present mailing consists of 775 newsletters. *(Ed note: As of July 2014 the Violette Family Association latest member number is 2955 and mailing list includes 830 by email and 490 by mail.)*

In August of 1984, our fourth reunion will be held in East Windsor, Connecticut, with Mrs. Gerald Violette (Sandra Pronsky) of Enfield, Connecticut, and Richard Violette of West Hartford, Connecticut, as Co-Chairpersons. It is at this particular event that the Violette Genealogy-"The Descendants of Francois Violet" will be made available to the membership. *(Ed note: Subsequent Reunions have been held in*

Portland ME (1987), Grand Falls NB (1990), Lewiston ME (1993), Shelburne Falls NH (1996), Westford MA (1999), Edmundston NB (2002), Gorham NH (2005), Windsor Locks CT (2008), and Van Buren ME (2011 and 2014).)

The first reunion was definitely the stepping stone to the formation of our Violette Family Association. Subsequent reunions provided the stage for its rapid growth. The formation of an Association has indeed been very rewarding to all. Bonds have been formed which otherwise never could have materialized. Acquaintances, which lay dormant for 30, 40 and even 50 years, have been renewed. Friendships between brothers, sisters, aunts, uncles and cousins have been deepened and strengthened.

It is with much pride in our heritage and with a deep sense of gratitude to our ancestors that we can truly say: **We Are One**".

(End of Rita's section "The Birth and Growth of the VIOLETTE FAMILY ASSOCIATION")

CHAPTER 7 - THE VIOLETTE FAMILY, PART 1, MAURICE VIOLETTE

(Note to the Reader: This work was written by Maurice Violette (1921-2004) and first published by Letter Systems, Inc, 52 Water Street, Hallowell ME, 1990. It is republished here by permission. The original publication was written in two parts, and this is Part 1; Part 2 is in the next chapter. The editors have added some comments to help in understanding as well as to update the text with more recent information. The editors also added the maps.)

Figure 7-1: Maurice's booklet, "The Violette Family – A History", was published in 1990

Maurice's *A History...*

The very first mention of our ancestors on this continent coincides with the arrival of the ship LE VESSEAU DU ROI L'INTREPIDE in Louisbourg, Nova Scotia on 29 June 1749. Listed as passengers on the ship were Charles Violet, his wife Marie David and their son, Francois. They were put ashore on the 23rd of July at which time Captain Charles des Herbiers, the new Commissioner and Governor of Cape Breton Island received the keys of the city from the British.

Charles Violet and Marie David were married on December 6, 1741 in the church of St. Vivien city of Saintes, France. Charles was born on February 13, 1716 in the commune of Villejesus (formerly known as Paroise de Jesus), France, son of Louis Violet and Marie Doux. Marie David was born on May10, 1705 in Saintes, France, the daughter of Jean David and Marie Gaindet. Sources in France reveal that the David family originated in Villejesus and thus the connection between Charles and Marie David occurred much earlier. Three children were born to this couple: Elie, born July 22, 1743 Saintes and died September 2, 1746 Rochefort, France; Francois, born October16, 1744 Saintes, France and died April 10, 1824, St. Basile, New Brunswick; Marie, born January31, 1747, Rochefort, France and died October 14, 1747, Rochefort, France. *(Ed note: For more details about these people, events, and places consult our Chapters 1 through 5.)*

Prior to Charles departure for New France, the North American continent was embroiled in competition between France and England for control of the entrance to the St. Lawrence Seaway. Since 1711, these countries vied for dominance of the areas resorting to piracy on the high seas and direct attacks against each other resulting in huge losses of lives and materials. The Treaty of Utrech *(Ed Note; Utrecht)* 1713 agreed to by both countries, gave Newfoundland (Terre Neuve) to England the French received control of Isle Royale which we know as Cape Breton Island. All fortifications from Placentia NFLD were transferred to Louisbourg. This, however, did not solve anything as both countries continued to harass each other throughout the world.

Thus it was in 1744 when Governor Shirley of Massachusetts induced Colonel William Pepperrell to head an army and ships to invade and capture the fortress of Louisbourg which was a thorn in the British sides, guarding the entrance to the St. Lawrence Seaway. The English defeated the French in 1745 and after deporting most of the French and Swiss Mercenaries back to Europe took over the control of Louisbourg. The New Englanders would not be staying very long in Louisbourg as the harshness of the weather, pestilence, diseases of epidemic proportions, decimated the occupying forces. Thus control of the Island was returned to France in 1749. King Louis XV of France called for the expatriates from Louisbourg to return and asked for volunteers in France to become pioneers and compliment the city of Louisbourg. He offered 150 French Pounds for each family. Charles Violet having lost two children to epidemics in France accepted the king's offer and thus we found them arriving in Louisbourg on June 29, 1749.

Soon after his arrival, Charles faced a huge tragedy. Marie David died on May 26, 1751. Her death records do not reveal the cause but when reviewing the history of Louisbourg in terms of the harsh weather, epidemics of typhus and typhoid, one can assume that she probably succumbed in one of the epidemics. One month later we find Charles in the Royal Court of Louisbourg, petitioning the court to authorize the assignments of Alexis Hilaret, son of Marie David by a previous marriage (age 18) stepson of Charles (Court request #486, June 26, 1751) and of Francois Violet (6 ½) son of Charles and Marie David (Court request #487, June 26, 1751) concerning the appointment of subrogate guardians in each case ... and further, to receive a judgement in bankruptcy. An inventory of Charles possessions was completed and attested to be worth a total of 458 French Pounds including the 150 Pounds owed by the King of France *(Ed Note: Charles and others who moved to Louisbourg were promised 150 French Pounds incentive to settle in the New World).* Thus, Charles, indebtedness to P Jauvain and Jean Bognais was dismissed since both had been appointed Subrogate Guardians respectively for Alexis Hilaret and Francois Violet. See Appendix I.

To truly understand what happened here one must refer to legal procedures. The hearings of June 26, 1751 were merely hearings in which the participants provided information to the court in support of Charles' request; to prove they were creditors; and to volunteer themselves to be "Subrogate Guardians" and as well to recognize Charles' rights of guardianship by "right of child." It appears that the inventory of Charles effects served to satisfy the debts to Jauvain and Bognais by their appointment as Subrogate Guardians of Alexis Hilaret and Francois Violet as decreed in a court decision of June 28, 1751.

Joy Francis Lareher, Distrainer *(Ed Note: to distrain is to take a debtor's property as payment for a debt)* to this case at the Royal Court of Louisbourg, ruled on the 28th of June "by virtue of the Governor of Louisbourg being in session at the bar of petitions since the 26th of the month, and at the petition of Charles Violet, resident of this city ... gives assignment to friends of the minor children of the deceased Jean Hilaret and Marie David, the father and mother, and to the son of Charles Violet and of the deceased Marie David, his wife, their father and mother, assign said children firstly to Jacques La Boyer de la Buissiere, Jean Senat, Pierre Jovin, Antoine Maitue, Pierre Barbreau, and Jacques Reneaut, et al, all residents living in this city and all common friends of the minors. Brought themselves and appeared jointly this day, nine o'clock of the morning in our office of the Department of the Distrainer of the Royal Court of Louisbourg to give their consentment to be subrogate guardians for Alexis Hilaret minor of the first bed of Jean Hilaret and Marie David and for Francois Violet, child minor of Charles Violet and of the Marie David, to govern and administer their persons and goods, declaring to them that even without their joint appearance, they will be bound to carry out this decree and they have been given to each a copy of this writ separately to which they will sign. Thus Acted Lareher." Decree issued on cases #486 and #487 petitioned on June 26, 1751 and ruled June 28, 1751. (See Appendix I)

Notwithstanding the agreement which appears to have been made between the friends and neighbors and Charles, The Distrainer of the Royal Court placed the two under the guardianship of the "friends and neighbors" with a final swoop of his signature. Of the "friends and neighbors" in court that day all but one had crossed the Atlantic to resettle Louisbourg on the Intrepide. Pierre Jauvain had been a long time resident of the city and in this particular case he was referred to as "Brother Jovin" indicating that he was a member of the legal profession. In the Archives of Louisbourg, it was discovered that in 1743 this particular Jauvain had been in the Royal Court involved in the "sale of a person." To further add corroborating information to properly evaluate the status of Francois Violet and Alexis Hilaret, the word "Subrogate" in legal terminology means "substitute ... to substitute a person or thing by or for another when attributing or assigning rights ... in law, the putting of a person who (as a surety) has paid the debt of another in the place of the creditor to whom he has paid it ..." There is the irrefutable evidence that Charles and Alexis were delivered by the father Charles to "friends and neighbors" as surety for a paid debt ... in other words, they were delivered in bondage and Charles left the court free of debt, free of family, free to remarry again which he did on June 29, 1751 to Marie Anne Sudois knowing full well the result of his petition to the court which was issued the previous day.

Marie Anne Sudois had originated from LaRochelle daughter of Pierre Paul Sudois and Anne Deniot. Five children were born of this marriage: Therese, born April 22, 1752 Louisbourg; died January 31, 1753 Louisbourg; Jerome, born June 31, 1753 Louisbourg; Marie Anne Francoise, born August 21, 1755 Louisbourg; Charlotte, October 10, 1756 Louisbourg; Marianne, born December 9, 1759 Rochefort, France. The baptism record of Marie Anne Francoise in Louisbourg shows her Godfather to be none other than Alexis Hilaret, the stepson of Charles. This was four years after the assignment of subrogate guardians for Alexis and according to his age he would now have been 22 and relieved of his obligation to serve "friends and neighbors" as appointed by the Royal Court in June of 1751. No information can be found concerning Francois Violet following the court appearance of June 1751. No information can be found that he was a passenger for France after the surrender of Louisbourg nor before. It is almost as if Francois had completely disappeared until he resurfaced in Ecoupag, N.S. in 1770.

The lack of evidence that he was even in Louisbourg ... i.e. no court appearance ... nor any other document involving Francois can be found, adds credence to the "Legend of the Violettes" in which a "cabin boy" had jumped ship in Ecoupag, had met an Acadian girl (Marie Luce Thibodeau). The legend says this young boy had been taken in by monks, had been taught to read and write and provided instruction in the faith and he participated in the rituals of the church with a very fine "singing voice". Why not? This seems a wonderful manner in which to fill a void of over 19 years. Why shouldn't Francois have run away from his guardians ... after all a life of bondage is not conducive to the pursuit of happiness.

Meanwhile, in 1756 England declared war against France and "the reduction of Louisbourg was their first objective, and lavish preparations were made for its success ... fourteen thousand troops were provided ... a fleet of twenty-three ships under the command of Major General Amherst to attack the city and lay it under siege as early as April next year ... (1757)." Among others in command was Major General Wolfe (victor over Montcalm at Quebec City). The armada converged on Halifax to prepare for the assault and ten more ships were added to the fleet. There in Halifax was Edward Cornwallis who would play a prominent part in the American Revolution who was now Governor of Nova Scotia. *(Ed Note: Louisbourg was important because it guarded the entrance to the Gulf of the St. Lawrence River, an important route for commerce with the interior of the continent. See Map 7-1. See the chapter on La Rochelle for more info.)*

Map 7-1: Louisbourg Guards the Entrance to the Gulf of the St. Lawrence River

Map 7-2: Cape Breton Island

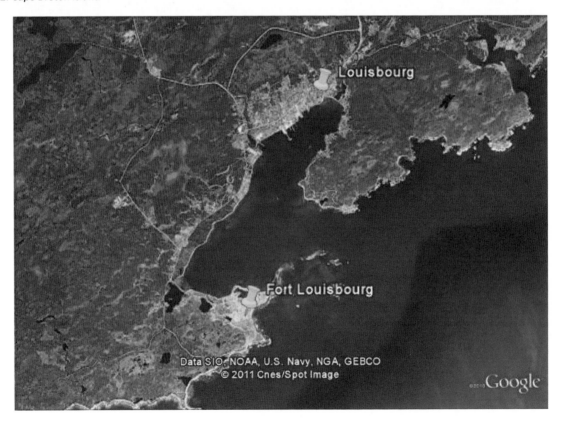

Map 7-3: The Louisbourg Area Today

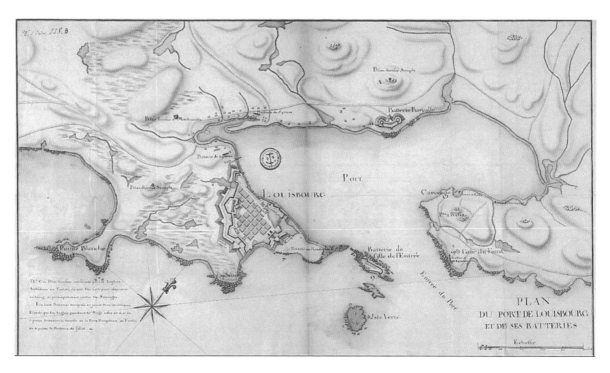

Map 7-4: Plan of the Port of Louisbourg and Its Batteries, circa 1751

The Siege of Louisbourg for all purposes began at the beginning of May 1757 and would last for two months, both sides prodding each other for an advantage. The heavy weather and seas did not provide the necessary "easy" approach for General Wolfe. During those two months, the fleet bombarded the city with over 330,000 10-12-24 pounders and rocket bomb. To illustrate the ferocity of the battle, the British expended 780,000 musket balls during this period. How the inhabitants could survive such an onslaught, devastating as it was, is amazing. There was no bomb shelters ... every building was damaged ... the hospital was the first to go and it was a neighbor of Charles on Rue D'Orlean. The wounded and injured were tended to in the Citadel inside the walkway through the fortification ... it was the only safe place in the city of Louisbourg. The children were allowed to fend for themselves during this bombardment. There was a sad and moving sight during this time. McLennon writes: "The few casemates (these were vaulted chambers in the fortification, a bombproof shelter, from which guns fired through openings) are placed in the inner part of the citadel, in them were shut in the ladies and some of the women of the town, and one was kept for wounded officers. There was every reason to fear that the fire (caused by the bombardment of the British) would reach the protection which had been placed in front of these casemates, and by the direction of the wind the smoke might stifle the women shut up in them, so that all the women and a great number of little children came out, running to and fro, not knowing where to go to the midst of bombs and balls falling on every side, and among them several wounded officers brought out on stretchers, with no safe place to put them."

On August 1, 1758, the siege of Louisbourg was over and the British occupied the town. The French troops were promptly dispatched to France. General Wolfe approved the expulsion of the town population and all were offered the opportunity to leave for France or the Islands of St. Pierre and Miquelon. We find Charles Violet and Marie Ann Sudoit his wife applying and negotiating for passage to LaRochelle. No children are listed in their request. Thus Charles returned to France with his wife and they arrived early in 1759. They arrived in LaRochelle and later moved to Rochefort-sur-Mer where Charles had gone to settle having been well acquainted the military in Louisbourg, this would seem natural for him to do so as Rochefort was strictly a military city. Thus we know that Charles although deported in accordance with General Wolfe's dictates, was offered a chance to go elsewhere if he had preferred. *(Ed note: Charles was also familiar with Rochefort, having lived there prior to moving to Louisbourg; see Chapter 3.)*

In France, Charles' situation did not improve. Marie Anne Sudois delivered another child Marianne. A year late Marie Anne Sudois died on November 16, 1760 in Rochefort. Five months late Charles married a Catherine Ytier, the widow of Jean Poinsot, Charles died on November 13, 1765 of unknown causes and his wife, Catherine, delivered a boy, Jean Nicholas Violette, on January 8, 1766 in Rochefort. Charles' funeral was sung at the old St. Louis Church in Rochefort and his remains are somewhere in the general area of that church. (Now Signal Tower)

Meanwhile, let us return to Louisbourg and the life of Charles after his arrival. From the available records and documents as well as the condition of the city of Louisbourg on his arrival it can be ascertained that his trade was very much in demand. 97% of all the buildings needed repair having been left unattended by the New Englanders who occupied that town between 1745 and 1749. However, Charles was an ordinary roofer and had to secure work with others who were masters of the trade. After the death of Marie Sudois, Charles became much more successful at his work for in 1753 records indicate that he was now contracting for himself and rather successfully. He contracts for a house on Rue D'Orlean in 1757 in the immediate vicinity of the Citadel which denotes the better section of the city in close proximity to the seat of government. Meanwhile there is no information on the whereabouts, disposition, or what is happening to Francois. Lack of information seems to confirm that Francois is no longer in Louisbourg.

However we are now able to definitely conclude that Charles came to New France at the King's request for tradesmen, soldiers and others to repopulate the city of Louisbourg in 1749. We can certify that the Royal Court of Louisbourg did assign Alexis Hilaret and Francois Violet to "friends and neighbors" as subrogate guardians in June of 1751. We know that Alexis Hilaret was Godfather to one of

Charles children in 1755 and later he would be found in Cayenne. *(Ed Note: Cayenne, West Indies, now French Guiana. Alexis died there July 2, 1765 at age 32.)* According to McLennon in his history of Louisbourg, he mentions that many of the expatriates from Louisbourg were offered an opportunity to resettle in Cayenne after they had returned to France. Apparently, Alexis Hilaret took advantage of that opportunity. Everyone else who returned to France were granted a pension for life.

The saga of Charles Violet continues in Part II *(Ed note: see Chapter 8)*. However, it would not be surprising if some item could show up in the future because he was a very interesting individual and provides the Violet Family of the Americas an exciting, vibrant, and fascinating heritage. The search still goes on in Louisbourg.

Francois' history is much closer to us as Rita Lippe has performed an almost miraculous task in assembling so much data and history to afford us a unique, almost intimate, closeness to the past when we thumb through her book The Descendants of Francois Violet. This book now rests in the municipal libraries of the cities in France where Charles and Francois left their tracks, available to modern day cousins in those cities to ponder on the evolution of the Violet/Viollet of France. *(Ed Note: Rita's story is found in Chapter 6 in this book.)*

Francois was married officially on May 5, 1770 at Ecoupag, N. B. to Marie Luce Thibodeau. Actually the marriage had occurred earlier but it was blessed on this date. It was the custom in those days due to the absence of clergy that of families "married" the couples in the interim pending the arrival of the visiting missionary. The evidence of this custom is seen in the Baptism of Francois' three oldest children: Marguerite born July 25, 1770; Augustin born September 15, 1771; Marie Genevieve born March 15, 1774 as all were baptized on September 15, 1774.

Francois received a land grant, registered in Frederickton on April 12, 1787. It is a ten-page document in which 6,888 acres of land were divided into 42 lots. *(Ed Note: this grant was along the Hammond River in lower New Brunswick. See our Chapter 12 for more details.)* Francois received Lot #14 mixed in with Loyalists who owned the lots abounding his property. This did not satisfy the Acadians who again and again petitioned for land below "Madoueska". Finally, Francois' petition was approved on December 24, 1789 (quite a Christmas present) effective December 21, 1789. As to the date he left for Madoueska is unknown but it is noted that it had to be by 1791 since his son, Alexandre, born September 29, 1789 at Kennebeccasis, was baptized on July 23, 1791 in St. Basile, Madawaska Territory.

The land grant was located in St. Basile Parish on both sides of the St. John River in what is known today as St. Leonard, N.B. and Van Buren, Maine. *(Ed Note: This grant was in the Upper St. John River Valley, and we will learn much more about this in later chapters.)* Two families, the Violettes and Cyrs settled these lands. Francois built and operated a grist mill, the first one, in the area on a small brook called Violette Brook, the precursor of the town of Van Buren.

The rest is history. With such dedicated people as Rita Lippe at the helm with assistance coming to her from every quarter, the Association *(Ed Note: the Violette Family Association.)* grew in leaps and bounds as evidenced with the results of the original reunion in Methuen, MA, 1978; followed by get togethers in Augusta, Maine, 1979; Van Buren, 1981; Winsor Lock, CT *(Ed Note: Windsor Locks)*, 1984; Portland, Maine, 1987; and Grand Falls, N.B. 1990 *(Ed Note: Since 1990 the Association has had Reunions in Lewiston ME, 1993; Shelburne Falls NH, 1996; Westford MA, 1999; Edmundston NB, 2002; Gorham NH, 2005; Windsor Locks CT, 2008; Van Buren ME, 2011; and Van Buren ME, 2014)*. The Association, in 1990, has grown to almost 1600 Registered Members. Originally under the Leadership of President Rita Lippe, it is now under the direction of Irene Violette Petit of Hudson Falls, N.Y. who was elected President of the Association in 1987 during the Portland Reunion. *(Ed note: As of July 2011 the Violette Family Association latest member number is 2873 and mailing list includes 980 by email and 592 by mail. For more history of the Violette Family Association and it leadership over time refer to the section titled The Violette Family Association in the front matter for this book.)*

(Ed note: The following pages contain translations of the petitions for guardianship of Alexis Hilaret and for Francois Violet and the judgment document granting those petitions.)

Petition for Guardianship of Jean Hilaret

ROYAL COURT
LOUISBOURG, ISLE ROYALE
NEW FRANCE
26 June 1751 Court of Requests

No. 486 Guardianship of Jean Hilaret

Violet — Roofer

THE PETITION

To the Bailliff of Louisbourg, Isle Royal

Humbly petitioning, Charles Violet, Resident of this city.

Since a certain time, he has had the misfortune to lose Marie David in death. She had a child of her deceased Jean Hilaret her first husband, named Alexis Hilaret, age now eighteen years, and one other child conceived and from the petitioner, named Francois Violet, age of six and a half years, and being important to the petitioner to have elected a guardian and subrogate guardian for the minor children and to accomplish this submits to your authority in order for you to please permit the petitioner to assign some friends and neighbors of the two minor children in sufficient numbers due to the lack of relatives in this country to be named guardian and subrogate guardian for the minor children. In order to accomplish this deed, the petitioner will take such action which he will be adjudged necessary to serve the ends of justice.

Allowed and ordered assigned to neighbors and friends minor children in numbers required, due to the lack of relatives in this country. To be heard Monday morning at nine o'clock in the morning in our office to conclusion.

The election of a guardian, a subrogate guardian for the minor children to Louis Brossiere this 26th June 1751.

Meyraig

THE PROCEEDINGS

In the year 1751, the 28th of the month of June, the two guardians appeared at this bench at the request of Charles Violet, roofer and resident of this city, father and guardian by right of child, the issue of his marriage with deceased Marie David. Pierre Jauvin guardian named by act of Guardianship this day for Alexis Hilaret, the issue of the first marriage of the said deceased Marie David with Jean Hilaret. We, Laurent D. Domenge, Meyraig Counsellor of the King, Bailliff, Civil and Criminal Judge at the Royal Court of Louisbourg, were transported with the Prosecutor of the King accompanied by the Clerk of Court and agreed to by the guardian of the court to the house occupied by the said Charles Violet in this city on rue in order to process the inventory and description of the furniture belonging to the first possession between the said deceased Jean Hilaret, and the said David, that those of the latter (union) with the said Violet, which inventory we have processed in presence of Jacques La Bognais La Brossiere, subrogate guardian of the children of said Jean Hilaret with the said David, and the said Prosecutor of the King after which the said Violet has sworn to as required in this case to present everything to the Clerk of Court.

The furniture and effects of the said two joint possessions to which he has returned none, such furniture were appraised and estimated by Louis Marie Etienne De Casignale, residents of this city, appreciator named by us for that office, which appreciators have sworn as required in this case and in their souls and conscience have appraised the furniture and effects which were required to be appraised at their just value without invention which they have promised to do. They have, the said appraisers, signed as well as the friends of the King, the said La Bognais and Senat subrogate guardians.

FIRST

One child's bed, curtains and bed cover of green serge in which were found a small feather bed, a double mattress with worn covers. All estimated at a sum of forty-five pounds 45.00

Item: Two chests estimated at ten pounds 10.00

Item: One work blanket of coarse wool with a bolster of old feathers estimated five pounds 5.00

Item: One pot hook, two andirons, one shovel for fire, one trivet, one grill, one tongs, one poker, all of steel, estimated at eleven pounds ten sols 11.10

Item: One stove of steel with exhaust flue pipe estimated at twenty-five pounds 25.00

Item: One pot with cover, one kettle with cover, together estimated at six tee pounds 16.00

Item: Two cauldrons, average to small, one stew pot and two candlesticks with one small drip pan. All of brass estimated at twelve pounds 12.00

Item: One folding table of which wood with three chairs stuffed with straw estimated at eight pounds 8.00

Item: Two axes, one hand saw, one chimney plaque, one spit, two small hammers, two small hatchets, all estimated at seven pounds ten sols 7.10

Item: Approximately two cords and a half of wood for burning which has been estimated at thirty-three pounds 33.00

Item: One coaster, four plates of ceramic, four small earthenware platters the more of the same (Idem), one pair of corset stays of tin, two huguinotte earthenware, one beer mug of ceramic, four glass bottles, two small bowls, two thin spoons and five forks of steel estimated all together of seven pounds 7.00

Item: In the attic, three flour barrels containing some six hundred and sixty-seven books estimated at ten pounds per Quintal which makes the sum of sixty-six pounds and fourteen sols 66.14

Item: Two small mirrors estimated at twenty-five sols 1.50

Item: One cape with its brown camelot hood estimated twelve pounds 12.00

Item: One skirt of new wool ten pounds 10.00

Item: Five worn corselets of cotton, of soft cotton, estimated at five pounds 5.00

Item: Three worn petticoats estimated at nine pounds 9.00

Item: Eight large bed sheets estimated at sixteen pounds 16.00

Item: Eleven chemises for use by women estimated at sixteen pounds 16.00

Item: One tablecloth and two towels very worn estimated at forty sols 2.00

Item: Two pairs of women's stocking with one pair of slippers estimated at forty sols 2.00

Item: Twenty-nine pieces for hairdressing, all of horn. Good for dressing hair only and are estimated together at nine pounds 9.00

Item: Two pairs of poches for women's use estimated at 20 sols 1.00

And not having found more to inventory we have in this place, affirmed the said Violet to declare to us if he had any papers or promissory notes in favor of this joint possession as well as active and passive debts which he is responsible to this proceedings. He declared having no paper nor notes but it was due him by the King a sum of one hundred and fifty pounds and by Mister Jovin that of nine pounds for these proceedings. Due to these proceedings he owes three months for the house which he occupies for reasons of expediency of twenty pounds, not of thirty pounds, that he has no knowledge of any other debts active or passive. Following these proceedings, we have processed and delivered to you a true presentation which has been found amounting without error to the sum of four hundred and eighty-eight pounds and nineteen sols and, including that of one hundred and fifty pounds due by the King, of nine pounds for the said Brother Jauven for the two joint processors appointed to these proceedings. Reducing that of thirty pounds which the said Violet will cease to pay for the place acquired by the King. Thus the present will remain net for that of four hundred and fifty-eight pounds nineteen sols. Consequently the present inventory remains closed and the proceedings halted. The proceedings have been for us Bailliff been concluded for the dismissal of debts to the Said Jovin hence the said Jauvain, Le Bognais, Senat Guardian Subrogate as well as Inquisitor Louie Marie and Etienne de Casignale, appreciator, signed

Petition for Guardianship of François Violet

ROYAL COURT
LOUISBOURG, ISLE ROYALE
NEW FRANCE
26 June 1751 Court of Requests

No. 487 Guardianship of Francois Violet

Louis La Cotte

B

In the year 1751, the 28th of the month of June since ten o'clock in the morning in our office came to us, Laurent De Dominge, Meyraig Counsellor for the King, Bailliff for the Royal Court of Louisbourg, Isle Royal, the Prosecutor for the King, present in our office has appeared jointly, Charles Violet, resident of this city, widower of Marie David, who has delegated as a result of our order of the 26th current session of these proceedings consciously placed at the end of his request presented to us the right to assign the named Jacques La Bossiere, Jean Senat, Pierre Jauvain, Antoine Maitue, Pierre Barbereau and Jacques Ranaeu, all residents of this city, friends and neighbors of Francois Violet, and the late deceased Marie David, his wife, due to lack of relatives in this colony to name a Guardian and a subrogate Guardian for the said minor child following the use of sequestor, for a revue, to be sworn by Lareher, Process Server, awaits that which the friends and neighbors, all present, will require of said Violet, that he will please proceed to the nominations which are required by us, Bailliff on the bankruptcy act and discharge of debts act, and orders that it shall be for him at this proceedings at law. Nominees and assigner will permit and swear to God to give us a good and faithful oath on said nominations

The said Violet has stated that he reports to justice and to the oath of friends and neighbors to be joint possessors of guardian and subrogate guardian for his son and so assign for this session of the inquest.

The said La Bossiere has stated that he names for Guardian at this proceedings of Francois Violet minor, the present Charles Violet, his father, and for subrogate guardian at this proceedings Pierre Jauvin and so signs.

J. Bognais

The said Jovin has stated that he names for guardian at these proceedings of Francois Violet, minor, Charles Violet, his father, and for subrogate guardian the said La Bossiere and so signs.

P Jovin

The said Barbereau has stated that he names for guardian at the proceedings of Francois Violet, Minor of Charles Violet, his father, and for subrogate guardian the said La Bossiere and so signs.

Pierre Barbreau

The said Renaut has stated that he names for guardians at these proceedings of Francois Violet, minor,

Charles Violet his father, and for subrogate guardian the said La Bossiere and so signs.

Jacques Renaud

The said Senat has stated that he names for guardian at the proceedings of Francois Violet, Minor, Charles Violet his father, and for subrogate guardian the said La Bossiere and so signs.

Senat

The said Le Maitre has stated that he names for guardian at the proceedings of Francois Violet, Mino Charles Violet his father, and for subrogate guardian the said La Bossiere and so signs.

L. Maitre

The said nominees to us Bailliff on the act of bankruptcy and dismissal of debts act in consequence, orders the consentment of the Prosecutor for the King that he Charles Violet shall remain guardian of the said Francois Violet his minor child, for the purpose of administering his person and goods and the said La Bossiere for subrogate guardian according to the oath of the friends and neighbors in order that will obtain homologue and homology and await the presence of said Charles Violet and La Bossiere that they will voluntarily accept the said charge. We have taken and received their oath to the case as required by these proceedings and in their souls and conscience will and faithfully fulfill the duties of their said charge. To each having provided by law and have signed and the said La Bossiere that which the said Violet did not do provided at this session of this inquest.

Meyraig J. Bognais

In the year 1751, the 28th of the month of June since ten o'clock in the morning in our office came to us, Laurent de Dominge, Meyraig Counsellor for the King, Bailliff for the Royal Court of Louisbourg, Isle Royal, the Prosecutor for the King, present in our office has appeared jointly, Charles Violet, resident of this city, widower of Marie David, who has delegated as a result of our order of the 26th current session of these proceedings consciously placed at the end of his request presented to us the right to assign the named Jacques La Bossiere, Jean Senat, Pierre Jauvain, Antoine Maitue, Pierre Barbereau, and Jacques Ranau, all residents of this city, friends and neighbors of Alexis Hilaret, age of eighteen years, minor of said late Jean Hilaret and of the said deceased Marie David, his wife, due to the lack of relatives in this colony to name a guardian and a subrogate guardian for the said minor child following the use of sequestor, for a revue, to be sworn by Lereher, Process Server, awaits that which the friends and neighbors, all present, will require of said Violet, that he will please proceed to the nominations which are required by us, Bailliff on the bankruptcy act and discharge of debts act, and orders that it shall be for him at this proceedings, the friends and neighbors will permit and swear to God to give us a good and faithful oath on said nominations.

The said Violet has stated that he names for Guardian for the said Alexis Hilaret, minor the person of the said Jovin and for subrogate Guardian the said Jean Senat and signs for this session of this inquest.

The said Jovin has stated that he names for Guardian for the said Alexis Hilaret, minor the person of the said Ranau, and for subrogate Guardian the said Senat and signs.

P. Jovin

The said La Bossiere has stated that he names for Guardian for the said Alexis Hilaret, minor, the person of the said Jovin and for subrogate Guardian the said Senat and signed.

A. Maitue

The said Barbereau has stated that he names for Guardian for the said Alexis Hilaret, minor, the person of the said Jovin and for subrogate Guardian the said Senat and signs.

Pierre Barbreau

The said Renaud has stated that he names for Guardian for the said Alexis Hilaret, minor, the person of the said Jovin and for subrogate Guardian the said Senat and signs.

Jacques Renaud

The said Senat has stated that he names for Guardian for the said Alexis H ilaret, minor, the person of the said Jovin and for subrogate Guardian the said Renaud and signs.

J. Senat

The said nominees to us Bailliff on the act of bankruptcy and dismissal of debts and act in consequence, orders the consentment of the Prosecutor for the King that the said Jovin shall remain Guardian of the said Alexis Hilaret, minor child, for the purpose of administering his person and goods and the said Senat for subrogate Guardian according to the oath of the friends and neighbors in order that will obtain homologue and homology and await the presence of the said Jovin and Senat that they will accept voluntarily the said charge. We have taken and received their oath to the case as required by these proceedings and in their souls and conscience will and faithfully fulfill the duties of their said charge. In each having undersigned.

Jovin   Senat   La Bossiere

Meyraig

Judgment for Guardianship of Jean Hilaret and François Violet

ROYAL COURT
LOUISBOURG, ISLE ROYALE
NEW FRANCE

28 June 1751 Court of Requests

No. 486/487 Guardianship of Jean Hilaret and Francois Violet

Violet — Roofer

THE JUDGEMENT

In the year 1751, the 28th of June, in the morning by virtue of the order of the session at the bar of petitions since the 26th of the month, and at the petition of Charles Violet, resident of this city, Joy Francois Lareher, Distrainer to this case at the Royal Court of Louisbourg IDEM. Rue perty into judicial custody; deposit into the hands of a third party, pending deter- des Rampartes Louisbourg gives assignment to friends of the minor children of rnination of ownership. the deceased Jean Hilaret and Marie David, the father and mother, and to the son of Charles Violet and of the deceased Marie David, his wife, their father and mother assign said children firstly to Jacques Le Boyer de la Buissiere, Jean Senat, Pierre Jovin, Antoine Maitue, Pierre Barbreau, and Jacques Reneaut, et al, all residents living in this city and all common friends of the minors. Brought themselves and appeared jointly this day, nine o'clock of the morning in our office of the Department of the Distrainer of the Royal Court of Louisbourg to give their consentment to be subrogate guardians for Alexis Hilaret minor of the first bed of Jean Hilaret and Marie David and for Francois Violet, child minor of Charles Violet and of the Marie David, to govern and administer their persons and goods, declaring to them that even without their joint appearance, they will be bound to carry out this decree and they have been given to each a copy of this writ separately to which they will sign.

Thus acted

Lareher

CHAPTER 8 - THE VIOLETTE FAMILY, PART 2, MAURICE VIOLETTE

(Note to the Reader: This work was written by Maurice Violette (1921-2004) and first published by Letter Systems, Inc, 52 Water Street, Hallowell ME, 1990. It is republished here by permission. The original publication was written in two parts, and this is Part 2; Part 1 is in the previous chapter. The editors have added some comments to help in understanding as well as to update the text with more recent information. The editors also added the maps.)

(Start of Maurice's text)

Charles Violet in Louisbourg, Isle Royale, New France.
Circa 1749-1759.

The Saga of Charles Violet of Villejesus, France, Department of the Charente goes on. Charles left his mark in many places and little by little, we are piercing that genealogical curtain which contains so much colorful and historical information providing us with a better understanding of his life and times.

In the beginning, we were very "young" in our approach to find our ancestors and much speculation had to be employed in order to arrive at the real truth … eventually. Still, we are seeking more and more information and as it comes in dribbles much of it is disconcerting. However, we should be very proud of our heritage as it is very unique … filled with those events that leave us groping for more.

Several years ago, I spent a week at the Fortress of Louisbourg in league with Eric Krause, the Superintendent of Historical Records, who provided me with myriads of information concerning the days of the French pioneers who arrived there in June of 1749 … including among them, Charles Violet of Rochefort-sur-Mer, Saintes, and Villejesus, France. Thus in order to provide a full picture of our ancestor, it is necessary to review the politics and the history of the area and the reasons which brought Charles, his wife Marie David, and his son, his only remaining child, Francois, as participants in the great struggle for the control of

North America between France and England. Charles had lost all his other children as a result of epidemics and famine which was the scourge of France in those days.

War between England and France had gone on with brief intermissions from 1689 and 1712. The war of the Spanish Succession, in which Europe formed a coalition to resist the pretension of the Great Louis, had left France exhausted. Many treaties, signed at Utrecht, settled the terms of the peace, but certain clauses in the one between France and England alone concern this narrative. It was agreed that the French should evacuate Placentia, Terre Neuve (Newfoundland), unhappily with indeterminate limits, it should be yielded to England, but that France should hold with full sovereignty the islands lying in the Gulf of St. Lawrence and its outlets. These included St. Jean (P.E.I.) and Cape Breton. *(Ed note: Map 1 below shows the extent of French holdings in North America around 1750 and depicts the status reported in Maurice's text. Note that while France retains a strong presence in the interior, Britain gained a stronghold around the Gulf of St. Lawrence. But France still retained Cape Breton Island, where Louisbourg is located, and other small islands in the Gulf.)*

Map 8-1: North American holdings around 1750 (from Nouvelle-France map-en.svg. Wikimedia Commons.)

But in order to complete the history about the "life and times" of Charles in Louisbourg, I had to first go back to 1713 and even before that to 1613 when Louisbourg was known as "Le Port des Anglois." This information is contained in Part I of the Violette Family History. *(Ed note: See Chapter 7 in our work)* It is included as the forerunner of this excerpt.

Picture world powers competing for supremacy in trade, commerce and world wide recognition as the major powers, Spain, France, England and the Dutch were all vieing for that positioning and were making bridgeheads in the New World, especially in the northern hemisphere. In the New World, the trade of such importance was that of the North Atlantic fisheries. It had been rigorously followed, at all events, from the beginning of the Sixteenth Century as Portuguese, Basque from the Spanish side, those in their French ports, Bayonne and St. Jean de Lus the fishermen of the Bordeaux, of Normandy, as well as the West Country English, visited the teeming waters of the "Western Coasts" of the North Atlantic. New England too, about the mid-Seventeenth Century, turned with far reaching affect on her people, from the demoralizing fur trade. Thus the scene was set for the upheavals which would lead to the conquest of Canada. The English controlled Halifax … the French, Cape Breton Island (Isle Royale) and Terre Neuve (Newfoundland) ... the Spanish were ensconced in Sydney known as "Le Baie de Espagnols".

During this period, the Indians were used by both the British and French alike to scour and raid and terrorize as far South as the Virginias and the Ohio territories in the West. The Treaty of Utrecht (1713) established rights for the individual powers but mainly for the French and English. Finally the French gave up Newfoundland, then took control of Cape Breton Island. The French and Indian Wars provided the catalyst that vaulted the French and English into a final confrontation which would be made in favor of the English in 1758.

Harassment of British shipping by the dominating position of the French who controlled access to the St. Lawrence Seaway and the Indian massacres against the English, which directly affected the New England Colonies to the South, provided the incentive for Governor Shirley of Massachusetts to appoint Colonel William Pepperell of Kittery and Portsmouth to lead an army and an armada of ships to attack and capture the city of Louisbourg in 1744.

Although Newfoundland and Nova Scotia were in the hands of the British, French Cape Breton was a sentinel in the gateway of the St. Lawrence through which passed the traffic of Canada … through which in event of new hostilities, attack on that colony would be made. The value of Cape Breton as a naval base to protect Canada and French commerce in the Western Ocean is so obvious that we need not go further in this area.

From 1713 to 1745, conditions in Louisbourg were very intermingled with corruption of officials and the politics of France. Bickering in the hierarchy prevented the full and proper defense to be provided to the city. However, irrespective of the many pitfalls Louisbourg became in 1726, with a population of 951, the major place of the colony.

The climate of Louisbourg was very dreary and disappointing. There are weeks in Autumn when a dull earth meets a leaden sea. In Winter, the ground is white and the sea is somber. In the Spring, the sea is white and glistening with drift ice and the land is dreary and dead of vegetation. In early Summer, sea and land are dank with fog and at any time occur gales of wind which are always blustering and often destructive.

The ocean was the only highway of important news. On it, mysterious sails appeared in the offing and pirates plundered. Each ship which worked in from its horizon might bring tidings of the adventure or of consequence to the onlooker or the community. With such prospect, life might be hopeless but it could not be permanently dull.

Thus with the encouragement from Governor Shirley of Massachusetts, the declaration of war with England was made on March 18, 1744, and expedited to Louisbourg by a merchant vessel from St. Malo which arrived on May 3rd of that year. As a result, privateering was encouraged against the English but still the New Englanders captured town after town. Canseau (Canso) was the first to fall. . .thence Annapolis. On the 17th of June 1745, Louisbourg surrendered to the New Englanders and over 2000 inhabitants of Louisbourg were prepared to be expelled to France aboard eleven ships. The French troops were allowed to retain their weapons and marched out of the city in an orderly and military fashion.

Now, General, Pepperell stayed in Louisbourg until the Spring of 1746. During this period his troops became dissatisfied with the conditions and many wanted to return to their homes. By September of that year, they were at a point of mutiny. Disease ran rampant and of epidemic proportions. The desperate situation was accented by the death of 890 men during the Winter of 1747 between December and April and due to the inclement weather, the living and the dead existed together. Local custom of billeting soldiers contributed to these epidemics as they slept two to a bunk and in some cases a dozen or more used one long, continuous bunk. It was probably such an epidemic of influenza, typhus, or typhoid which caused the demise of Marie David in 1751. *(Ed note: Marie David was the wife of Charles and had come from France with him in 1745)* The community was restricted in growing their own food which had to be mostly imported and many lacked proper diet which consisted mostly of fish.

The Treaty of Aix-la-Chapelle was signed on October 18, 1748 which returned the Cape Breton Island to France. This disappointed Governor Shirley bitterly as it denied the English from establishing the seat of the Colony which had been the goal of the New Englanders earlier. Thus we have now reached the point in time where Charles will enter and join in the historical events of the period with Marie David and son Francois *(Ed note: And stepson Alexis Hilaret).*

In Part I we have accounted for the reason Charles brought his family to the New World and how the tragic events of the day compounded just about everyone of his efforts to obtain the good life. *(Ed note: See also Chapters 4, 5, 6, and 7 in this work.)*

The former inhabitants of Louisbourg were recalled and as well, new ones were recruited from Canada and France. They found the houses in poor condition as but few of them had been repaired by the British during their occupation. The Governor of Louisbourg, Francois Bigot, provided 200 cows for distribution among the people, including Charles, and for two years they were supplied with rations from the king's stores. The newcomers were greeted by the 94 French-men who had remained under British rule during the occupation. However, the return of Louisbourg to the French did not stop the hostilities.

The order of the day was to continue the harassment of the British, repel force by force, Halifax to be attacked by Indians but to do so covertly. Acadians were encouraged to settle on the Isle of St. Jean (P.E.I) ... the English replied in kind and brought against them as many indiscreet obstacles as could be done without compromise and to take steps to protect against them.

Development to the West in the Ohio territories had a direct bearing on the plight of the French in Louisbourg ... the defeat of Lt. George Washington at Fort Necessity by the French (as retaliation for Washington's ambush and massacre of French troops earlier) provided the spark to encourage the English and the New Englanders to remove the French once and for all and to wrestle control from them in the north especially in Louisbourg and Quebec. *(Ed note: Refer to Map 1 to see the relationship between New England and New France. Though the Manifest Destiny concept was not formalized for another 75 years or so, even in the times reported here many New Englanders did not want to be hemmed in to the Atlantic coastal regions of the huge continent. In the times reported here New England was still a group of British colonies and not independent.)* General Braddock returned to the American continent with two regiments and the French were to be driven from the North American continent.

Meanwhile in Louisbourg, Charles and wife, Marie David, and son Francois *(Ed note: and stepson Alexis)* tried to arrange their lives in the best possible manner. Charles' presence was made possible by the fact that his trade was that of a roofer and just about every building standing in the city required repair especially the roofs. Much of this period has been covered in Part I of the History of the Violettes preceeding this addendum. *(Ed note: Chapter 7 in this work)* Suffice it to say that Charles had a most difficult time to make ends meet in as much as he was not a master roofer as yet and found it necessary to work for others. Income must have been very limited due to the adverse weather and short roofing season of the area. Although we do not know the exact location of his living quarters, the court of Louisbourg failed to indicate it in any of his court proceedings before 1755. This can be assumed that Charles lived in a more wanting area of Louisbourg and had not reached a level of economic success. Please review Part I of the family history which contains Charles' attempt to improve his lot petitioning for bankruptcy in the Royal Court. (See Appendix I) *(Ed note: Found in Chapter 7 in this work.)*

J.S. McLennan, author of the book LOUISBOURG writes on page 187: "The transfer of Isle Royale and its dependencies to France had been made without difficulty. Charles des Herbiers, Sieur de la Raliere, a naval captain of distinction, was chosen as French Commissioner and Governor. He had left France with the men-of-war Tigre and Intrepide, which convoyed transports from Rochefort-sur-Mer carrying about five hundred troops from Isle de Rhe, an island off the coast of LaRochelle and civilians from the Charente Maritime Department for Isle Royale. Charles, Marie David and son, Francois were aboard the Intrepide registered under 3rd Class Passengers. The French Flag replaced that of England over the Citadel and Batteries of Louisbourg and the English forces withdrew to Halifax.

Charles did not find the streets paved with gold and like all had to face the rigors and uncertainties of the period. Bigot, the Intendant for Governor of New France, had a reputation of being very harsh towards the British and he made everyone who resided or remained in New France sign an oath of allegiance to the King of France ... otherwise he would deport them. Expulsion was not invented by the British who deported the Acadians from the land as repayment in kind.

A search of Louisbourg records did not reveal much information about Charles and his family from 1749 through July of 1753 with the exception of his petition to the Royal Court to "give" Francois and stepson, Alexis Hilaret, to his "friends and neighbors" in June of 1751 following the death of Marie David and to obtain a ruling in bankruptcy.

According to the inventory of his personal effects at the time of his appearance in Court, Charles was about the poorest man in Louisbourg. *(Ed note: See Chapter 7 for the listing of the inventory.)* His furniture was badly deteriorated to almost the status of junk. The few tools were well worn and from the records, he was penniless as he petitioned the Royal Court to pay him the 150 pounds the King of France had promised him.

One can adduce any interpretation as one may desire from this but in the final analysis we find that Charles is for all legal purposes divesting himself of the two children as the judgement of the Magistrate has so specifically appointed the "friends and neighbors" as subrogate guardians of both Alexis Hilaret and of Francois Violet. However, I might add one statement to this session of the court which has been covered in Part I *(Ed note: Chapter 7 in this work),* as to why the Distrainer of the King, Lareher, ruled as he did. In the final judgement, he noted that all participants had signed the oath to carry out the dictates of the court ... all signed but Charles and this was pointed out by Mayreig, the Counsellor for the King, Isle Royale, and the Prosecutor for the King who wrote: "We have received their oath to the case as required by these proceedings and in their souls and conscience will and faithfully fulfill the duties of their said charge. . .which the said Violet did not do (sign the oath) provided at this session of this inquest."

In view of the fact Charles did not sign the oath, Lareher had no other choice but to assign the two children to them who did sign the oath. By the fact he was in court in petition for bankruptcy, we can assume that Charles owed a lot of money. . that Jauvain and Senat cancelled Charles' debt and in return Alexis Hilaret and Francois Violet were thus placed in their charge as collateral for repayment by Charles. This was a common practice during colonial days. By this action, Charles was now free to devote his personal life to new approaches. Nowhere could I find that Charles ever repaid his creditors nor that the two children had ever been relieved, officially, of their obligation to "serve" their subrogate guardians. Thus from this point forward, we can no longer find any information concerning Francois ... Alexis Hilaret does surface in 1753 as the Godfather of Charles' second child, Marie Anne. However, Francois is missing. It would have been natural, I feel, for him to have become a Godfather to one of the other two children born in 1755 and in 1756 had he been in Louisbourg. No such event occurred.

Four years after his arrival in Louisbourg, we find Charles in court again and in the ensuing years, he would be there quite a number of times for he had now become a Master Roofer and was thus self-employed in contracting work for the people of Louisbourg.

July 3, 1753. Charles has an audience with the Magistrate of Louisbourg in which he requests that Pierre Santier have installed by carpenters a part of the roof with new boards still to be covered in order to prepare the roof properly to receive slate shingles. The Magistrate gave Sentier 24 hours to do so. (Santier, according to a rental contract in 1755 would become Charles' neighbor).

August 21, 1754. In another case, Charles was a party to the event when a resident of the town asked the court to force a landlord to install a new roof. Charles was the contractor.

January 14, 1755. We find Charles in court once more. This time he is in the process of leasing a home on Rue D'Orleans (about one block away for the Citadel). This indicates that he is now a successful business man in Louisbourg and the property is needed for him to expand in business in the form of a boutique as well as to rent an apartment in keeping with his new status. The contract reads as follows, in French, and taken from the script retains the colorful grammar then in use. Translating into English would not do justice to the intent and meaning of the various aspect of the lease.

"VIOLETTE, Charles (apparently name corruption by Le Gras)
14 Janvier 1755, AFO G3, carton 2044, no. 6 (Archives of Louisbourg) Bail (lease)
a loyer dune maison. Allain Le Gras a Charles Violette.

Nous allain Le Gras habitant de Cette Ville Et Charles Viollette maistre Couvreur Et Marchand ausy demeurant En Cette Ville sommes Convenus de Ce qui Suit Scavoir que moy allain Le gras ay par les present Loue Et afferrn au dit Viollette Le bout de ma maison quo jocupe Se Consistant En une grande Cave Situee Sous le grand Corps de la ditte ma/son Avec Celle Sous le Cuisine du mesme bout Vers M. Santier, plus la boutique, Salle, Cuisines, Cabanneau, au bout, Cornmoditte de Court Et fontaine, Latrinne, La Chambre Sur la Salle, Le Grenier Sur la ditto Chambres, ainsy que Celluy de Sur La Cuissine, generalement la moitie de la maison Le bout Ver le dit Santier a la Reserve do la Chambre Et Grennier a Lempost (?) dicelle quocupe Monsieur badesse La quelle nest point antandu (?) du presant marche, 1 souffrira Monsieur Badesse sier son bois a feu dans le Court, mesme passage de fontaine Et Latrinne, La dit loyer Convenu pour le temps Et Espace de sinq annee parfaitte Eta Complique qui commenceront le dishuittome du presantmois, Etfinirons a pareil jour Et La ditSieur Viollette Soblige paier au dit La gras par Chaquon an La Somme do Six Cents Vingt Et sinq Livres paiable En quatre Cartiers qui Est de trois mois En trois mois, Se montant a la Somme de Cent cinquante Et Six Livres sinq Sols, pour quelle Est Promaitant Remettre a ditto maison avec ses apartments, Sans Degradation, mesme no tireraucune (bords fly Cloux, (mises ?) pour suspendre des marchandises dautant que le ditte Le gras Los Luy Laissera de a mesme fasson ainay que les bords de boutique deux armoires Vitres deux tables do boutiques Ettableau une Clochette En Letat quil Est presentement la maison Vitree suivant La detail que nous En feron Le jour do son Entree au dos du presant ... (la maison est situe sur la Rue D'Orleans)"

It appears that Charles has at this point expanded his role as a businessman in the City of Louisbourg in which he now is the owner of a "boutique" and has made arrangements with Monsieur Le Gras to rearrange it into a store or place in which he can display his wares for sale. Boutique as used in French can mean many things. A dress Shop. A frivolous boutique which would involve items used for almost anything from knitting needles and cloth goods, or even a place of hardware sales. It would seem natural that his trade as a Master Roofer would not require the use of a display to sell his trade. However, the key word in the lease "to hang his merchandise" does indicate that the boutique must have been for use as a Dress Shop and possibly accessories. Marie Anne Sudois apparently belonged to a well-to-do family in LaRochelle who were engaged in the manufacture of Carriages and would have a definite knowledge of styles and must have been a qualified seamstress. One must also consider the adverse weather condition of Louisbourg located on a promontory extending out into the sea guarding the St. Lawrence Seaway, in a natural breezeway causing unpredictable and unnatural storms made roofing a very short season at best. A boutique would have compensated to fill the gaps when work in the open was impossible.

Earlier in 1754, Charles was again in court for having assaulted a customer. It seems a contract fell through and Charles lost the job. He had delivered all the materials for the work to the job site and had gone back to pick up his supplies and tools. It is assumed this would be slates delivered earlier and scaffolding. The tenant came out of the house and forbade Charles to remove the materials. He physically assailed Charles, knocking him to the ground. Charles got up and took a two by four piece of lumber and promptly clobbered the tenant thereby disposing him from discussing the deal any longer. Charles removed his materials and the court ruled in his favor in this case. We can conclude that Charles, like all Violettes, did not take a back seat to anyone ... he was apparently able to fend for himself quite well.

July 14, 1766. *(Ed note: Probably 1756)* Charles is again in court sued by Pierre Letourneur Le Lorembec in that Charles abandoned a half-completed roof and thus by this action has caused the roof to rot completely. I did not have time to find out the rest as reading old script can be mind boggling and eye blinding as this was a lengthy case. However, Charles did not lose too much from this episode. This delay in completing the job might have been caused by inclement weather and thus an "Act of God."

May 6 and 9, 1757. Charles is suing a German resident of Louisbourg for having killed his cow according to his allegations. You will remember that Francois Bigot, the Intendant of New France, had given all the newcomers to Louisbourg in 1749 a cow to help them feed their children. The case was resolved and the German, Benedit Moyhun, was acquitted from any such action. It seems that the cow was in foal and the German neighbor had attempted to help the cow but it died in the birth of a calf which survived.

As Charles and his family forged ahead and were prospering, war was declared in 1756 and thus the blockade of the Fortress of Louisbourg by the British began and would last until the fall of the city in 1758. The siege did not cause much concern to the inhabitants of Louisbourg in the beginning because there was enough food to feed the city for two years. Life continued. The main fare was codfish and the normal pasttime was gambling and drinking, especially by the Army. However by 1757, time took its toll and the food supply began to dwindle. Famine began. One is appraised that there was a great deal of corruption in the local government. As the Siege of Louisbourg has been well covered in Part I *(Ed note: See our Chapter 7)*, this narrative will move ahead to 1758.

After the surrender of Louisbourg in 1758, the British occupied the city. General Wolfe carried out his pledge to reduce Louisbourg to rubble and after the expulsion of all the inhabitants, he began his destruction. Every building or what was left of them were put to the torch, burned and levelled to the ground in 1760.

During the siege, the British lost 195 men but the French lost much more ... between 700 and 800 perished counting civilians as well mostly due to the merciless pounding of the city by a bombardment of the city from the English fleet. The actual casualties were never tabulated nor ascertained as no such list was ever found and no funeral service was held for the dead. There are monuments in the newer cemetery located on the Southern tip of Louisbourg on a point of land extending into the ocean, commemorating the dead from the siege of Louisbourg. A comment about the cemeteries. There are two of them. The old sits next to the demolished home of the Town's Executioner and contains the dead of Louisbourg up through 1744 and the new one honors the dead after that date. They are overgrown with thick grass and wild flowers. The grass resembles that found near salt water sand dunes. There are very few monuments as the original markers undoubtedly made of wood and have long ago deteriorated due to the adverse weather conditions. As one walks through these areas especially on a rainy day with the wind blowing in from the sea, an eerie feeling comes over you as the fog and the heavy clouds blot out the sun and the visibility becomes that of late twilight.

When I arrived around noon, there were a few tourists pouring over the remains but without realizing it, the rain had increased and the wind was much stronger and all the tourists were now gone. It was two o'clock in the afternoon but it looked and felt as if it was nine o'clock in the evening. By now the long grass tugged at my feet as if trying to hold me back. I felt that something or someone wanted me to stay and a feeling of almost panic overtook me. I knew that under my feet in those depressed and sunken graves rested Marie David and Charles' three children by a second marriage. *(Ed note: Probably Maurice was referring to Therese, born 1752; Hierome, born 1753; and Marie Anne, born 1755)* The cold rain pelted down on me and I began to run up Rue D'Orleans towards the Citadel. I was the only "tourist" left in the entire city as the rain had discouraged all including the "soldiers" and "inhabitants" and the busses had stopped running and thus had to find my way back to the Administration Building. My sojourn and search of records in the archives had kept me too busy to visit the ruins. Having spent so much time alone with the old records, the ghosts of Louisbourg had affected my mind!

I ran through a deserted city truly in panic? I felt I were in a Twilight Zone where unknown tentacles were pulling and calling me back. I had been isolated too long with the microfilm machine. Running through the deserted city past the rubble of the destroyed convent of Notre Dame located across the street from the hospital where Charles house is to be found, I sensed an outcry from those who lay beneath the surface for compassion, sympathy and solace ... I felt invisible hands tugging at my legs in a gesture that I should not leave. Having stood there in the cemetery with the rain beating down on me from the sea, the roar of the pounding surf gave me time to reflect and to ponder about the dead. I was in total communion with them and I was scared. I was alone! A comment about the cemeteries. They are situated about thirty feet from the ocean. Every year, much topsoil is eroded by the pounding waves. The dead of Louisbourg throughout history were buried only two to three feet below the surface because of the saturation of the land from the sea. During violent storms, the area has been compromised and periodically human bones have been found.

My search of the archives of the Fortress of Louisbourg from 1756, the year after the war was declared, through 1759 for traces of Charles' children proved fruitless. None could be found except for birth records. The French kept meticulous records. Each sailing list was scrutinized for traces of Francois and Alexis as well. None was found. Charles and Marie Ann Sudois did negotiate to return to LaRochelle and left Louisbourg in December of 1759 without the children. *(Ed note: We have since learned that Charles and Marie were deported from Louisbourg in 1758 along with the other French and returned to France in French ships. Also, Maurice mentioned above that three children were buried in the cemetery at Louisbourg but they also had a fourth born in Louisbourg – Charlotte, in 1756. Another child, Marianne, was recorded born in Rochefort December 9, 1759. See chart that follows.)*

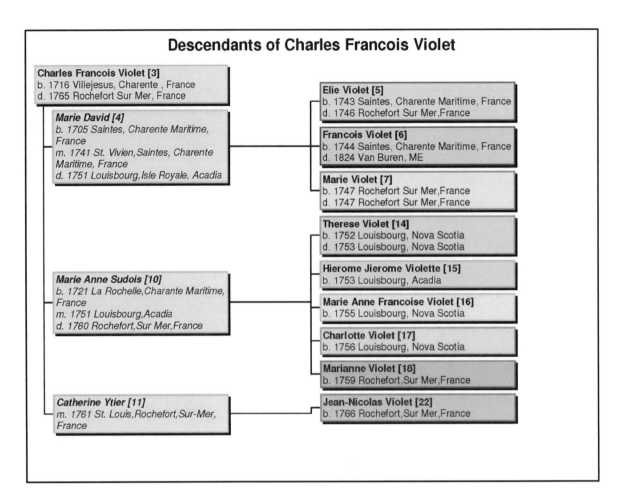

Descendants of Charles Francois Violet

Charles Francois Violet [3]
b. 1716 Villejesus, Charente , France
d. 1765 Rochefort Sur Mer, France

Marie David [4]
b. 1705 Saintes, Charente Maritime, France
m. 1741 St. Vivien, Saintes, Charente Maritime, France
d. 1751 Louisbourg, Isle Royale, Acadia

Marie Anne Sudois [10]
b. 1721 La Rochelle, Charante Maritime, France
m. 1751 Louisbourg, Acadia
d. 1760 Rochefort, Sur Mer, France

Catherine Ytier [11]
m. 1761 St. Louis, Rochefort, Sur-Mer, France

Elie Violet [5]
b. 1743 Saintes, Charente Maritime, France
d. 1746 Rochefort Sur Mer, France

Francois Violet [6]
b. 1744 Saintes, Charente Maritime, France
d. 1824 Van Buren, ME

Marie Violet [7]
b. 1747 Rochefort Sur Mer, France
d. 1747 Rochefort Sur Mer, France

Therese Violet [14]
b. 1752 Louisbourg, Nova Scotia
d. 1753 Louisbourg, Nova Scotia

Hierome Jierome Violette [15]
b. 1753 Louisbourg, Acadia

Marie Anne Francoise Violet [16]
b. 1755 Louisbourg, Nova Scotia

Charlotte Violet [17]
b. 1756 Louisbourg, Nova Scotia

Marianne Violet [18]
b. 1759 Rochefort, Sur Mer, France

Jean-Nicolas Violet [22]
b. 1766 Rochefort, Sur Mer, France

(Ed note: The chart above shows the families of Charles Violet. At the time of the account in this chapter he had not yet married Catherine Ytier and all of his children with Marie David and Marie Anne Sudois except Marianne had been born. Our next chapter will describe Charles's return to France and what happened there.)

Eric Krause, Superintendent of Historical Records for the Fortress of Louisbourg agreed with me that the children must have perished during the bombardment of Louisbourg as Charles' house, located near the Citadel was in the immediate range of fire from the British. It was located next to the hospital which received the first hits. No record was found anywhere of any mass burials and it is quite possible that some of the dead still remain in the rubble of what was once Louisbourg. No funeral record for those who died during bombardment can be found as the Chapel Saint Louis in the Citadel was completely destroyed during the siege.

It is a great feat of construction that the Canadian Government was able to reconstruct over 20% of the Citadel and nearby Port area to scale and the city today comes to life every Summer as "French" soldiers occupy the Fortress and many citizens from nearby modern Louisbourg dress in the style of 1744 when the city capitulated to the New Englanders. The descendants of Charles and

Francois have a stake in this city and we should all take the time to visit Louisbourg, find the hospital on Rue D'Orleans and the lot next to it on the Citadel side of the hospital was the house belonging to Allain Le Gras from whom Charles leased his boutique. Only the Foundation walls remain and have been filled with rubble from the devastation of the city in 1760. The reconstruction of the city, unfortunately, stopped but a short distance from the Le Gras home.

Today the ruins of Louisbourg are completely overrun by the Angelique plant. The plant is to be found throughout the old city, modern Louisbourg, and halfway to Sydney. It grows wild, impossible to stop, and it is cursed by the local inhabitants which is made up mostly of descendants from Scotland who have settled the area. The origin of the plant, according to Eric Krause, was from a French resident of Louisbourg during the siege. He had used the plant to provide an improved taste for his gin. After the fall of Louisbourg, the plant was allowed to propogate and it did because the area was left unattended for so many years. The plant tentacles reached out and covered every inch of the city with thick stems and flowers about three feet high everywhere you look. This seems to be fitting and poetic justice for the suffering of the inhabitants of old Louisbourg who withstood so much from the British. The Angelique plant stands as a reminder that Angels still watch over the city.

Many of us sometime wonder just what role Charles might have played during the battle for Louisbourg. McLennon tells us that all able bodied men participated in the defense of the city ... be it a member of the Home Militia, as Damage Control people who tried to repair damage caused by bombs and the shelling by the British, or to render and provide health and comfort for the wounded or injured. Charles was there and thus did participate in the Damage Control group. We can state with certainty that one of our ancestors did participate in the struggle between France and England for control of North America.

Charles Violet was a most interesting individual. It was rather educational to learn how this man could circumvent problems. He never ceases to amaze me in his wheeling and dealing and his mode of life. He was certainly ahead of his time as he seemed to live his Eighteenth Century under the accepted life style of the Twentieth Century. He has provided for us a most interesting legacy and a challenge to discover more if it can be found. Most of all, be very proud of your heritage. . .don't be afraid to acclaim it to the world because it is colorful, full of mystery, of intrigue, and with the aspect that in time, all will be resolved. We are the envy of all our Acadian friends!

Be proud of Villejesus! The final word is not in as yet as to the actual origin of the Violet/Viollet/Violettes. Some say it is Fontenille but records fail to provide the information although the Viollets of that town outnumber the Viollets of Villejesus. *(Ed note: Subsequent research has found documents reported in earlier chapters that show Villejésus was the place of origin of the family.)* Maire Montussac of the Commune of Villejesus told me that the commune was among the first Christian settlements in France during the days of the Romans. We don't go back that far but isn't it great that we have a connection to the beginning of Christianity. Think about that!

In France, a book written by Chateaubriand finds a M. Violet who plays a pocket violin and is the "maitre de danse" for the Iroquois Indians. He is reported to have served with the troops of Rochambeau during the war for U.S. Independence at Yorktown. There is no first name and research in France should provide the answer ... who knows, probably one of Francois' Sons or a Violet conscripted from the Charente — his future is unknown. Under Rochambeau, he was a kitchen helper. More later. *(Ed note: This turned out to be the end of Maurice's published writings.)*

(End of Maurice's text)

CHAPTER 9 - CHARLES, BACK TO FRANCE
Time Span: 1758-1760

Charles may have been glad to leave the New World behind, after all the troubles he had there! He came to Louisbourg with a wife and two children, his wife died while there, he had to declare bankruptcy when his business failed, and as part of his bankruptcy he had to assign his children to his creditors. He did remarry within a month after Marie David Violet died, this time to Marie Anne Sudois. This second Marie appears to have been a fairly wealthy woman.

Marie Anne Sudois was born in La Rochelle, France, on November 30, 1721. We do not know how or why and when she came to Louisbourg. She was 29 years old when she married Charles on June 29, 1751 and Charles was 35. Charles and Marie Anne Sudois had four children born in Louisbourg: Therese, April 22, 1752; Hierome, June 17, 1753; Marie Anne Francoise, August 21, 1755; and Charlotte, October 10, 1756. Therese died in Louisbourg January 31, 1753; she was only eight months old.

But then another blow struck with the fall of Louisbourg to the British in July 1758. All French occupants were transported to France. We know the last ship left Louisbourg at the end of September 1758, so it is fair to say that Charles and his second wife Marie Anne Sudois arrived at La Rochelle in the fall of that year. No children were listed on the manifest, so we are left to speculate what happened to Charles' children from his marriage to Marie Anne Sudois. We know from Louisbourg records that Therese was born and died in Louisbourg. But what happened to Hierome, Marie Anne Francoise, and Charlotte? There is no record of them arriving in La Rochelle nor is there any subsequent record of them in France.

We know from Rita Lippe's book that Alexis Hilaret married Cecile Caissie on July 2, 1765 in Cayenne, West Indies. Alexis was the natural son of Marie David and was adopted by Charles. We'll drop Alexis from our story at this point and, of course, we'll tell no more about our "Mémère" Marie David Violet except to thank her for our heritage.

And we know of course that François next showed up in New Brunswick at Hammond River. We'll be hearing much more about our ancestor François in the next several chapters of this book.

Louisbourg did not fall peacefully, and Maurice Violette speculated that the others may have been killed in the bombardment during the siege by the British. The following is an excerpt from Maurice Violette's history P.15.

(Start of Maurice quote)

"My search of the archives of the Fortress of Louisbourg from 1756, the year after the war was declared, through 1759 for traces of Charles' children proved fruitless. None could be found except for birth records. The French kept meticulous records. Each sailing list was scrutinized for traces of Francois and Alexis as well. None was found. Charles and Marie Ann Sudois did negotiate to return to La Rochelle and left Louisbourg in December of 1759 without the children.

(Ed note: We have since learned that Charles and Marie Anne were deported from Louisbourg in 1758 along with the other French and returned to France in French ships.)

Eric Krause, Superintendent of Historical Records for the Fortress of Louisbourg, agreed with me that the children must have perished during the bombardment of Louisbourg as Charles' house, located near the Citadel was in the immediate range of fire from the British. It was located next to the hospital, which received the first hits. No record was found anywhere of any mass burials and it is quite possible that some of the dead still remain in the rubble of what was once Louisbourg. No funeral record for those who died during bombardment can be found as the Chapel Saint Louis in the Citadel was completely destroyed during the siege."

(End of Maurice quote)

Document 9-1 Research on Charles' return to France. Translation of written text: "I find the families of Charles Viollet, roofer, as follows: Charles Violet, has taken rations at LaRochelle up until January 31, and was removed February 1ˢᵗ; Marie Anne Sudois, his wife, idem, was at Rochefort with her husband from March 1, 1759." Translation of printed text: "On this document no mention of the return to France in 1759 of 3 children born at Louisbourg (Canada). Hierome, born June 17, 1753; Marie-Anne-Françoise, born August 21, 1755; Charlotte, born October 10, 1756." "Idem" means the same as ditto, which we interpret as saying she followed the same pattern as Charles.

And, our poor Charles did not leave his trials and tribulations in Louisbourg as misfortune followed him back to France.

Shortly after arriving in La Rochelle, Charles moved his family to Rochefort where he had lived prior to sailing for Louisbourg. On December 9, 1759, Marie Anne Sudois had her fifth child, Marianne, in Rochefort. Less than one year later on November 16, 1760 Marie Anne Sudois died, leaving Charles once again with young children.

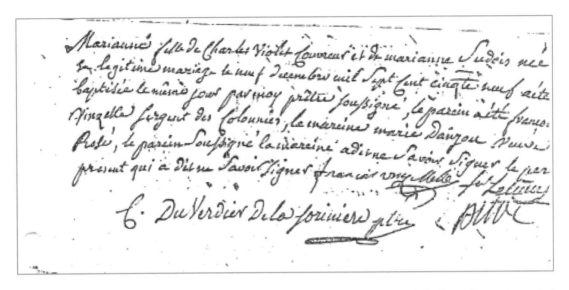

Document 9-2: Birth record for Marianne Violet. Translation: "Marianne, daughter of Charles Violet, roofer, and of Marianne Sudois, born of a legitimate marriage on 9 December 1759 and baptized the same day by me, priest undersigned, the godfather was Francois Vinzelle, Sergeant of the Colonies, the godmother Marie Danjou, widow Rose, the godfather undersigned, the godmother said could not sign, the father presnt who said he did not know how to write." (Signatures follow.)

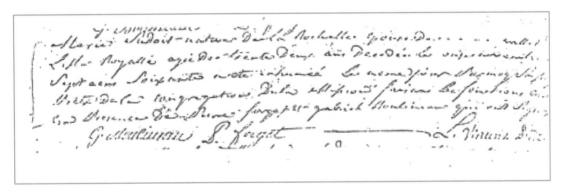

Document 9-3: Death record for Marie Sudois Violet. Translation: "Marie Sudoit, born in La Rochelle, spouse of Charles Violet of the Ile Royale 32 years old, died the 16th of November 1760 and was buried the same day by me the undersigned priest of the congregation of the mission performing church functions, in the presence of Pierre Forget and Gabriel Moulineau, who have signed." (Signatures follow)

Charles married for the third time, on April 13, 1761 to Catherine Ytier, the widow of Jean Poinsot. There was a son Jean-Nicolas born of this marriage on January 8, 1766. Unfortunately, Charles died on November 13, 1765, two months prior to the birth of his son, leaving Catherine Ytier a widow. So, we now have all the people in Charles' genealogy on stage, and the chart that follows is complete.

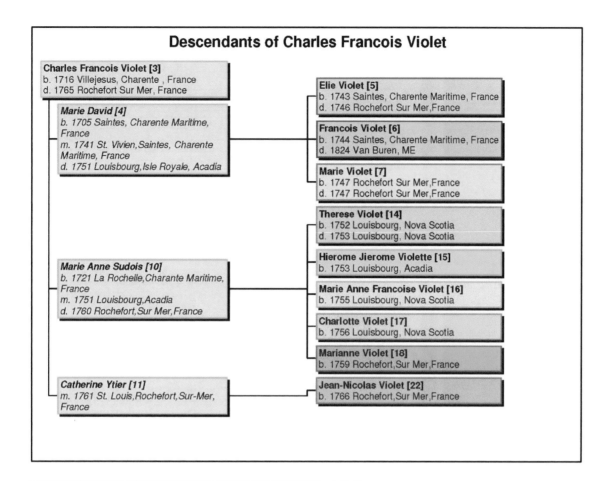

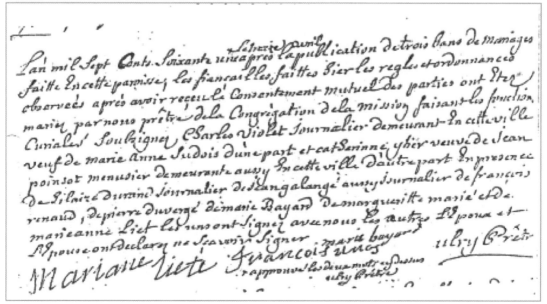

Document 9-4: Marriage record, Charles Violet and Catherine Ytier. Translation: "The year 1771, the 13th of April, after the publication of three banns of marriage made in this parish, the fiancailles made yesterday, the rules and laws observed after having received the mutual consent of the parties were married by us, priest of the congregation of the mission doing the curatorial duties, undersigned, Charles Violet, journeyman, living in this city, widower of Marie Anne Sudois, the first party, and Catherine Ytier, widow of Jean Poinsot, carpenter, also living in this city, the other party, in the presence of Hilaire Durand, journeyman, of Jean Galange, also a journeyman, of Francois Renaud, of Pierre

Duverge, of Marie Bayard, of Margueritte Marie, and of Marieanne Liet, the ones who signed with us, the others, the husband and wife have said they do not know how to write." (Signatures follow)

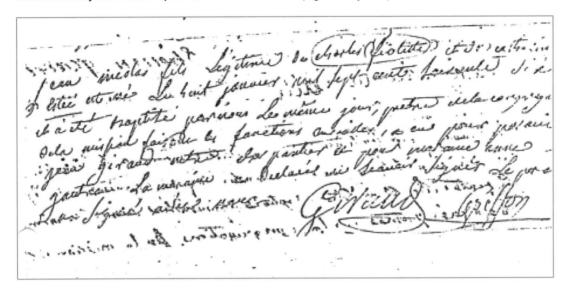

Document 9-5: Birth record of Jean Nicholas Violet. Translation: "Jean Nicolas, legitimate son of Charles Violette and of Catherine Estie, was born the 8th of January 1766 and was baptized by us the same day, priest of the mission, doing curatorial duties, has for godfather, Jean Giraud, Master Carpentier, and for godmother Anne Gautreau, the god-mother having declared she did not know how to sign, the godfather having signed with us." (Signatures follow)

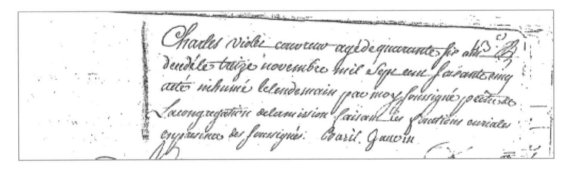

Document 9-6: Death record for Charles Violet. Translation: "Charles Violet, roofer, 46 years old, died the 13th of No-vember 1765, and was buried the following day by me undersigned priest of the congregation of the mission doing curatorial duties in the presence of the undersigned." (Signatures follow)

We can find no records subsequent to the death of Charles with regard to his heirs. So, the chapter on Charles' life comes to a close. Perhaps sometime in the future, his heirs, if any, will make contact with their North American cousins.

CHAPTER 10 - SOME VIOLETTE LEGENDS – SOME SPECULATIONS

Time Span: 1758-1770

An early family oral tradition once described how the name Violet/Violette came to be applied to young François; this was prior to the research reported in our earlier chapters that shows the name was found in 17th century France. And remember that François was assigned to subrogate guardians in Louisbourg in 1751 and we have no record of his ever being part of his father's family again. When his father Charles returned to France in 1758 there is no record that any of his children returned with him. While today we know that the name came from France through his parents, and have the records to show this, you can imagine how early people without this knowledge could come up with a story to explain a child on his own and without parents.

Another family oral tradition holds that François at some time was apprenticed to or raised by a missionary. We explore this legend as well.

The name Violet/Violette

No there is nothing definitive about the name's origins. It could be the color, or it could be the flower. Old church records spell it different ways: Louis Viollet, Charles Violet. Records found by Rod Violette, our Genealogist, did not have it spelled Violette until about 1753 in Louisbourg i.e. Hierome Violette and the early 1800's in St. Basile, NB.

The French dictionary describes *violette* as a plant, and *violet* as a color.

Explaining François' "Missing" Years – Some Speculation

One early family oral tradition holds that François was at some time apprenticed to or raised by a missionary. He had some education and could at least sign his name, but that literacy could also have come from a school at Louisbourg, for there were nuns teaching there before 1758. If he was associated with a missionary, there is no record of which one. It seems hard to believe that a roving missionary could afford to have a youngster tagging along, and missionaries were expected to move frequently from community to community. We could construct a scenario where François left his family when his father remarried in 1751. Remember that François' mother died when he was 6½. He was assigned to subrogate guardians at this young age shortly after, but we do not know if he lived with them or with his father still. His father remarried within a month after his 46-year-old mother died, and his new stepmother was 30. New children started appearing within a year; Francois had been living in a household as an only child with only his father and mother for the last 4½ years and now suddenly there were little ones coming every year. When his father and the new family left for France in 1758 we can well imagine that François did not feel sufficiently a part of this group to go with them, if in fact he was free to do so under his subrogate guardianship. In fact, we can also imagine an estrangement beginning even earlier if François' new mother did not accept him as part of "her" family; picture a Cinderella story but with the father's child being male instead of female. If François did, indeed, become attached to a missionary we can also imagine his father accepting this because he was too busy with his work to take charge of an "orphan" boy and glad to have someone responsible do it, or maybe it was simply a way to avoid the turmoil if an estrangement occurred because of his second marriage.

That last paragraph contains elements of both oral tradition and speculation and may be pure fantasy. But while there is often some element of truth in oral tradition it is also very difficult to prove in any rigorous way. We leave it to the reader to construct their own explanation of that twelve-year period in François' life between the ages of 14 (1758, when Charles returned to France) and 26 (1770, when François shows up in records in southern New Brunswick)!

CHAPTER 11 – FRANÇOIS LEAVES ÎLE ROYALE

Time Span: 1755-1769

We now move on in our narrative from our "grand-père" Charles to his son, our "père", François. Remember that François was the son of Charles and his first wife, Marie David, who died in Louisbourg in May 1751. François had an older brother, Helie, and younger sister, Marie, who had both died while the family was still in France. He also had an older step-brother, Alexis Hilaret, who was with the family when they moved to Louisbourg in 1749. After François' mother, Marie David, died Charles remarried and with his second wife, Marie Anne Sudois, had four children born in Louisbourg between 1752 and 1756 (Therese, Hierome, Marie Anne, and Charlotte). In Chapter 9 we related that Charles and his second wife Marie Anne had sailed from Louisbourg to La Rochelle in the fall of 1758 and settled in Rocheford, France. The port of La Rochelle's records do not show any children accompanying them. So, we are left to wonder if Hierome, Marie Anne, and Charlotte were killed in the bombardment associated with the siege of Louisbourg (Therese died before her first birthday). The Superintendent of Historical records at Louisbourg, Eric Krause, and Maurice Violette, VFA #14, (1921-2004), have come to that conclusion.

So that leaves Alexis Hilaret and François still in the New World. Alexis was 25 when Charles left Louisbourg and François was 14. We have records that Alexis was married to Cecile Caissie in Cayenne, West Indies, in 1765 (Cayenne, West Indies is now known as French Guiana and was a Dutch possession at the time Alexis moved there). We also have records that François was married to Marie-Luce Thibodeau, their marriage being blessed by Abbott Bailly, May 6, 1770. François' marriage was registered at Ecoupag (Ekoupahag), now known as Springhill, New Brunswick.

Acadia: A Long, Rich Heritage Brought to a Disastrous End

No honest history of the Violette family should fail to mention the events that caused many of the trials and tribulations of the Acadians. François was not an Acadian by birth, but when he married Marie-Luce Thibodeau on May 6, 1770, he became part of one of the oldest Acadian families, their forefather having arrived at Port Royal in 1654. So it is important to learn something of the Acadian history.

So far we have related history from the viewpoint of France and Great Britain. And certainly those two world powers greatly defined the events and the culture of Île Royale/Cape Breton Island/Acadia. The strategic importance of Fortress Louisbourg at the entrance to the Gulf of St. Lawrence resulted in the area coming under one rule or the other as the two powers struggled for dominance in the region. Both were invading forces who wanted to control the area because of its importance to a major fishing industry as well as its importance as a gateway to the vast continent beyond to the west.

But while the French and British came and went there remained a constant local non-indigenous population, who had settled the area many generations before. These were the Acadians. And our "mère", Marie-Luce Thibodeau, was of this stock. Rod Violette, VFA #12, our Genealogist, has been able to trace her ancestry back six generations so we know where her family came from (France) and when they arrived in Acadia (1654). The two-page chart at the end of this chapter shows what Rod has been able to learn about Marie-Luce's heritage. Her father, mother, grandfathers, and grandmothers were all born in Acadia. On her mother's side, her great-grandparents were also born in Acadia but their parents came from France in the 1640-1660 period. On her father's side, her grandfather's parents were born in France while her grandmother's parents were born in Acadia, but their parents were born in France. So, Marie-Luce was at least a third-generation Acadian.

The Acadians had left a feudal system in France where land ownership was denied them. By relocating to a place with abundant land available for ownership they could establish their free enjoyment of their land and their efforts and the Acadians had done this for more than a century at the time of our account. When the first settlers came to Acadia in the mid-1600s they were located away from active commerce and communication channels and were more-or-less in isolation. Neither the French nor the British were able in those early years to establish an active foothold in the region.

As the fishing industry on the Atlantic shelf grew and as the French explored and settled the interior of the continent (New France) via the St Lawrence River and the British established colonies in New England to the south, the Acadians found themselves holding some lands very desirable to others. The value was not necessarily in what the land could produce but in the strategic location of the lands in controlling the commercial and communication corridors of the North Atlantic. The Acadians were fiercely independent and developed a stateless society. Historian Carl Brasseux wrote in *The Founding of New Acadia*:

> For example, from 1655 to 1755, the century before the Grand Dérangement (as the Acadian dispersal is popularly known), the Acadians did not hesitate to protest the actions of local administrators and clergymen to higher authorities in Quebec and France. When appeals proved ineffective, the colonists resorted to procrastination, subterfuge, and other forms of passive resistance to foil unpopular administrative policies.
>
> [. . .]. Though paradoxical on the surface, Acadian contentiousness clearly reflects the eagerness of the frontiersmen to protect their newly acquired and highly prized personal liberties from encroachment on any level.

But because of their location the Acadians were constantly forced between the two world powers who struggled to control the region.

The French and Indian War was fought for control of the North American continent between 1754 and 1763. However, in 1756 it erupted on a larger scale and became one theater in the Seven Years War. When Britain retook Île Royale/Cape Breton Island/Acadia in 1758 they demolished the fortifications at Fortress Louisbourg so the French could not reestablish themselves there. The rout of the French continued after the fall of Louisbourg, and in 1759 they lost control of Québec as well and in 1760 they lost Montreal and the whole of New France.

A critical period for our family came in 1755, when the British brutally deported the Acadians from their homes and lands in what has become known as the Grand Dérangement. Briefly, at this time the

British drove out all the Acadians, took their lands, destroyed their homes, split up families, and generally tried to destroy a people.

Why did François end up in New Brunswick? François was French, but he was probably not deported with the rest of the French when Britain retook Île Royale/Cape Breton Island/Acadia in 1758. Perhaps, fearing the same fate as the Acadians who were exiled to the colonies, or were imprisoned in Great Britain when Louisbourg fell to the British in 1758, François may have decided to slip away and join some three to four thousand Acadians who evaded the British and escaped the Grand Dérangement. The Acadians dispersed north to Prince Edward Island and Île Royale (where Louisbourg is located), and to Memramcook, Petitcodiac, Miramichi, Caraquet, Baie des Chaleurs, Gaspé, the Madeleine Islands, or to the St. John River area. Map 11-1 shows these locations in relation to Acadia.

Map 11-1: Places the Acadians went (green) to avoid British rule

The Acadians were not isolationists, though they immigrated to Acadia to avoid mainstream life in France. They were known to be traders and traveled extensively along the Atlantic seaboard. As written in *Acadia: Peaceful, Prosperous, Stateless*, Chantal K. Saucier wrote:

> For one hundred years, the Acadians managed to live peacefully and to remain neutral in a disputed territory while Acadia remained stateless and became one of the most prosperous places in North America. Over the years, Acadians did make pledges of allegiance to England, but they always refused to take any oath that did not include the following (libertarian) provisions:
>
> - A recognition of their property rights;

- Freedom to keep and practice their Catholic faith;

- And an exemption from having to bear arms against the French and their allies (allies here meaning the Mi'kmaq people, neighbors and friends to the Acadians).

Acadians also were free traders and they traded with all regardless of the regulations the empires tried to impose on them (at some point, British officials even outlawed commerce between the Acadians and the Mi'kmaq in an effort to brake the alliance that had developed between the two communities). There are reports that Acadians traveled as far as the Caribbean islands, trading their products (which included what was considered some of the best whiskey in North America) for rum and other southern merchandise.

In addition, historians have written that Acadians found all sorts of means to evade taxes and some refused to answer censuses. In the 1671 census, for example, we find that Pierre Lanoue, cooper, "sent word that he was feeling fine and he did not want to give his age."

It may have been in conjunction with the trade in the Caribbean and beyond that Alexis Hilaret relocated to the West Indies.

Around 1755 there were as many as 18,000 Acadians living in the English territory then called Nova Scotia. Nova Scotia at that time referred to both the island called Île Royale/Cape Breton as well as the remainder of the Acadian Peninsula plus the contested lands in what is now called New Brunswick, on the other side of the Bay of Fundy (see Map 11-2).

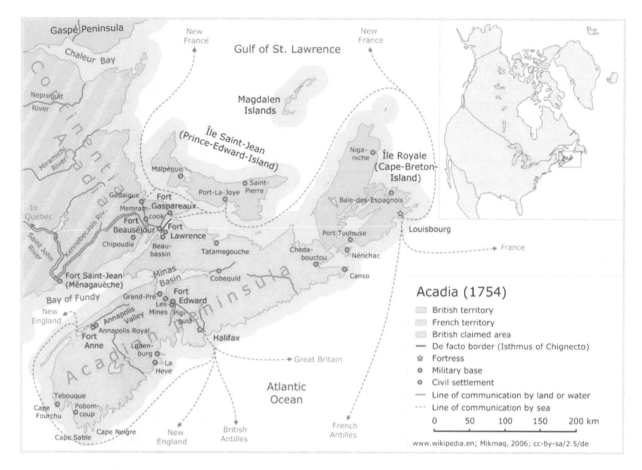

Map 11-2: Status of lands in Acadia in 1754 (from Wikimedia Commons, Image made by Klaus Mueller, Germany, 2006)

The pretext for this deportation in 1755 was that the Acadians refused to take an unconditional oath of allegiance to the English King and were thus considered enemies. The major objection the Acadians had to the unconditional oath was that they would have to renounce their Catholic religion and might be obliged to fight against their own former countrymen, the French. Back in 1727 the Acadians had signed a conditional oath exempting them from these provisions.

Even though the Acadians had been loyal to that 1727 oath during the fighting in 1748, in 1754 Lt. Gov. Lawrence insisted that they sign an unconditional oath, which they refused to do. Enraged by their refusal, Lawrence put into effect his "final resolution". This may sound like Hitler's "final solution" to his Jewish problem, and to the Acadians it turned out to be just as devastating. So, on the afternoon of August 6, 1755, *A Great and Noble Scheme* was put into operation (*A Great and Noble Scheme: The Tragic Story of the Expulsion of the French Acadians from their American Homeland.* W. W. Norton & Company, 2005, ISBN 9780393051353 is the title of the latest book written by John Mack Faragher about the plight of the Acadians). The deportations started after the Battle of Beauséjour, first from Chignecto, then from Grand Pré, and finally from Port Royal (Fort Anne).

The following contains excerpts from *The History of Madawaska* by Fr. Thomas Albert: English translation by Sr. Therese Doucette and Dr. Francis Doucette, Northern Graphics, Madawaska ME, 1985, pages 31-32.

> Breaking up by armed force the families of an honest and peaceful people consti-
> tutes one of the darkest pages in the history of British conquests. England has
> tried to regain some honor by disavowing the event as it has recently disowned

its conduct towards its own colonies of New England before the Revolutionary War.

The exile of the Acadians was a mistake because it lacked sufficient cause. It was a crime against humanity in its mode of execution: confiscation of belongings and separation of families. It was a crime because of its results: suffering of spouses, mothers, innocent children and, intended or not, deprivation, misery and death in large numbers. Even if the Acadians had been guilty of all that they have been accused, the punishment would still have been disproportionate to the crime.

The deportation did not end with the Grand Derangement of 1755. The inhabitants of New Brunswick and Isle St. Jean were not spared. Military expeditions were sent against the different settlements of these regions to complete the work of Lawrence and Shirley. In the St. John the task was confided to Colonel Monckton. This valley had many settlements from Fort Latour (St. John) to Ste. Anne-des-Pays-Bas (Fredericton). The principal ones were Grimrose with a population of 350, Villerai, Jemseg, Robichaud, Belle-Isle, Nashwack, and Ecoupag. The village of Ste. Anne had 250 inhabitants.

Within two months Monckton, with his twelve hundred rangers, accomplished his task very well. Wherever he passed there was nothing but smoking ruins. However, the advanced season prevented him from going further up the St. John River to burn the beautiful village of Ste. Anne. Most inhabitants of the ravaged areas had fled into the forests or had taken refuge in Ste. Anne. Monckton returned to Halifax with a few captives. Ste. Anne however would have its turn. During the winter of 1758 a detachment of Rangers under Moses Hazen was sent by land to complete the destruction of the settlements on the St. John.

During the horrible night of January 28-29, 1759, Hazen's soldiers charged the unsuspecting village of Ste. Anne, burned the houses and massacred those who refused to join the burners in hastening the destruction of their village. Tradition has it that two women, Anastasia Bellefontaine, wife of Eustache Pare, and the wife of her brother Michel, were massacred with their four children after having offered heroic resistance to the British soldiers. The Rangers took twenty-three prisoners. The other refugees went further into Canada or fled into the forest.

The Acadians who were not caught by the British were constantly harassed by soldiers until after the end of the war. Even after the end of hostilities, in the spring of 1763, Lieutenant Gilfred Studholm, on orders of Governor Belcher of Nova Scotia to purge the province of Acadian presence, ordered the refugees at Ecoupag to evacuate the village. When Studholm learned that a hundred Acadians had taken refuge not far from Ecoupag, he promptly chased them away. He would hear nothing of their pleas or promises to leave the province in the spring. So these inhabitants also went to the shores of the St. Lawrence.

After the fall of Québec in 1759, two hundred Acadians who had taken refuge there, after being expelled from the St. John River between 1758 and 1763, decided to take the oath of allegiance. They were given a copy of the Act along with a statement by General Monckton permitting them to return to their homes on the St. John River. They traveled from Québec to Fort Frederic in October 1759. Upon their arrival, they presented their documents to Colonel Arbuthnot, who referred the matter to the Governor in Halifax, Charles Lawrence, the very person who had ordered the expulsion of the Acadians from all of Nova Scotia in 1755. Lawrence asserted that the statement granting them permission had been obtained under false pretenses. Furthermore, he maintained that the Acadians in question must have been from another St. John River Valley in Canada, and that Monckton had made a mistake in granting his permission for them to settle there!

But Monckton knew the St. John River very well. He had expelled the French from it and burned the village of Ste. Anne (Fredericton). He could no more have made a mistake about it than Lawrence could claim that Monckton had made a mistake.

So poor was the treatment of the Acadians by the British in 1755 that 250 years after the fact, in 2003, a Royal Proclamation was issued apologizing for their actions. Both Lawrence's Deportation Proclamation (Appendix 11-A) and the text of the 2003 Royal Proclamation (Appendix 11-B) are found at the end of this chapter.

A Repatriation of Sorts

Until the close of the Seven Year's War of 1757-1763, the Acadians or French persons had been regarded as enemies. Some had been deported; others had fled to territory still held by the French - first to Île St. Jean (Prince Edward Island) and Île Royale (Cape Breton Island) and later Québec. Following the Treaty of Paris in 1763 all these places of refuge became parts of British North America and the status of the Acadians changed from that of "enemies" to "subjects".

For the British, the problem of what to do with these new subjects remained. Antonine Maillet's 1979 book *Pélagie-la-Charette* (Pélagie-the-cart) presents a fictional yet quite historically accurate portrayal of Acadian repatriation from the American south to Nova Scotia, though some of the deportees chose to repatriate themselves in the French held Madeleine Islands. The title character, Pélagie Le-Blanc, a widow, leads her fictional people back to Grand Pré from which they had been deported in 1755.

In reality, in 1766 Joseph Dugas led the return of the Acadians to Nova Scotia, though they were not allowed to re-establish on the same estates they had lost during the war. They settled in the more westerly portion of the province of Nova Scotia and also in Cheticamp on the north side of Cape Breton Island.

There was also a New England (pre-Loyalist) migration into the lower St. John Valley at this time. These pre-Loyalists set up the rudiments of Paartown (named after the Governor of Nova Scotia, John Paar) at the mouth of the St. John River. Among them were the merchant traders, William Hazen, Richard Simonds, and James White in whose merchant establishment we will find a record of François Violet's buying activity in 1782.

François and Marie-Luce at Hammond River

The Hammond River is a tributary to the Kennebecasis River and joins the Kennebecasis about 18 miles (28 km) above its mouth. The Kennebecasis is tributary to the lower St John River and joins the St John River about four miles (6.7 km) from where it empties into the Bay of Fundy.

We know that François and others who left Cape Breton Island/Île Royale made their way to the St John River, eventually settling on the Hammond River, a short distance from the main Kennebecasis River (the Hammond used to be called the Little Kennebecasis). They may have been chased from their initial St John River location because of raids conducted by Monckton, Hazen, and Studholm between 1758 and 1763. We think that they settled there because the Hammond River was off the beaten track, and the raiders of the St John River settlements never mention French squatters on the Hammond River. These raids were not just minor harassments: they were meant to destroy all property, both houses and animals, and, in some cases, resulted in the loss of life of the settlers.

We will learn more about life in the Hammond River settlements in the next chapter.

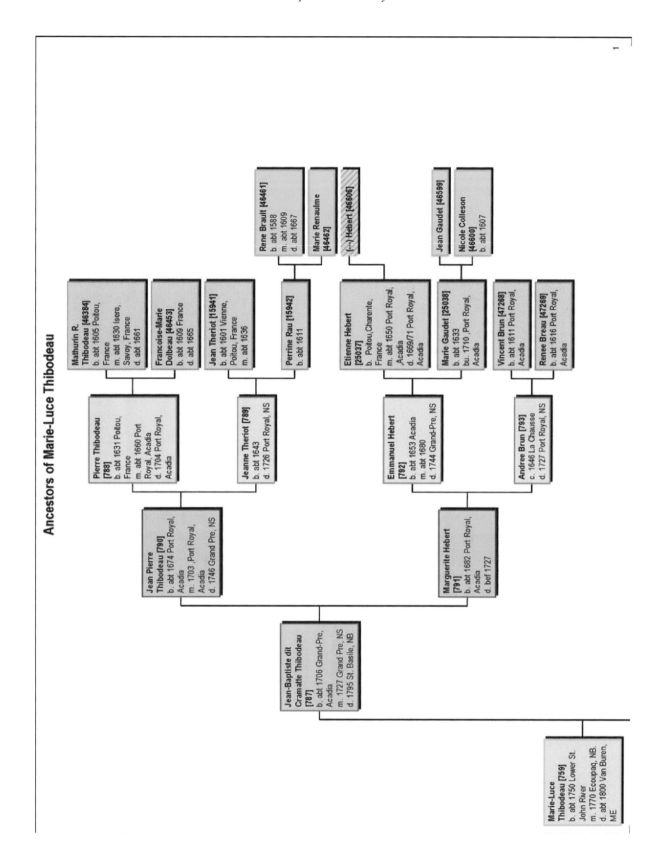

Ancestors of Marie-Luce Thibodeau

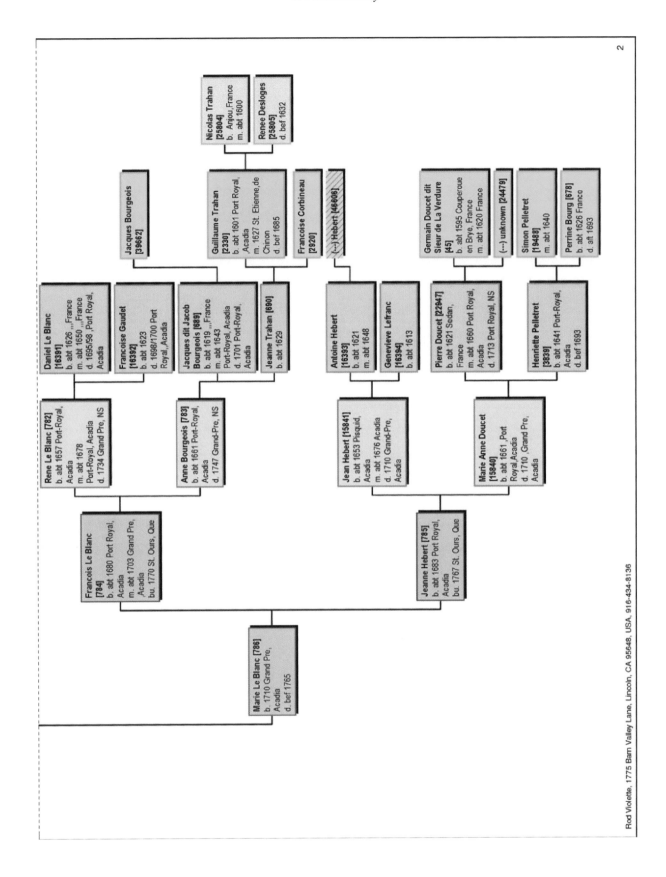

Appendix 11-A

Deportation Proclamation of Governor Lawrence in 1755

Gentlemen,

I have received from his Excellency Governor Lawrence, The Kings Commission Which I have in my hand and by whose orders you are Convened together to manifest to you His Majesty's final resolution to the French Inhabitants of this his Province of Nova Scotia, who for almost half a Century have had more Indulgence Granted them, than any of his Subjects in any part of his Dominions, what use you have made of them, you your Self Best Know.

The Part of Duty I am now upon is what thoh Necessary is Very Disagreable to My natural make and Temper as I know it Must be Grevious to you who are of the Same Species.

But it is not my Business to annimdvert, but to obey Such orders as I receive, And therefore without Hessitation Shall Deliver you his Majestys orders and Instructions, Vizt.

That your Lands & Tennements Cattle of all Kinds and Live Stock of all Sortes are Forfitted to the Crown with all other your Effects Saving your Money & Household Goods and you your Selves to be removed from this his Province.

Thus it is Preremtorily his Majestys orders That the whole French Inhabitants Of these Districts, be removed, and I am Throh his Majestys Goodness Directed to allow You Liberty to Carry of your Money and Household Goods as Many as you Can without Discomemoading the Vessels you Go in. I Shall do Every thing in my Power that all Those Goods be Secured to you and that you are Not Molested in Carrying of them of and also that whole Familys Shall go in the Same Vessel and make this remove which I am Sensable must give you a great deal of Trouble as Easey as his Majestys Service will admit and hope that in what Ever part of the world you may Fall you may be Faithfull Subjects, a Peasable & happy People.

I must also Inform you That it is his Majestys Pleasure that you remain in Security under the Inspection & Direction of the Troops that I have the Honr. To Command. and Then Declared them the Kings Prisoners.

And Gave out the Following Declaration

Grand-Pre September 5th 1755.

all officers and Soldiers and Sea Men Employed in his Majestys Service as well as all his Subjects of what Denomination Soever, are hereby Notifyed That all Cattle viz Horsses

Horne Cattle sheep goats Hoggs and Poultrey of Every Kinde, that was this Day So-posed to be Vested in the French Inhabitants of this Province are become Forfitted to his Majesty whose Property they now are and Every Person of what Denomination Soever is to take Care not to Hurt Kill or Distroy anything of any Kinde nor to Rob Or-chards or Gardens or to make waste of anything Dead or alive in these Districts without Special Order; Given at my Camp the Day & Place abovesd.

John Winslow

(End of 1755 Deportation Proclamation)

Appendix 11-B

The Royal Proclamation of 2003

The Royal Proclamation of 2003 — formally known as Proclamation Designating July 28 of Every Year as "A Day of Commemoration of the Great Upheaval", Commencing on July 28, 2005 — is a document issued by Queen Elizabeth II acknowledging and expressing regret concerning the Grand Dérangement, England's expulsion of French-speaking Acadian peasant farmers from Nova Scotia beginning in 1755.

Historical background

The proclamation's origin dates back to a 1763 petition submitted to King George III of Great Britain by Acadian exiles in Philadelphia, Pennsylvania. Because the King never responded to the petition, Warren A. Perrin, a Cajun attorney and cultural activist from Erath, Louisiana, resurrected the petition and threatened to sue England if it refused to acknowledge the illegality of the Grand Derangement.

After thirteen years of discussions, Perrin (now head of CODOFIL, the Council for Development of French in Louisiana) and his supporters in the United States and Canada persuaded Queen Elizabeth II, in her capacity as Queen of Canada, to issue a royal proclamation acknowledging the historical fact of the Great Upheaval and consequent suffering experienced by the Acadian people. The document itself was signed by Adrienne Clarkson

Text of the proclamation

Elizabeth the Second, by the Grace of God of the United Kingdom, Canada and her other Realms and Territories Queen, Head of the Commonwealth, Defender of the Faith.

To All To Whom these Presents shall come or whom the same may in any way concern,

Greeting:

Morris Rosenberg
Deputy Attorney General of Canada

A PROCLAMATION

Whereas the Acadian people, through the vitality of their community, have made a remarkable contribution to Canadian society for almost 400 years;

Whereas on July 28, 1755, the Crown, in the course of administering the affairs of the British colony of Nova Scotia, made the decision to deport the Acadian people;

Whereas the deportation of the Acadian people, commonly known as the Great Upheaval, continued until 1763 and had tragic consequences, including the deaths of many thousands of Acadians - from disease, in shipwrecks, in their places of refuge and in prison camps in Nova Scotia and England as well as in the British colonies in America;

Whereas We acknowledge these historical facts and the trials and suffering experienced by the Acadian people during the Great Upheaval;

Whereas We hope that the Acadian people can turn the page on this dark chapter of their history;

Whereas Canada is no longer a British colony but a sovereign state, by and under the Constitution of Canada;

Whereas when Canada became a sovereign state, with regard to Canada, the Crown in right of Canada and of the provinces succeeded to the powers and prerogatives of the Crown in right of the United Kingdom;

Whereas We, in Our role as Queen of Canada, exercise the executive power by and under the Constitution of Canada;

Whereas this Our present Proclamation does not, under any circumstances, constitute a recognition of legal or financial responsibility by the Crown in right of Canada and of the provinces and is not, under any circumstances, a recognition of, and does not have any effect upon, any right or obligation of any person or group of persons;

And Whereas, by Order in Council P.C. 2003-1967 of December 6, 2003, the Governor in Council has directed that a proclamation do issue designating July 28 of every year as "A Day of Commemoration of the Great Upheaval", commencing on July 28, 2005;

Now Know You that We, by and with the advice of Our Privy Council for Canada, do by this Our Proclamation, effective on September 5, 2004, designate July 28 of every year as "A Day of Commemoration of the Great Upheaval", commencing on July 28, 2005.

Of All Which Our Loving Subjects and all others whom these Presents may concern are hereby required to take notice and to govern themselves accordingly.

In Testimony Whereof, We have caused this Our Proclamation to be published and the Great Seal of Canada to be hereunto affixed. Witness: Our Right Trusty and Well-beloved Adrienne Clarkson, Chancellor and Principal Companion of Our Order of Canada, Chancellor and Commander of Our Order of Military Merit, Chancellor and Commander of Our Order of Merit of the Police Forces, Governor General and Commander-in-Chief of Canada.

At Our Government House, in Our City of Ottawa, this tenth day of December in the year of Our Lord two thousand and three and in the fifty-second year of Our Reign.

By Command,
Jean-Claude Villiard
Deputy Registrar General of Canada

CHAPTER 12 – FRANÇOIS AT HAMMOND RIVER

Time Span: 1769-1789

The previous chapters showed that the latest record of a young François Violet in Louisbourg was in 1751 at age 7 and that we have no record of him leaving Louisbourg in 1758 at age 14 when his father, Charles, returned to France. Our next record of François occurs in 1769 when his name appears on payroll records at St John. Then in 1770, at age 26, his marriage to Marie-Luce Thibodeau was recorded on May 6ᵗʰ. In Chapter 10 we provided some possible insights into how and why he may have relocated from highly-developed and long-established Louisbourg to an untamed spot on a small tributary to the mighty St John River. In this chapter we will explore what was happening in the lower St John River valley at the time and how François fit in there.

Acadians on the Move

Acadia was historically at the center of competition between the British presence in New England and the French presence in New France. The British had gained control of Acadia in 1628 but lost it to the French in 1632. The British took it over again in 1654 and the French took it again in 1670. The British retook it in 1710, renaming it to its present-day name of Nova Scotia, and the French ceded Acadia to Britain for good in 1713. The French retained control of Cape Breton Island (Île Royale) where Louisbourg is located. However, as all these changes in power took place Acadians started leaving their peninsular home starting in the early 1700s and relocated to areas on the mainland in what is now New Brunswick, some probably seeking to be away from the conflict and others just to find lands for growing families. During the early part of the period just described the tension between the two major world powers was probably to maintain communications between their New World holdings and their European base. But as time went on more and more commercial operations (fishing, etc.) developed in the New World and tensions grew as the value of the region grew. The Acadians were not French but an independent group by this time, having lived in Acadia for more than six generations by the mid-1700s, but they probably had more affinity for the French because of language, religion, and national origins. And being fiercely independent the Acadians probably had more antipathy to the British because the British tried to force them to pledge allegiance to the British Crown whereas the French largely let them go their own way. As we saw in Chapter 11 the Acadians started migrating to various locations on the mainland; see Map 12-1.

Map 12-1: The Acadians migrated to places on the mainland and nearby islands.

Around 1701 the population of the St John River settlements was around 50 people, but this grew in 1732 after the British took over Nova Scotia/Acadia and by 1755 there were approximately 500 Acadians living in scattered settlements along the lower St John River. Map 12-2 shows where most of the St John River Acadians were living at that time (green markers).

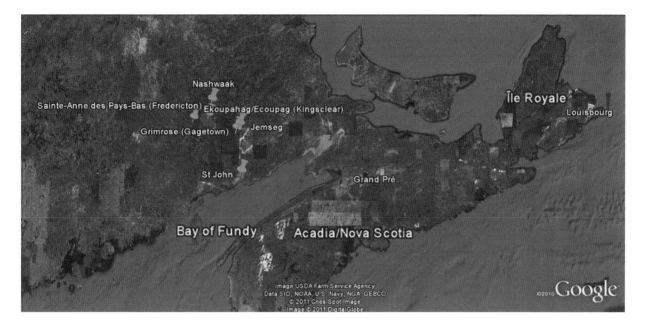

Map 12-2: Acadian relocations in lower St John River valley in early 1700s (green).

Bringing our family into the picture shown in Map 12-2, the place we next find François after Louisbourg (yellow marker) is in the lower St John River valley around St John (marker on the map). We don't know exactly when he moved but it was sometime after 1751, when he was assigned to a guardianship while in Louisbourg, and before 1769, when we next have a record of him around St John. He probably moved in 1755 or before, since all Acadians remaining in Acadia were displaced from there in the Grand Dérangement of 1755. Marie-Luce Thibodeau was born somewhere around St John about 1750 but her family had moved there from Grand Pré (pink marker) sometime after 1738; her sister Marguerite was born in Grand Pré but we don't know where the three children born after Marguerite and before Marie-Luce were born.

We'll move in a little closer to the family location later in this chapter.

Innovative Acadians: Masters of Their Environment

The Acadians who left France in the 1600s to live in the New World on a large peninsula (now Nova Scotia) in the Gulf of St Lawrence brought with them skills learned in their homeland, which helped them to master their new environment. Picture an isolated land with forests and sea marshes at its edge. The growing season was very short and the weather could be harsh much of the year. But these people came from the Poitou region of France at roughly 45° latitude and their new lands were also at 45° latitude, so many conditions were similar. In Poitou the people had perfected a system for using marsh lands to grow crops and they brought this technique to their new home.

Agricultural techniques such as crop rotation, using fertilizers, and soil amendments were to come far in the future for these folks and even the early agricultural revolution in Britain was just barely starting at the time those Acadians began their new homes. The practice at the time was to cut timberland to open fields for crops and then to grow crops until the land "wore out" due to loss of nutrients for plants and then cut more timberland for new crop fields. Not only was this highly labor-intensive, but they would soon run out of new timberlands to clear living in a confined area. The idea of planting grass to raise hay for a field crop to store for winter feed had not developed, so farmers usually slaughtered their livestock in the fall because they had no way to feed them during the long winters.

But in Poitou they learned to farm the marsh areas and create renewable fodder resources. The marshes had a natural coarse grass crop that was constantly replenished and the soil did not wear out because nutrients were constantly being replenished by the tides. So they figured out how to build dikes to drain and dry out the marshlands so they would not be as affected by tidal fluctuations. They often built the dikes by driving 5-6 rows of logs into the ground and then laying more logs horizontally between the rows in stacks. They would then fill the spaces around those log lattices with clay material well packed, since water does not easily drain through a clay material. They would then cover the whole structure with sod cut from the marsh grass itself, and the sod cover would help protect the dike from erosion by tide and weather. These dikes thus formed areas protected from tidal surges and the protected land soon became drier. This new environment supported finer grass species, which then grew in abundance in the fertile soil in the diked areas and provided a nutritious feed for cattle. But they still needed a way to let fresh water from rainfall and snowmelt off their new lands, so they invented a one-way valve that allowed fresh water to drain from the land during low tides but pre-vented sea water from entering the lands during high tides. This valve, called an aboiteau, was hinged so that accumulated fresh water would open it and drain away when the pressure of the sea water was reduced on the other side due to lowering tides and would close again when the pressure of the sea water was greater than the pressure from the freshwater side. The aboiteau concept is still in use today and is called a flap gate, and modern engineers have developed many different flap gate designs. Figure 12-1 shows an illustration of the dike and aboiteau system.

Figure 12-1: Building a dike and aboiteau valve system. Painted by Azor Vienneau for use in the production of an educational film series on pre-expulsion Acadian life called <u>Première Terres Acadiennes</u> Courtesy museum.gov.ns.ca.

Those early Acadian settlers recognized immediately that this system would provide them with a constant source of grass hay to feed their cattle, and the crop could be harvested and stored to use as winter feed. This made them much less dependent on the short growing season typical of dry-land crops grown on cut forested land. While the soils thus exposed were high in salt content at the start and not as productive, after two or three years of allowing the soils to become flushed with fresh water from rain the salts were reduced enough to make the soils very productive.

They also continued to cut the salt grasses for hay on the seaward side of the dikes, where the marshes were covered by at least the higher seasonal tides and in some places even the daily tides. They would cut the hay when tides were out and carry and stack the hay on wooden platforms called staddles on dry land to season. This salt grass hay then allowed them to feed cattle during the long winters – this helped to provide stability to life in this land and would not have been possible without the combination of wet-land/dry-land farming they developed. As described at the web site for the

Nova Scotia Museum *Info Sheets* in *The Acadians 2* (http://museum.gov.ns.ca/arch/infos /in-foaca2.htm):

> Before 1755 the Acadians lived largely self-sufficient lives on their marshland farms. They tilled the soil and it yielded abundant crops of wheat, oats, barley, rye, peas, corn, flax and hemp. They also kept gardens in which they grew beets, carrots, parsnips, onions, chives, shallots, herbs, salad greens, cabbages and turnips. Cabbages and turnips seem to have been particularly important in their diet.
>
> The Acadians kept cattle and sheep. Pigs roamed freely in the forest behind the houses and also fed on kitchen scraps and, in winter especially, on leaves and peelings from the cabbages and turnips which the Acadians often stored covered with straw in their gardens until they were needed. They seem to have eaten a lot of pork but relatively little beef, preferring to keep their cattle for milk, as working animals (i.e. as oxen), and for trade.
>
> The Acadians supplemented what they produced on their small farms by hunting and fishing. They even brewed their own spruce and fir beer.
>
> Theirs was a hard life but a good one, lived in a landscape which they understood and which they made work for them.

The British, French, and other settlers made fun of the Acadians, calling them lazy because they used these methods rather than clearing upland forest land for planting The Acadians were referred to as défricheurs d'eau – clearers of water – by comparison with the other method of being clearers of land. But we know today that the Acadians developed a system that was far more productive and with less overall effort than continuously clearing land for planting.

In their new land they had, of course, to clear some lands by cutting timber. Timber grows on the higher lands not subject to tidal and storm effects and these lands provided stable areas in which to build houses and other permanent buildings.

After Louisbourg François' name first appears in 1769, on the payroll of Simonds and White, the founders of the first permanent English settlement at St. John (the city). At age 25, he was employed along with other Acadians to dike the marshes east of the city, a technique at which the Acadians were quite skilled since they had been doing it for more than eight generations. Map 12-3 shows the area around St. John; while we don't know exactly which marshes François worked on, today's landscape shows many constructed works along the east side of the bay that could have been formed by diking. There was probably a lot of dike building to do and no shortage or work for the builders! And the Acadian défricheurs d'eau contributed greatly to the development of sustainable agriculture in the area.

Map 12-3: St. John area

A Wedding and then a Marriage

In that period of Nova Scotian administration, government authorities limited the presence of Catholic missionaries to but two roving and itinerant French-Catholic missionaries - Father Charles Bailly and Father Joseph Mathuring Bourg, both of whom would provide us with substantial evidence of François Violet in New Brunswick.

Rev. Bailly, whose mission headquarters was at the Old Indian Village of Ecoupahaq left us a 1769-1770 mission register in which at the date of May 6, 1770 we find record of his nuptial blessing of the wedding vows of François Violet and Marie-Luce Thibodeau.

Whereas Fr. Bailly was an itinerant missionary covering all of the province and even trekking into Nova Scotia, it is as likely that the nuptial blessing took place at French Village on the Hammond River at the time of Fr. Bailly's travel to Halifax. However as this missionary kept all his records at Ecoupag (Ekoupahag), this entry in his register has given the impression that the marriage of François Violet and Marie-Luce Thibodeau took place on the St. John River.

How great it would be if we had photos of bride and groom at the wedding of François and Marie-Luce! We only have the marriage records of Abbott Bailly which show that on May 6, 1770, François married Marie-Luce Thibodeau. He notes that François was a native of Louisbourg and Marie-Luce was born in the St John River ("Marie-Luce Thibodeau était née en la Rivière St-Jean"). He says that those present at the marriage were: "Jean Thibodeau, father of the bride Olivier Thibodeau, Ignace

Caron, Joseph Cire, and the parents of the bride". *(Ed Note: While we don't have Bailly's actual documents we can rely on the excellent work of Prudent L. Mercure, who researched the history and genealogy of the early settlers in the Madawaska Territory and documented his work in a 2200-page handwritten manuscript titled Papiers: Histoire de Madawaska. The Madawaska Historical Society published those papers in book form by Roger Paradis in 1998. The spellings given above are directly from Mercure's work; the name Cire is often used in earlier texts instead of the more common Cyr today. The first name given is probably the bride's oldest brother, Jean-Baptiste dit Chairon Thibodeau (1727-1823). The bride's parents were Jean-Baptiste dit Cramatte Thibodeau and Marie LeBlanc, so Baily's notation of father of the bride Olivier Thibodeau probably actually refers to her older brother Olivier (1732-1801).)* This was undoubtedly a reconstituted marriage, as their first child, Marguerite, was born July 25, 1770.

In those days not every community had a priest – in fact priests were so scarce that they were forced to cover very large areas, even by today's travel standards. A community might only see a priest once or twice a year. However, life had to go on and they could not wait for a priest to perform ceremonies such as marriages and baptisms. Instead, the community held their own ceremonies and a couple would stand with family and friends and declare their marriage and then the priest would formalize and record it on his next trip to their community. This is referred to as a *reconstituted marriage.*

The marriage was recorded in Ecoupag (or Ekoupahag; Kingsclear NB today), though it probably took place further south and in the St John area. Ecoupag was the parish from which Bailly operated and where the parish records were kept. We know François was in the St John area in 1769 from his employment record mentioned previously but their first twelve children are recorded as being born in Kennebecasis as shown in Figure 12-2 to the right.

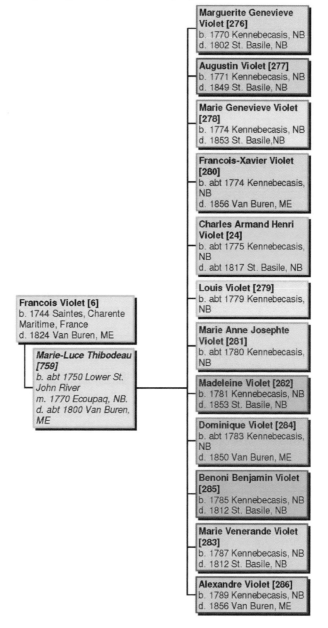

Figure 12-2: First 12 children of François and Marie-Luce

We don't know where the marriage took place, nor do we know when and where the couple actually was wed earlier, but it must have been some months prior and was probably at a home in the Kennebecasis area or in the French Village in the Hammond River area.

In the next record of an itinerant missionary, Rev. Joseph-Mathurin Bourg on Sept. -- 1774 at Kennebecasis, we have the baptismal record of four of the Violet couple's eldest children.

Baptêmes faits à Quanabequechis [Kennebecasis] en 1774.		
15	Marguerite Violette, fille de François et M. Luce Thibodeau	25 juil., 1770
15	Augustin Violette, fils de Fran. et M. Luce Thibodeau	15 sept., 1772
15	Genev. Violette, fille de Fran. et M. Luce Thibodeau	15 mars, 1774
		40
En quelle année ces familles allèrent elles s'établir au Madawaska; c'est ce que j'ignore.		

Figure 12-3: Excerpt from Mercure, Tome 1, Page 17

Note in Figure 12-3 that the last name is given as Violette, not Violet. This shows that even back then there was some ambiguity about how the name should be spelled.

The Kennebecasis River and the Hammond River

The Hammond River is a tributary to the Kennebecasis River, which joins the St John about four miles (6.7 km) above the mouth of where the St John empties into the Bay of Fundy. The Hammond River empties into the Kennebecasis about 18 miles (30 km) above its mouth. See Map 12-4.

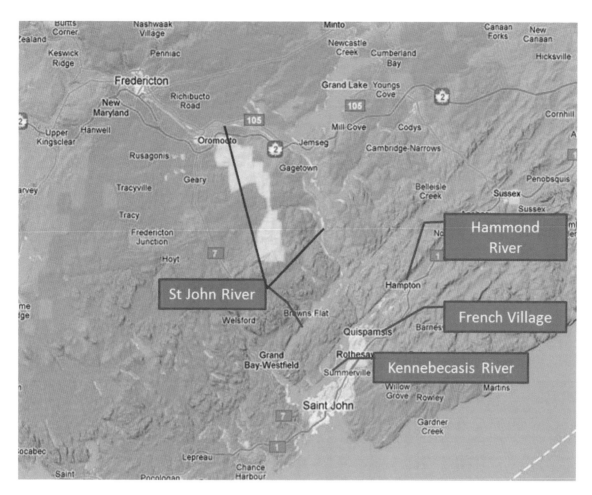

Map 12-4: Rivers in St John area

Acadians had been aware of the St. John River since the time of Samuel de Champlain, who had named it in 1604. Several forts had been constructed in the area. One of the first was Fort Jemseg, built around 1632, by Charles St. Étienne de Latour. It is located a short distance south of Fredericton, on the east side of the St John River. Later, St. Étienne de Latour would build another fort at St John.

François and other Acadians made their way to the town of St John along the St John River and he may have lived there for a while. But eventually he and others settled on the Hammond River, also called the Little Kennebecasis. The lower St John River area was receiving increasing interest by British subjects as more and more moved to the continent and came to the region. Monckton, Hazen, and Studholm conducted raids along the St John between 1758 and 1763 to rid the area of French and Acadian settlers in order to make room for the Loyalists moving in even before the Treaty of Paris. We think that the Acadians settled along the Hammond River because the Hammond was off the beaten track, and the raiders of the St John River settlements never mention French settlers on the Hammond River. These raids were not just minor harassments: they were meant to destroy all property, both houses and animals, and, in some cases, resulted in the loss of life of the settlers.

On January 7, 1689, Pierre Chesnet, Ecuyer, Sieur de Breuil obtained from the crown of France a seigneury of about 24,000 acres on both sides of the Hammond River. Seven years later a grant of 8,000 acres was given to Bernard D'Ameur, Ecuyer, Sieur de Pienne. See Map 12-5. So this part of the lower St John River area had a strong French presence and influence for many years before François and the other Acadian families decided to move into the area. By the time François and Marie-Luce were married in 1770 61 Acadian families totaling 341 people had moved into the Hammond River area, though we do not think that they had title to their land from the French seigneurs, and those seigneurs had largely not sought to develop their holdings. Mercure reports (Tome 2, pg 57) that according to Allison the French Village settlement was probably formed in 1767, which was almost 80 years after the French land grants were made . We do not have maps showing the layout of lots under the French grants, so the boundaries shown in Map 12-5 are a best guess based on various pieces of evidence.

We have described before that the war that started over conflicts in the New World as the French and Indian War, ended up expanding as the Seven Years War in Europe as well. On this continent it pitted French against British for control of much of the continent. It ended with the Treaty of Paris in 1763 that ceded the entire continent to Britain except for Île Royale, where Louisbourg is located, and the Madeleine Islands east of the Nova Scotia peninsula. But the signing of the Peace Treaty created problems for the Acadians, as they did not have title to their lands from the French seigneurs. Perhaps the Acadians could not see a world where the French did not hold power and so did not worry about gaining title. So, they were considered squatters on what was now English soil.

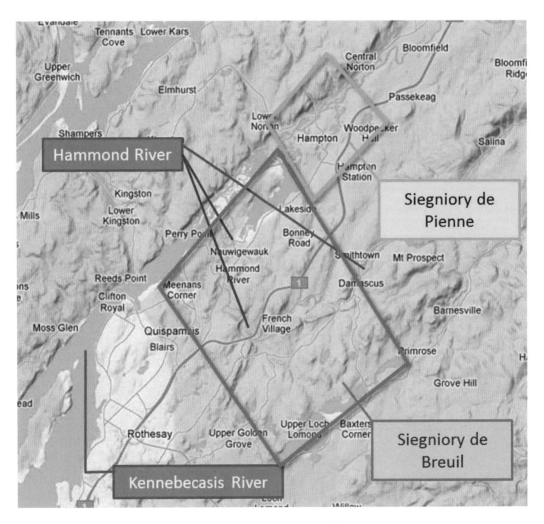

Map 12-5: French land grants, prior to 1763, approximate sizes and locations

The Influx of Loyalists

Soon after the Treaty of Paris, pre-Loyalist British started moving into the area around the Bay of Fundy. By the spring of 1764 Simonds, Hazen, and White established their trading post at the mouth of the St John River and others settled further up the river. Oromocto was established as the shire town of Sunbury County in 1765 and by 1768 the British removed all the Acadians from along the St John River up to Sainte-Anne de Pays-Bas (Fredericton). These Acadians were chased off their land. Some went to Québec and some to the Miramichi area (see Map 12-1 above). But some families had chosen to move to the Hammond River area where they probably felt safe from British raids since this took them away from the St John River and its major tributary the Kennebecasis, which were accessible by British ships.

Matters were made worse for the Acadian settlers during and after the American Revolution, as British Loyalists in what had now become an independent country and were no longer British colonies fled New England for British lands in the north. The British crown made many land grants so that their subjects could have land to own and build on, and the earlier French land grants were abandoned or ignored.

The accommodation between English merchants and Acadian settlers proved be more easily reached than that of those same people as land settlers. There was already well documented accommodation between merchants and French clients by 1782 but it would take another five years for the New Brunswick government to first define itself, and then get on in resolving the settler's claims. François Violet would then acquire actual title to what came to be called Lot 14 on the Hammond River of the Kennebecasis valley in 1787.

There was also a New England (pre-Loyalist) migration into the lower St. John Valley at this time. These pre-Loyalists set up the rudiments of Paartown (named after the Governor of Nova Scotia, John Paar) at the mouth of the St John River. Among them were merchant traders, William Hazen, Richard Simonds, and James White in whose merchant establishment we find a record of François Violet's merchant activity in 1782.

In that era of Nova Scotian governance of what later (in 1784) became the Province of New Brunswick, pre-Loyalist merchant traders occasionally hired services of newly-arrived Acadians. The Acadians had marshland dike building skills, and diking such readily available coast lands allowed for a quick acquisition of farm lands which did not have to wait for forest clearing and the difficulty of dealing with stumps and thick roots.

Merchant traders also hired Acadian settlers as loggers and river drivers to bring their "sticks" to the market areas of the masting industry, which provided the merchant marine with the masts for the sailing ships of the day. The exchange of work and services in this era of the barter economy resulted in the Acadians acquiring credit in the merchant-trader establishments. We show two pages of such merchant accounts for François Violet in Appendix 12-A. In the 1782 record of Hazen and White we find among François Violet's sundry purchases a debit for a half pound of chocolate on February 4, in time for what we now regard as Valentine's Day! Of course they also bought chocolate again in April.

Merchants were careful to keep government authorities informed of their activity. For example, at the same time as François Violet's' sundry purchases James White writes to Michael Francklin, lieutenant governor of Nova Scotia, informing him that the French on the Kennebecasis had driven their sticks to the market area of St. John.

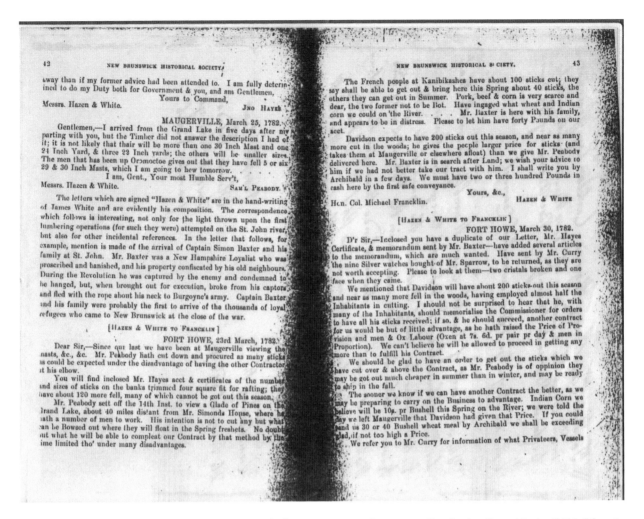

Figure 12-4: Excerpt from NB Historical Society records showing correspondence regarding the Acadians shipping "sticks" (mast logs)

In 1782 the lands of the earlier de Pienne and de Breuil French seigneuries were granted to Sir Andrew Snape Hammond, the Lt. Governor of Nova Scotia, and new lots were defined and surveyed. These new lots probably generally followed the layout of the earlier lots with short frontages along the river and great depths away from the river. This arrangement made sense since access to the rivers was important for travel and communication.

At the time of the Hammond grant mention was made that the land grant included a French settlement of fifteen families that had been there since 1768. (Ref: Mercure Part I pg. 13.) The list included the names Thibodeau and Violet/Violette. Map 12-6 shows where the Violette and Thibodeau lots were laid out under the succeeding British Hammond Grant, and Map 12-7 shows the same lot layout overlaid on a Google Earth image.

Map 12-6: Lots along Hammond River. Lot 14 (violet outline, east side) is labeled "Francis Violet, 210ac", Lot 12 (yellow outline, west side) is labeled "Olivier Thibodeau, Sr, 120 ac; Lot 13 (green outline, west side) is labeled "Joseph Terrieau, 133ac"; Lot 14 (from county maps)

Map 12-7: Lots along Hammond River. Lot 14 (violet outline, east side) is labeled "Francis Violet, 210ac", Lot 12 (yellow outline, west side) is labeled "Olivier Thibodeau, Sr, 120 ac; Lot 13 (green outline, west side) is labeled "Joseph Terrieau, 133ac"; Lot 14 (blue outline, west side) is labeled "J Terrieau & Olivier Tibideau, 160 ac". (overlaid on Google Earth image)

In 1786, the Hammond lands passed into the hands of the Loyalists, who immediately proceeded to dispossess the Acadians living there. Fortunately, two influential Loyalists, Edward Winslow and Ward Chipman, took up the cause of the Acadians and obtained from the government the restoration of some of their property. On April 12, 1787, grants of land were made to fifteen Acadians and twenty seven Loyalists. The lots were awarded such that the Acadians were dispersed among the Loyalists. François was awarded lot # 14 on the east bank, consisting of 210 acres. (See Maps 12-6 and 12-7 above) The subdivision into lots shown in Maps 12-6 and 12-7 was not from the original French grants but from the British grants to Sir Andrew Snape Hammond, mentioned above. Notice also in Map 12-6 the holdings of other family members on the west bank: Olivier Thibodeau, Sr, Marie-Luce's older brother, holds Lot 12; Joseph Terrieau (Theriault), married to Marie-Luce's older sister, Marie-Madeleine, holds Lot 13; and Olivier Thibodeau, Sr, and Joseph Theriault together hold Lot 14 – immediately across the Hammond River from François and Marie-Luce.

But those lots as they were laid out by the British did not exactly conform to the ones occupied by the Acadians already living in the Hammond River valley for several years. We find, for example, a petition by François from August 28, 1786 containing the following:

> To His Excellency Thomas Carleton, Esquire Captain General and Governer in Chief of His Majesty's Province of New Brunswick etc:
>
> The Petition of Francis Violet one of the French Settlers on Hammond River
>
> Humbly shewith.

That he was one of the first settlers in what is called the French Village on Hammond River and some years ago took the oath of Allegiance to his majesty at which time the Farm on which he now lives was sett off to him by M. Francklin one of his Majesty's Council for Nova Scotia, who give him a writing which he supposed to be a sufficient assurance of his farm.

That the manner in which the land has lately been laid out Your memorialist loses ten acres of his best improved interval on which he now has a Crop of Wheat –

That he has always strictly attended to his allegiance – has a large Family to support for whom he is with difficulty able to procure the necessaries of Life and should he be deprived of his improved Interval which has Cost him so much labour it will greatly distress his numerous family,

That the lot adjoining (No. 14) the one on which his House stands on the North side (which he supposes to be No. 13) includes said Ten Acres of Interval –

Your Excess Petitioner therefore humbly prays that said Lots No. 14 & 13 on the North side of Hammond River may be granted to him to enable him so to support his Family that they may instead of being a burthen, become usefull settlers in the Country – and in Duty bound he will be ever thankfull.

St John 28th August 1786   Francis Violet

We are not sure of the success of this petition.

Though the Loyalists only arrived in the French Village area in 1783, some of the Acadian families had been living in the Hammond River valley as their home as early as 1768. The families included: Robichaud, Thibodeau, Blanchard, Gireau, Terrieau/Theriault, Domenic, Levecon, Bourke, Cormier, and Violet/Violette. Due to the influx of the Loyalists, several of these Acadians found it necessary to leave the land that had been cultivated by several generations of their families, to seek homes in another part of New Brunswick.

The Studholm Report of 1783 enumerated all the settlers living along the St John River. Sixty three French families were found to have settled a short distance above Sainte-Anne des Pays-Bas (Fredericton). In his report, Studholm listed the number of family members in each family, the improvements they had made to the land, and how long they had been on the land. The list of those living above Sainte-Anne includes Olivier Thibodeau and Olivier Thibodeau, Jr, Marie-Luce's brother and nephew but did not include François, who apparently elected to stay on his land at Hammond River. There were a total of about 370 settlers. We know the last of the original French settlers along the lower St John River were chased off the land in 1763, by Studholm himself. These settlers either escaped into the forest, or returned after the signing of the Peace Treaty of Paris in 1763. This 1783 report does not mention the families settled south of Ste. Anne and it did not include the French Village of the Kennebecasis where François had settled.

Having given up hope of ever obtaining deeds for their lands near Fredericton François and the Thibodeaus, along with others, applied for land grants farther up the river. On June 21, 1785, the Acadians from the Ste. Anne (Fredericton) area were given a license to occupy lands in Madawaska Territory, later known as the Mazerolle Concession. This grant extended on both sides of the St John

River from the Madawaska River at present day Edmundston, N.B. to the Riviére Verte (Green River) about 10 miles (16 km) above today's Van Buren ME and St Leonard NB. After a ten-day canoe trip up the St. John River, the first settlers arrived the latter part of June 1785, in what is now St. David (Madawaska, Maine); The Madawaska Historical Society celebrates the anniversary of that event every year. This first group was followed in 1790 by families from the French Village area, who opened what was called the Soucy Concession just downstream from the Mazerolle. We will cover more about that migration in Chapter 13.

The photos in this chapter were taken by two of the authors – Rod Violette, VFA #12, in 2002 (Photos 12-1 through 12-3) and Dave Violette, VFA #621, in 2011 (Photos 12-4 through 12-9). Rod's personal account of his visit is contained in Appendix 12-B and Dave's in Appendix 12-C.

Photo 12-1: Rod Violette with Hammond River and François' Lot 14 in background. Taken in 2002.

Photo 12-2: Existing French Village Bridge over the Hammond River, approximately ½ mile (805 m) upstream from Lot 14.

Photo 12-3: Lots 14, 15, and 16 as seen from south of the Hammond River, in 2002.

Photo 12-4: Looking up at the farm buildings from the lower level below the brook

Photo 12-5: Looking down on the farm buildings from the upper field

Photo 12-6: The Steele farm (former François lands) as seen from the Thibodeau property across the Hammond River

Photo 12-7: Lots 14, 15, and 16 as seen from south of the Hammond River, in 2011.

Photo 12-8: The Steele farm setting as seen from the Olivier Thibodeau property across the River

Photo 12-9: Looking across the brook and river to the former Thibodeau and Theriault lands on the west side

Appendix 12-A

Merchant Records of François Violette

This Appendix contains copies of two pages of the merchant records of Hazen & White, St John NB, from the period June 1780 through early 1783. They show a string of transactions for "Francis Violet". Note that the 8 in the year and elsewhere is written to lie sideways. The cost amounts are shown in pounds : shillings : pence. The pages have been marked up in red to try to make clear what was recorded in that ancient script, made more difficult by copying.

It was common for people to run such accounts and work off amounts owed by working under contract. We know that Hazen & White had contracts to construct dikes and other contracts to deliver cut timber for masts and as François and others would work on these contracts their balance would go down; as they bought things on credit the balance would go up.

Francis Violet
to Hazen & White

1 Pig Tail ?@6/1, Hat@3/6,
?@3/8

June, 1780

? Jo Terrio

Mar ?, 1781

Feb 4, 1782

?@, 2 yds Flannel@5/6

1 Blankett ? Damaged@1:2:6

6 ?@2/6, 2 lb Bacon@13/4

½ nails@6/6, 1 Dozen ?@10/

12 ?

1 lb Tea@5/, 3 lb Sugar@5/, 1 lb Chocolate@5/3

1 pair Hose@6/6, 1
Dozen Spoons@6/

? ?@4/9, cloth@1/

1 lb Tobacco@2/6, Buttons@2/11

Twist ? ¾ yd Sattin@2/6

Silk & cat gut@4/3, ½ yd Lace@4/3

1 ? Coat

1 ¾ yd Ribbon

1 ¾ yd ?@5/

1 ? Coat@35/, ?@3/4
Lace@1/, ?

11 :10 :9

11 :17 :9

Sum carried forward

Francis Violet Dr.

To John Hazen

1782

Feb 26 To 174 9d Strand 31/ £ 12.6
Feb 26, 1782

Month 16 1 Tea 6/ 1 Hatt 3/6 Melof 3/9 — 13.3
Mar 16, 1782   1 Tea@6/1, Hat@3/6, ?@3/8

2 2 Wine 5/ 1 Comb 6d 5.6
       2 ? Wine?@5/1, Comb@/5

2 Tobacco 5/ 1 Rum 4/ ? Indigo 7
       2 Tobacco@5/12, Rum@4/2 Indigo@ ?

20 2 Gallons Molasses 15/ 1 Tea 6/ 1.1
Apr20, 1782   2 Gallons Molasses@15/1, Tea@6/1

1 2 Brandy 4/ 1 Tea 6/ 3 Sugar 5/ — 15
       1 l Brandy@4/1, Tea@6/3, Sugar@5/

2 2 d 7/6 1 Blankett 15/ Chocolate/5 1.4:3
       2 ?@7/6, Blankett@15/, Chocolate@1/5

3 6 Axel a 2/6 5/4 Iron & 1 Ax 15/ 1.7.10
       3?@2/6, Iron Ax@15/

6.16.4

1783

Feb 25 To 1 Tea 7/6 1 Hatt 5/6 £ 13 —
Feb 25, 1783   Tea@7/6, Hatt@5/6

1 2 Paper 2/6 1 Gimblet 8d — 3.2
       ?@2/6, Gimblet@/8

1 Gallon Rum 15/ Pins 1/8 — 16.8
       1 Gallon Rum@15/, ?@1/8

Sile Soy 2 10
       ?@10/

2.2.10

1783
Jan 4 Cr By Mr Hayes £10 —
Jun 4, 1783   Credit by M Hazen £10/0/0

Fort Howe 1st March
1783 & Excepted
       Fort Howe 1st March
       1783 & ?

Appendix 12-B

A Personal Story by Rod Violette, VFA #12

Ever since Rita Lippe published *The Descendants of François Violet* I was interested in Lots #14 and #15 in the Kennebecasis region that she described in her book. The lots in question are in fact on the Hammond River, formerly known as the Little Kennebecasis. The land is now legally described as New Brunswick Property identifier #196626 in Hampton Parish.

Prior to the Violette Family Association Reunion in 2002, I made a trip to the region and located the lots described in Rita's book. I took some photos *(Ed Note: Photos 12-1, 12-2, and 12-3 in this chapter)* and spoke to the current owners. I did not have the time to research the history of the property myself, but a friend, Florine Theriault, who lives in Fredericton, undertook to do the research for me, for which I am very grateful.

After persistently following many leads ending in dead-ends; she was able to get in contact with someone who provided her with the answers we were looking for.

Lot #14, which consists of 210 acres, was granted to François by the "Widow Sarah Hunt and others land grant" of April 12th, 1787, as registered in Fredericton, New Brunswick.

On January 15th, 1790, François signed a contract to buy Lot #15 from Henry Darling, for £100. However, no records show that lot #15 was ever deeded to François. He must have signed that contract not knowing that the requests for lands in Madawaska had been granted.

On February 4th, 1790, François sold lot #14 to John Ford for £100.

On April 27th, 1791, Henry Darling sold the north half of lot #15 to John Ford for £60 and the south half to Andrew Sherwood for £30 and 10s.

In 1982, lot #14 was subdivided for the use of Mr. Joseph Steele. The remainder belongs to Meadow Brook Farms Ltd., whose directors are members of the Steele family. A portion of the north section was expropriated in 1990 for the construction of Highway #1 between St. John and Moncton, New Brunswick.

An interesting aside is that François' signature appears on this contract, but not on the request for the land grant in Madawaska. The Mercure Papers indicate that he signed with an X. I see no reason why François was not able to sign his name. Having grown up in Louisbourg, from the age of 5 to 14, he must, surely, have attended school there.

Appendix 12-C

A Personal Story by Dave Violette, VFA #621

I took the opportunity during our travels following the Violette Family Reunion 2011 to visit the Hammond River area to see where my ancestors had lived. Actually I had at least six ancestors that lived in that area:

My Violette grandfather was Cyr Regis Violette and among my great-great-great-great grandparents on his *father's* side were **François** and **Marie-Luce Violette** and among my great-great-great-great grandparents on his *mother's* side were **Olivier** and **Madeleine Thibodeau**. My grandfather Violette's mother was a Cyr. Olivier and Madeleine's daughter **Madeleine** was born in 1771 so she also lived there and my grandfather's maternal line comes down through the daughter Madeleine. And Francois and Marie-Luce's son **Charles** was born there in 1775 and also lived there and my grandfather's paternal line comes down through him.

My Violette grandmother was Adeline Soucy/Soucie and among my great-great-great-great-great grandparents on her *father's* side was the same **Olivier** and **Madeleine Thibodeau** and among my great-great-great-great-great grandparents on her *mother's side* were the same **François** and **Marie-Luce Violette**! My grandmother Violette's mother was a Lebel. Olivier and Madeleine's daughter **Madeleine** was born in 1771 so she also lived there and my grandmother's paternal line also comes down through the daughter Madeleine. And Francois and Marie-Luce's son **Charles** was born there in 1775 and also lived there and my grandmother's maternal line comes down through him.

Notice that the generations on my grandfather's and grandmother's sides are offset by one generation, so the same people who are g-g-g-g grandparents on my grandfather's side are g-g-g-g-g grandparents on my grandmother's side. This can be so confusing it is hard to follow without pedigree charts, but that is beyond this story.

Though Joseph Theriault was married to Mari-Luce and Olivier's sister Marie-Madeleine, I am not directly related to the Theriaults.

I drove down Porter Road off Hampton Road (NB 100) since that appeared from the Google map to lead to François Violette's Lot 14. Starting as a two-lane blacktop road as I neared the end it became a narrow farm lane gravel road. Suddenly I arrived at a farmhouse on my right and I was right in their dooryard. There were three people sitting on the porch – two men and a woman. I stopped and got out, went up to the porch, and told the group that I believed that my great-great-great-great grandparents had pioneered this property. One of the men asked my name and I told him and he became excited and rose and introduced himself as Mike Steele, an owner of the property. He said he had heard a long time ago that a Violette had lived there but had never gone to check out the records to be sure. As I described to him what we had learned about the property and its history he became more excited.

Mike told me that his family had bought the property around 1960 from the Porters. His father had run the farm during his life and Mike had been running since. Mike's mother still lives on the property on a lot that had been subdivided from the farm.

Map 12-8 shows a closeup of the farm buildings, with the lot overlay in place. The Steeles have purchased not only Lot 14 but 15 and 16 as well and perhaps some of Lot 13, so they own and farm much more than did François.

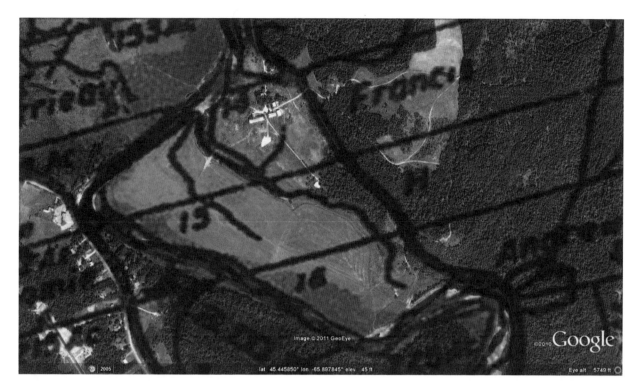

Map 12-8: Existing farm buildings on Lot 14

Map 12-9 shows a closer view of the farm buildings without the lot lines in place. The area where the buildings are located is on ground about 30 feet (9.1 m) higher than the Hammond River, so it is less subject to flooding. And the land continues to rise going away from the River, to about 300 feet (91.4 m) higher at the far east end. The long, skinny Lot 14 scales at around 990 feet (301.8 m) wide, which is 60 rods (one rod measures 16 ½ feet, or 5.03 meters). The map shows that Lot 14 contains 210 acres (85 ha) so the average length of the lot is around 9,240 feet (2,816 m).

Mike Steele said that they have never found any signs of earlier buildings or their foundations, so likely the existing buildings were built over where François had built.

The lands along the River and the brook that runs through the property are fairly level and appear to be productive for growing hay for cattle feed. No doubt they were also productive for François to grow grains for his family as well. The higher ground would have provided all the wood and timber needed for construction and heating.

Map 12-9: Closeup of existing farm buildings

Mike took me on an extended tour of their property on his four-wheeler. You can see a network of roads and trails in the aerial photos, and I think we may have been on every one of them! But his gracious tour gave me the opportunity to take the many photos shown in the main body of this chapter. Photo 12C-1 below shows us at a stopping point.

Photo 12C-1: Mike Steele and Dave Violette touring Francois' lands on a four-wheeler

Photo 12C-2: Mike Steele and one of his dogs in front of the camp his father built using lumber from the old Sherwood barn from Lot 16.

It was fascinating to me to explore the lands that 220-230 years ago were pioneered and farmed by my ancestors. As I rode and walked on the land I tried to imagine the families living there in sight of each other but yet spaced apart, close enough for easy communication but yet having their distinctive lives.

How great those lands must have seemed to them! Here they had lands along a river to provide water for people, animals, and crops – lower lands made fertile by periodic inundation, and higher bench lands overlooking the bottoms. The soils appear to be rich and suited to supporting crops of all kinds. The woods on the properties provided a source of building materials and fuel for heating, cooking, and farm operations. Though I don't know what the Thibodeau's lives were like in Grand Pré, after the turmoil years that François spent in his early life moving from France as a young boy, losing his mother, having his father remarry, being set out with a surrogate guardian, and moving from Louisbourg being settled on some good lands along the Hammond River must have been like a dream come true.

He married Marie-Luce and they started raising a family. They had 12 children during those 20 years on the Hammond River, and probably planned on spending the rest of their lives on the place they had built. By the late 1780s the first of their children were grown and approaching adulthood themselves. No doubt François and Marie-Luce were hoping their children would settle nearby – maybe they would even subdivide their lands to include the kids – and they would be able to grow to old age on familiar grounds with grandchildren around them.

But the turmoil found them again. The American Revolution forced major changes in the region and suddenly there were new people moving in and demanding lands for themselves, and the former settlers under the French struggled to maintain their rights. And where they had sought peace in a community of people of similar backgrounds and customs that community was now being splintered with the newcomers.

The 20+ years they spent along the Hammond were probably good years. Those were the formative years for a young family, challenging to provide for their growing brood but satisfying in knowing they had some good lands that would provide for their needs. And they had other families nearby who were also raising families as they were. The Olivier Thibodeaus had 6-8 children and the Joseph Theriaults had four, all living within a mile or two of each other. If they got together for holidays and celebrations over the years that would have been a rousing group of as many 30 family members by the time they left the region in 1790!

Those years along the Hammond River were the formative years, especially for their children. The children learned from an early age what it took to provide for and support a family. They were largely self-sufficient in raising much of what they needed, but as we know from the merchant records in this chapter they also traded with commercial enterprises as well. We don't know if they sold crops to raise the cash needed for purchases, but we do know that they cut timber and sold or traded it for the supplies they needed. The records show that they cut logs and floated them down the river. Whether they did this under contract or independently we do not know. But the kids would have learned what must be done and as they got older they would have participated in the farming and logging activities to a greater extent. We know from later information that after relocating to the Upper St John River valley not only were the parents industrious and enterprising but their children were as well. So the lessons they learned growing up on the Hammond River gave them a great base from which to grow.

While touring the property with Mike Steele I got a chance to view the property from a number of different vantage points. In each place I tried to look at the property from how I thought François might have seen it, and I could imagine a sense of pride he might have felt when overseeing his domain. A home established on grounds safe from river flooding but close enough to take advantage of the river. Lands under cultivation and growing to feed his family and his stock. Timber lands behind him to provide an almost endless supply of wood and timber. Relatives close by to provide companionship and help when needed. I don't know if those who lived in those times took time to reflect and enjoy, but I suspect that is a natural characteristic of us humans. And from what I saw on the Steele farm during my visit François would have had much to be proud of and he could have enjoyed a great sense of satisfaction in what he and Marie-Luce had created.

CHAPTER 13 – FRANÇOIS MOVES TO MADA-WASKA SETTLEMENT
Time Span: 1789-1824

Francois [1] {6} and Marie-Luce {759} had lived on their "hideaway on the Hammond" for at least 15 years when their lands passed from French title to British title around 1786. These were the lands on which they had settled, cleared, built, raised a family of (at that time) ten children, and made many improvements. In that long time, life must have settled into a routine of following the seasons and the tides of family. François was a teenager when he left Louisbourg and a young man of 26 when he married Marie-Luce in 1770. Now, he was 42 and probably considered himself well-established on his land and in his place. The title to his land, however, was granted under the French establishment and so was in question when it came under the British. He and his neighbors had thought that their move to Hammond River took them out of sight and out of mind of the British pre-Loyalists who were flooding into the area along the St John River, as we reported in Chapter 12. During and after the American Revolution the area further became a target for the Loyalists who were leaving the lower colonies in droves, especially after the British defeat and the American independence. As reported in the last chapter, François was awarded Lot #14 in 1787.

François and his family found themselves with new neighbors, none of whom shared their heritage, language, religion, and culture. These new neighbors were English-speaking, non-Catholic, British subjects. François had pledged allegiance to the British Crown in order to avoid deportation to France and to be able to hold lands *(Ed Note: See the petition by François on page 151 in Chapter 12, where reference is made to his taking an Oath)*, but was only able to hold title to his lands with the help of two influential Loyalists. Edward Winslow and Ward Chipman took up the cause of the Acadians and obtained from the government the restoration of some of their property. That Francois did not receive all his property back is indicated by that petition shown in Chapter 12, dated 28th August 1786.

When the French in the Ste. Anne (Fredericton) area and other settlements along the St John River were forced to move north to the Madawaska Settlement in June of 1785, the fifteen French families along the Hammond River at French Village did not follow. They were finally granted deeds to their lands on April 12, 1787, having been on those lands since about 1768. However, when the lands were granted under the British, the lots were assigned so that Loyalists were interspersed with the Acadian settlers. While these families probably felt comfortable where they were, having spent almost 20 years of toil improving their property, they soon became uncomfortable being increasingly a minority in the region.

But by 1789 there were other pressures on François and Marie-Luce. Their children were growing older and would soon need lands of their own to settle on and develop. By now they had twelve children living with them, and quarters must have been cramped, to say the least. We know nothing about their house and how large it was or if they had to keep expanding it, but certainly any house they built when they first started living there in 1760 would have become too small several times over! The oldest was Marguerite (19) and the youngest was Alexandre, 3 months old. In between were Augustin (17), Genevieve (16), François-Xavier (15), Charles (14), Louis (10), Marie Anne (9), Madeleine (8), Dominique (6), Benoni (4), and Marie Venerande (2).

From a different point of view, the New Brunswick government was anxious to have settlements in the upper St John River valley as a way to improve and secure a communication route with Québec. In addition, the Governor of New Brunswick did not wish to rid himself of the Acadians and did not want to lose them to the Province of Québec. He knew the Acadians were anxious to establish settlements where they could exercise their Catholic religion and Québec was beckoning to them to come there. By granting them lands within his province he succeeded in more than one desire. *(Ref: Papers of Prudent Mercure, Tome 2, page 16)*

So, on August 28, 1789 some French settlers along the Hammond River petitioned for grants of land in an unspecified portion of the upper St. John River; see Appendix 13-A. On December 21, 1789 another request was made, this time for lands below the original Mazerolle Concession; see Appendix 13-B. And on December 24, 1789 this second request was granted. We don't know why the second petition was necessary, but it contained much more detail and covered many more points than the first so we have to assume that the petitioners had been advised to enhance their petition by adding these points. The petitioners became part of what was called the Soucy Concession.

Three Main Groups Move North

While there were some early settlers in what was to become known as the Madawaska Settlement or Madawaska Territory, there were three major groups that petitioned for land grants and settled there in the early years. There were four land grant documents issued by the New Brunswick Provincial Government: one, in 1787, two in 1790 and one in 1794. *(Ref: Early Land Grants in Madawaska - 1787, 1790 & 1794; http://www.upperstjohn.com/madawaska/earlygrants.htm)*

Lists of those granted lands in those periods are included in Table 13-1. Note: the June 1790 grant included only Pierre Duperré, 213 acres. The 1787 grants were actually licenses to occupy, so this did not provide title to the landholders.

Table 13-1: British (Province of New Brunswick) Land Grants, 1787-1794

January 1787 Grants	October 1790 Grants	August 1794 Grants
ALICOTE, Alexander	AIELLICOT, Accarie 227 acres	CIRE, Aaron 200 acres
DAIGLE , Joseph, junior	AIELLICOT, Alexander 230 acres	CIRE, Fierement 0 acres
DAIGLE, Joseph, senior	AIELLICOT, Joseph 252 acres	CIRE, Joseph 292 acres
DUPEREE , Piere	ALBERRE, Francis 189 acres	CIRE, Joseph Jr. 0 acres
FURNEAUX, Baptiste	AUBEAR, Simon 252 acres	CORMIER, Alexis 0 acres
MERCURE , Lewis	AUCLAIR, Joseph 194 acres	CORMIER, Baptiste 0 acres
MERCURE , Michael	BOULLE, Maturin 253 acres	CORMIER, Francois 0 acres
POTIE , Paul	CERE, Alexander 174 acres	CORMIER, Pierre 0 acres
SANFACON, Louison	CERE, Alexis 234 acres	LEBLOND, Louis 0 acres
SIRE , Anthony	CERE, Anthony 234 acres	MICHEAU, Joseph 0 acres
	CERE, Fereman Jr. 217 acres	SHERRIT, Baptiste 0 acres
	CERE, Fereman Sr. 254 acres	SOUCI, Germain 0 acres

SIRE , Fereman	CERE, Francis 288 acres	SOUCI, Joseph Jr. * 200 acres
SIRE , Francis	CERE, Francis Jr. 194 acres	TERRIO, Joseph 0 acres
SIRE , James	CERE, James 227 acres	TERRIO, Joseph Jr. 0 acres
SIRE , Oliver	CERE, John Baptist Jr. 346 acres	TIBIDEAU, Baptiste 0 acres
	CERE, John Baptist Sr. 269 acres	TIBIDEAU, Fierement 0 acres
SIRE , Paul	CERE, Joseph Jr 226 acres	TIBIDEAU, Gregoire 0 acres
SIRE , Piere	CERE, Michael 212 acres	TIBIDEAU, Jean 0 acres
TIBBIDO , Baptiste	CERE, Oliver 423 acres	TIBIDEAU, Oliver 0 acres
	CERE, Paul 192 acres	TIBIDEAU, Oliver Jr. 0 acres
	CERE, Peter 195 acres	VIOLETTE, Augustin 0 acres
	COSTIN, Thomas 220 acres	VIOLETTE, Francis 200 acres
	DAIGLE, John Baptist 319 acres	WILLET, Louison 0 acres
	DAIGLE, Joseph Jr. 246 acres	
	DAIGLE, Joseph Sr. 223 acres	
	DAIGLE, Maria Margaret 180 acres	
	DUBE, Augustin 188 acres	
	FOURNIER, John Baptist 231 acres	
	GAGNIE, Antoin 207 acres	
	LISOT, Pierre 182 acres	
	MARTAIN, John 184 acres	
	MERCURE, Joseph 174 acres	
	MERCURE, Louis 234 acres	
	MERCURE, Michael 224 acres	
	MUZERALL, Joseph * 200 acres	
	MUZEROLL, John Baptist Jr. 220 acres	
	POTIERS, Paul 207 acres	
	SANSFASON, Louison 277 acres	
	SAUNDERS, John 1646 acres	
	SAUSSIERS, John Marie 166 acres	
	SAUSSIERS, Joseph 237 acres	
	TARDIFF, Jean 257 acres	
	TEMONG, Joseph 211 acres	
	TIBIDEAU, Etienne 227 acres	
	TIBIDEAU, John Baptist Jr. 270 acres	
	TIBIDEAU, John Baptiste Sr. 223 acres	
	TIBIDEAU, Joseph 220 acres	
	VASSOUR, John 209 acres	

When studying the names in Table 13-1 one has to remember that names were often or usually written phonetically, and so some variations become evident. For example: Sire, Cere, and Cire most certainly are the same name, today spelled Cyr. Alicotte and Aiellicot probably both refer to today's Ayotte. Micheau became Michaud. Terrio becomes Terriault. Tibbido and Tibideau become Thibodeau. Willet is probably Ouellette. Sanfacon and Sansfason are the same name. And so on. Similarly with first names: Fereman and Fierement show up later as Phirmin or Firmin. François was shown as Francis or sometimes Frank. Jean Baptiste was shown as John Baptist, John Baptiste, and sometimes just Baptiste.

Also notable in Table 13-1 is the presence of large families, such as the Sire/Cire/Cere/Cyr family and the Tibbido/Tibideau family, which appear in all three columns in Table 13-1. These families will play a large part in our narrative as will the Terrio/Theriault family and, of course, the Violet/Violette family. In Chapter 14 we will trace how these families intermarried and played important roles in the Upper St John River region. But for now, their importance to our narrative is about the Violettes moving upriver and the sequence of events that led to that move.

(Ed Note: We are introducing genealogical references starting here and continuing in Chapter 14 as we start discussing individuals. These references are for those who want to trace genealogical aspects of the discussions. References in square brackets [] are to the genealogical index in Descendants of François Violet, *by Rita Violette Lippé, 1984 [809c] {654} (1). References in curly brackets {} are to the Record Identification Number (RIN) in Rod Violette's [798a] {34} (12) ongoing genealogical database. The references in parentheses () indicate Violette Family Association VFA member numbers.)*

The Cyr and Thibodeau families started it off

The sequence of events presented in this part of this chapter is based on conclusions drawn from the information presented in Table 13-1 as well as from other references.

In the **January 1787 column** of Table 1 we see seven Cyrs (Sires) and one Thibodeau (Tibbido). We think that Baptiste Tibbido refers to Jean-Baptiste dit Cramatte Thibodeau {787}, born in Grande Pre about 1706 and married there in 1727; he died in the Madawaska Territory in 1795. We also think that the Sires in that same column refer to the children of Jean-Baptiste dit Croc Cyr {722}, born in Beaubassin about 1710 and married there in 1734; he died in Fredericton NB in 1785, before the family moved upriver.

(Ed Note: Marriages shown below in italics occurred after the year of the grants)

The seven youngest of Jean-Baptiste Cyr's nine children (all sons) are in the **January 1787** column:

- Paul {3754}, who married Charlotte Ayotte {22736} in 1783
- Jacques? (James?) (Lt) {1856}, who married Elisabeth Ursule Belanger {1857} in 1779
- Pierre {3756}, who married Madeleine Hayot Ayotte {22737} about 1780
- Francois (Capt) {3757}, who married Marie-Anne Guilbeau {1885} in 1770 and then Josephte Ayotte {65832}
- Olivier {3759}, who married Anastasie Lebrun {22740} in 1779 and then Marie-Madeleine Thibodeau {22741} *in 1803*
- Firmin {3758}, who married Marie Josephte Ayotte *in 1787*
- Antoine {1876}, who married Genevieve Violet *in 1792*

Then in the **October 1790 column** we see the two older Cyr children:

- Joseph {724}, who married Marguerite Blanche Thibodeau {725} in 1760
- Jean-Baptiste {1853}, who married Marie Judith Guerette-Dumont {737} in 1767

Along with Joseph Cyr's children:

- Joseph Jr {3497}, who married Marie Marguerite Daigle {3525} *in 1795*
- Firmin {3500}, who married Euphrosine Cyr {30361} *in 1795* and then Ursule Roy Desjardins {32329} in 1792
- Anne Marie {3502}, married to Jean-Baptiste Daigle {23888} in 1791
- Theotiste {26134}, married to Joseph Daigle {26133} in 1790
- Marguerite Genevieve {36049}, who married Joseph Soucy Jr {36795} *in 1806*
- And maybe others

And Jean-Baptiste Cyr's children:

- Jean-Baptiste Jr {1852}, who married Marguerite Genevieve Violet {276} *in 1793* and then Catherine Dufour {31072} *in 1803*
- Michel {22739}, married to Madeleine Thibodeau {23196} in 1786
- Marguerite {705}, who married Pierre Lizotte {704} *in 1794* (he is also on the 1790 list)
- Euphrosine {30361}, who married Firmin Cyr {3500} *in 1795* (he is also on the 1790 list)
- Marie Rose {28298}, who married Simon Theriault {28299} *in 1803*

And Francois Cyr's children:

- Alexis {30602}, married to Victoire Theriault {10686} in 1804

As well as Jean-Baptiste dit Cramatte Thibodeau's children:

- Jean-Baptiste Jr {15926}, who married Anne Francoise Babin {668} in 1753

But we also see some other Thibodeaus, who may be children of Jean-Baptiste's son Olivier {10669} and Josephte Cormier {10670}:

- Jean Baptiste {1933}, who married Marie Anne Cormier {1934} in 1791

We don't have records in our genealogical database that help us identify Etienne or Joseph Thibodeau from that October 1790 column.

Finally in the **August 1794 column** we see more Cyrs:

- Hilarion? (Aaron?) {726}, who married Marie Charlotte Tardif {727} in 1795
- Firmin (could be {3500}, same as above?)
- Joseph (could be {724}, same as above?)
- Joseph Jr (could be {3497}, same as above?)

Among the Thibodeau family at that time are:

- Olivier {23198}, son of Jean-Baptiste, married to Madeleine Pothier (23199} (sister of Paul Pothier {23207}, shown in the January 1787 column)
- Jean Baptiste (could be {1933}, from above?)

And children of Olivier {23198}:

- Firmin {23886}, who married Marie Euphrosine Cyr {24833} in 1795
- Gregoire {10695}, who married Madeleine Levasseur {10696} in 1794
- Jean Baptiste? {36092}, who married Marie Anne Tardif {36093} in 1810
- Olivier Jr {10669}, who married Josephte Cormier {10670} in 1792

And, of course, the Violettes:

- François [1]{6}, who married Marie Luce Thibodeau {759} in 1770
- Augustin [2a] {277}, son of François, who married *Elizabeth Cyr {1855} about 1800*

(Ed Note: Marriages shown in italics occurred after the year of the grants)

From the foregoing we draw the following narrative:

After the death of Jean-Baptiste Cyr {722} in Fredericton in 1785, his children were ready to move out of the conflicts developing in the lower St John River valley and petitioned, along with others, for land in the Madawaska Territory. There were nine sons, and the younger seven moved first and into the Mazerolle Concession shortly after that. They may have made a grant request even before the death of the father.

And Jean-Baptiste dit Cramatte Thibodeau {787}, married to Marie LeBlanc {786}, was among those early movers.

Likely others of those families made at least one visit to the Madawaska Settlement to see conditions there and returned to tell the remaining family members. The elder two Cyr sons applied for grants and moved around 1788-9, and more of the Thibodeaus moved then as well. François Violet [1] {6}, married to Jean-Baptiste Thibodeau's youngest daughter, Marie Luce {759}, also visited the area for we have evidence that he was in the Madawaska region in 1789. His presence is mentioned in the Kennebecasis petition and François is reputed to have sent word to his wife that **"tout est hors de prix au Madawaska"**. *(Everything is priced out of sight in Madawaska).*

These moves and visits resulted in many more of the Cyr and Thibodeau families applying for grants and moving around 1789-90, including our ancestors François [1] {6} and Marie Luce [2] {759}. This third group received their grants in August 1794.

So, while certainly each of the people mentioned in Table 13-1 had to make their own decision to make the move, the fact that others of their families were moving must have made it easier to move and may have, in fact, prompted the move. And obviously there were others, especially minor children, who had no decision to make; they went where their parents went. While all of them felt pressure to move, having so many family and friends moving to one location made the decision to go there easier, though some did go to other places

The January 1787 Grants/Licenses

As mentioned above, this action on the part of the New Brunswick government simply granted the individuals on the list in Table 13-1 the right to occupy the lands, but did not set up a way for them to gain title to those lands. Also, if you look carefully at the names in this column of Table 13-1 you will see that each of them except Pierre Duperré is also listed in the October 1790 column. But he was the sole subject of a June 1790 land grant that was not included in Table 13-1. We think that those who got those 1787 licenses to occupy then perfected their title in the October 1790 grants, along with many others who had become attracted to the area by that first group.

Mazerolle Concession – the October 1790 Grants

The second of the group of land grants by the New Brunswick government in the Madawaska Territory was the Mazerolle Concession. By the way, these "Concessions" were named after one of the individuals on the list. This grant of land was made formal in the Act of October 1, 1790. The families had moved onto the land in 1785 and the lots were allocated by Louis Mercure, acting as Settlement Agent for the Acadians. This grant "included 16,000 acres of land starting just below the Indian reserve at the mouth of the Madawaska River and extended on both sides of the main river, down as far as Rivière Verte (Green River), a distance of 9 miles (14.5 km)." The grant was made to Joseph Mazerolle and 51 others. ***(Ref: Papers of Prudent Mercure, Tome 2, page 18)***

Individual lots were marked by the settlers themselves by notching or felling trees to mark the corners. They were granted their dwelling permit in February 1787, as shown in Table 13-1 above, and an official survey was made by G. Sproule that summer; that's the Surveyor General, Honorable George Sproule. See Map 13-1; the mentioned limits along the river of the Mazerolle Concession are shown in green.

Soucy Concession

This second grant of land was made to Joseph Soucy Jr. and 23 others and lies southeast and downstream from the Mazerolle Concession limits at the Green River (Rivière Verte in Appendix 13-B) and includes the portion of the St John River having seven islands. This would extend the downstream portion to somewhere above the Grand Falls, though those falls were not mentioned in the petition, and actually the lower of the seven islands is just above the Grand River and above Van Buren/St Leonard today. Descriptions were given for six new tracts and restated three tracts from the earlier Mazerolle Concession. The Soucy Concession also included Les Trois Isles (The Three Islands) in the St John River just upstream from Van Buren/St Leonard. These petitioners started taking their lands in 1791 (see the petition of François Violet, Joseph Cyr, Joseph Theriault, and Oliver Thibodeau in **Appendix 13-A** and that of François Violet, Joseph Cyr, and Oliver Thibodeau in **Appendix 13-B**) and the Concession was formalized in 1794. The land record details from the Provincial Archives of New Brunswick for François are shown in Figure 13-1; this gives the information for those searching the records, including Volume and Page, and Microfilm number. Those lots would later be surveyed so they could be formally granted. See Map 13-1; the mentioned limits of the Soucy Concession along the river are shown in violet.

The Soucy Concession tracts are shown in Map 13-2. The Concession consisted of 5,234 acres (2,118 ha) of land situated between the Green River and Grand River on both banks of the St John River. The land was to be meted out with 200 acres (81 ha) going to each head of family with the usual front of 60 rods (990 ft, 302 m). Among the recipients were François Violet (Sr.) [1] {6}, and his son, Augustin Violet [2b] {277}.

Name	VIOLETTE, Francis
Volume	B
Page	421
Grant number	292
Place	Madawaska Settlement
County	York
Date	1794-08-16
Accompanying plan	No
Acres	200
Microfilm	F16302
Comment	--

Other names on this grant (23):

CIRE, Aaron   200 acres
CIRE, Fierement   0 acres
CIRE, Joseph   0 acres
CIRE, Joseph Jr.   0 acres
CORMIER, Alexis   0 acres
CORMIER, Baptiste   0 acres
CORMIER, Francois   0 acres
CORMIER, Pierre   0 acres
LEBLOND, Louis   0 acres
MICHEAU, Joseph   0 acres
SHERRIT, Baptiste   0 acres
SOUCI, Germain   0 acres
SOUCI, Joseph Jr. *   200 acres
TERRIO, Joseph   0 acres
TERRIO, Joseph Jr.   0 acres
TIBIDEAU, Baptiste   0 acres
TIBIDEAU, Fierement   0 acres
TIBIDEAU, Gregoire   0 acres
TIBIDEAU, Jean   0 acres
TIBIDEAU, Oliver   0 acres
TIBIDEAU, Oliver Jr.   0 acres
VIOLETTE, Augustin   0 acres
WILLET, Louison   0 acres

Figure 13-1: Listing from Provincial Archives of New Brunswick (PANB)

The terms of each concession were similar. The settlers were first given licenses to occupy the land and later, if they met the conditions of the grant, they would then be given title. The conditions to receive title under the grant are as follows:

- Payment of 2 shillings per 100 acres (40.5 ha) annually, (about one day's wages) due September 29th.
- Erect one good dwelling to be at least 20 feet by 15 feet (6.1 m by 4.6 m) within 3 years.
- Clear or drain 3 acres (1.2 ha) for every 50 acres (20.2 ha) of plantable land.
- Have 3 head of cattle for every 50 acres (20.2 ha).

Map 13-1: Early land grant limits in Upper St John River (Mazerolle Concession=green, Soucy Concession=violet) with today's place names

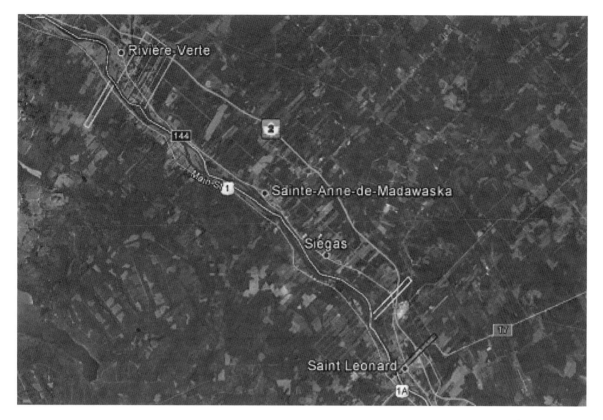

Map 13-2: Tracts in the Soucy Concession (Tract 1, blue; Tract 2, cyan; Tract 3, violet; Tract 4, red; Tract 5, orange; Tract 6, green)

Lands for François and his sons

The grantees were responsible for selecting and laying out their own lots, following the rules for lot dimensions set in the terms of the concession, as described above and in Appendix 13-D. The lots were to be 200 acres in area (81 ha) with the usual front of 60 rods (990 ft, 302 m). This would make the lots 8,800 feet (1.67 miles, 2.68 km) deep.

Island land would be especially desirable because due to spring freshets and flooding most islands would not have large trees, and they could be easily used to grow hay for feed.

François [1] {6} and his son, Augustin [2b] {277}, both received grants in the Soucy Concession. They each received one 200-acre (81 ha) lot in Tract 3, along with Joseph Cire {724}, Joseph Cire Jr {3497}, and Fierement Cire {3758}. And those five, along with Aaron (Hilarion) Cire {726}, were given grants on the three islands. *(Ed Note: Cire is also spelled Sear and Cyr)* Joseph Cyr {724} was married to Marie Luce's [2] {759} sister Marguerite Blanche {725}, also later known as Aunt Blanche (*Tante Blanche*), famed in history; we'll read a little more about her in Chapter 14. Joseph {724} was born in 1737 and they were married in 1760, so they would have been among the older of the grantees. Joseph Cyr Jr {3497} was born in 1764 so would have been around 27 when he settled in the area; he married Marie Marguerite Daigle {3525} a few years after the move. Firmin Cyr (Fierement Cire in the grant) {3758} was born in 1756 and would have been 35; he was married to Marie Josephte Ayotte {17703} in 1787, a year or so before the move. We don't have any information about Aaron Cyr, however. So, Marie Luce and her sister, Marguerite Blanche, settled on adjacent 200-acre (81-ha) lots in the new country, and Marie Luce's son Augustin settled on the other side of her. None of the other children of François and Marie Luce were old enough at that time to become settlers in their own rights.

We'll learn more about the families and where they settled in Chapter 14.

Selling out at Hammond River

Before leaving the Hammond River François had some business to complete. First among these was sale of his Lot #14 land and improvements.

There's an old adage in the real-estate industry which says if you intend on selling, your neighbors may well turn out to be your best buyer. Would this have been the case with François Violet? On the 15th of January after discourse with his neighbor we have the 100 pound note reading, "**I Francis Vilette of King's County, yeoman, am held and firmly bound unto Henry Darling of same county, yeoman, in sum of one hundred pounds of lawfull money to be paid to said Henry Darling, his Executors....**" The condition of the obligation contains legal points difficult to understand without a copy of the final sale of the lot #14. The document speaks of arbitrators Munson Jarvis, esquire; James White, esquire; and Christopher Sower, esquire; all of St. John.

White was already well known to François Violet, he having traded in White's store for over seven years. In looking at the Kings county map today one can see "Darling Island" in the Kennebecasis at the mouth of the Hammond River. So Darling might be noted as having owned more property and likely have greater capital, so he could advance the sum of 100 pounds to his neighbor.

We don't have any record of the sale of the Lot #14 property, so we do not know to whom it was sold, at what price, or when.

Our progenitor may well have used this loan to finance his move to the upper St. John River. Or was this capital to initiate construction of a grist mill on the Picquanositac (Violette Brook) at what later became Van Buren? We do not truly know. We have the 1831 testimony of his son, François Violet [2e] {280} to Agents of the State of Maine, John G. Deane and Edward Kavanagh, who wrote in their report about François: "**He said that his father, François Violette built a grist mill on that lot 40 years ago and that he has his rights from him.**" *(Ref: http://archiver.rootsweb.ancestry.com/th /read/ACADIAN-CAJUN/1998-09/0905202669)* This would have placed the building of the grist mill around 1791. The old mill was in operation into the 1950s, but fell in ruins sometime after that.

But even up-river there was conflict

We are sure that Marie-Luce and François Violet, Madeleine and Olivier Thibodeau, Marie-Madeleine and Joseph Theriault, and the other Acadians who left the French Village at Hammond River partially to get away from turmoil over land ownership rights, expected to have a more quiet time in their new lands along the upper St John River. But sadly, that was not to be. While they ended up in a three-way squabble over who would control their new lands; at least they did not have to worry about fights over ownership.

The Province of New Brunswick and the Province of Québec, part of British North America at that time, both claimed jurisdiction over the upper St John River area. Indeed, there were settlers in the Mazerolle and Soucy Concessions from both lower New Brunswick (the Acadians) and from Québec. Both provinces were still part of Great Britain. But both were concerned about the United States making claims on the territory, and thus it was an international conflict.

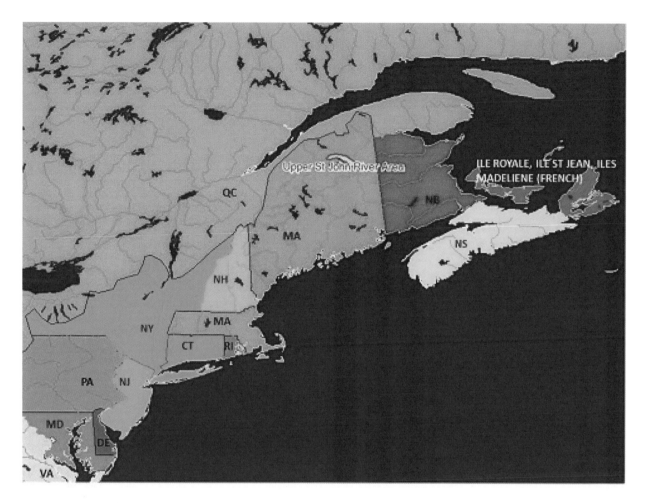

Map 13-3: Interests in Region 1789-90

Map 13-3 shows the various interests and defined areas around 1789-90. The states in the United States are shown; notice that what is now Maine was part of Massachusetts at that time. France still had control over Île Royale, Île St Jean, and the Madeleine Islands (blue). The Province of Nova Scotia had been established (yellow) as well as New Brunswick (red). At that time the rest of British North America shown in the map was in the Province of Québec (salmon) but this would soon be divided into Upper Canada (now Ontario) and Lower Canada (now Québec) – not to be confused with present-day Canada, which would not become created as a Confederation until 1867. The area of interest to François and his neighbors who moved from lower New Brunswick is shown in red-outlined yellow and labeled Upper St John River Area.

The area around where Maine is now was in dispute between the Provinces of Québec and New Brunswick as to where the boundary should be drawn. Québec said that since the settlers in the area mostly spoke French and practiced the Catholic religion it should be part of that province. New Brunswick said that since the land grants were made by the Governor of New Brunswick and many of the grantees came from lower New Brunswick it should be part of New Brunswick. But both were aware that U. S. had an interest in the area and the boundary between the two countries had not yet been defined. There were few, if any, settlers from what would become the U. S. in the Upper St John River area at that time. Both the Mazerolle and Soucy Concessions in the Madawaska settlement lay within the borders of this disputed territory claimed by both the United States and Great Britain since the Treaty of Paris in 1783. The boundary between New Brunswick and Québec was set in 1791, and the land grants were made by the Governor of New Brunswick in 1790 (Mazerolle et al) and 1794 (Soucy et al).

Maine became a state on its own in 1820, having been split from Massachusetts. However, the northern border of Maine was in dispute until the international boundary was fixed by the Webster-Ashburton treaty in 1842. Not until the national boundary was set did the settlers on the south side of the boundary receive the grants to their lands. They were also awarded automatic U. S. citizenship at the same time.

The logistics of the grand move

We don't know if the whole families (Violet, Thibodeau, and Theriault from the petition in Appendix 13-A in our story) moved all at once or if a small party went first, got houses built and some land cleared, and the rest moved later. Remember that for just those three families there were 38 people involved ranging in age down to three months (see the listing in Appendix 13-B). All three families had long-established homes (at least 20-30 years) in the French Village along the Hammond River and probably had provisions in place there for some to continue to live in that area. They would have also had some provisions for an advance party to take with them for use while getting started in the new land. We don't have deeds of sale for the properties along the Hammond River so we can't get the dates of moves that way. We do know that François borrowed £100 from Henry Darling against his Lot #14 property and maybe he used those funds to support the move and get started upriver.

We don't know the exact date when an advance party arrived; we have to assume they arrived in the spring, after the ice was out and spring flooding was over, for these reasons:

- They would not have made the move during winter because they had no shelter in place in their new lands.
- They would have slower currents to travel against – remember they were going upriver in small hand-propelled boats.
- They would have moved as early in the year as possible because they would have much work to do when they arrived to be prepared for the following winter.

How did they travel?

We can be fairly certain that they travelled upriver in boats, for that was the most common mode of travel where water routes were available. And we know that families erected settlement crosses along the river near where they first landed and established their lots, so they saw the river as their access frontage.

The boats had to have been hand-propelled using oars or paddles or poles.

How large were the boats? What did they look like? How was cargo stored? How many passengers could they carry? We don't have answers to those and the many other questions that naturally arise!

Pelletier and Ferretti *(Ref: Van Buren Maine History (by Martine A. Pelletier and Monica Dionne Ferretti, St John Valley Publishing Co, Inc, Madawaska ME, 1979, page 26)* suggest that an earlier group that fled the Fredericton area travelled to the Madawaska area by pirogue and canoe, and suggest that it took ten days to reach the Upper St John River area. The distance for that group was about the same – roughly 200 miles (320 km) – as for our families. We can then infer that it took the Violets, Thibodeaus, and Theriaults about ten days on the river.

The Grand Falls (Grand Sault) of the St John River presented a challenge to those moving upriver, just as it presented a barrier to British ships tracking down Acadians earlier. They would have to exit the river and carry their boats and all the contents around the falls in order to continue upstream. This partially dictated the size of boat they could use since they would have to carry the boats by hand around the falls. The Falls drop some 75 feet (23 m) and the portage around the falls was at least 1½ miles (2.4 km) of partially steep going. Since canoes are traditionally light weight, a canoe would take only one or two people to carry it, but canoes also provided a good way to carry the contents, and four people – two at the bow and two at the stern – could carry a loaded canoe to the upper river. A pirogue is either constructed from a single log as a dugout or constructed from boards, and pirogues are typically heavier than a canoe. Still, a pirogue could also be used to carry contents on the portage around the falls, though perhaps with less of a load each time and making multiple trips. For some assumptions and calculations on the possible size of these boats refer to Appendix 13-C.

We know that the Acadians were much at home on water, living as they did originally on a peninsula and doing much of their communication and commerce on water. The pirogue is an Acadian traditional craft and the canoe a traditional craft of the natives in the region, so the technology for boat-building was readily available. In fact, they probably had at least some of the needed boats already on hand for these craft were the pickup trucks of their day! (Thanks to Dave Wylie of St. David ME for that thought!) Some examples of what their boats might have looked like are shown in Photos 13-1 and 13-2 and Figure 13-2.

That must have been quite a sight! If we assume there were at least two people in each boat to provide propulsion (either an adult male or older girl or boy) and that the children were distributed among the boats as passengers along with household goods, it would have taken at least five boats for each of the three families. We can picture an arrangement such as the following (assuming the whole family moved in 1790):

- Boat 1: François Sr plus Benoni (5) plus household goods and provisions
- Boat 2: Augustin (19) and Louis (11) plus Marie-Anne (9) plus household goods
- Boat 3: François Jr (16) and Charles (15) plus Marie-Luce and Alexandre (6 months) plus household goods
- Boat 4: Genevieve (17) and Dominique (12) plus household goods and provisions
- Boat 5: Marguerite (20) and Madeleine (9) plus Marie-Venerande (3) plus household goods

If all three families moved at the same time there would have been a flotilla of at least 15 canoes or pirogues – quite a sight! But this is all pure conjecture, of course, since we have no actual record of the move.

Photo 13-1: An old boat found on an island in Acadia. Source: Wikimedia Commons, submitted by Antaya, commons.wiki-media.org/ wiki/File:Bateau_Acadien.jpg

Photo 13-2: A 20 ft Connors-St John river-driving boat ("bateau") used in re-enactments on the St John River and at the Acadian Festival in Madawaska. Similar to pirogues in common use. Courtesy Dave Wylie, St David ME

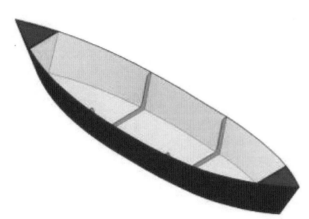

12' Pirogue canoe specifications
Main dimensions:
Length overall = 3,500 m / 11' 6"
Beam = 0,800 m / 2' 7"
Depth = 0,450 m / 1' 6"
Draft = 0,150 m / 6"
Displacement = 210 kg / 463 lbs.
Hull weight = 16 kg / 35 lbs.
Passengers = up to 2

From: www.boatplans.dk/boat_plans.asp?id=55

Figure 13-2: An example Pirogue Canoe you could make

They would have stopped each night and had to prepare an evening meal, probably a hot one. Breakfast would also likely be a prepared hot meal and lunch would be a cold one prepared before embarking for the day and eaten at a stop along the way without making camp.

Overnight camp stops probably had them erecting some hasty shelter; maybe they had some sail-cloth or similar to make a lean-to shelter or just used small trees to provide cover. No warm sleeping bags for them! They probably prepared a ground surface to sleep on using balsam fir tips and with blankets for ground cover as well as over them.

Their first homes

We know that François first built a log house along the St John River and near the mouth of what was called by the Indians as Picquanositac Brook. This stream is on the U. S. side (south side) of the St John River and has been renamed Violette Brook many years ago. *(Ed Note: In Chapter 14 we show in maps where the original grants were located and where François and other subsequently staked out land. The probable original location of the cabin and the location of the current house is not in François' original grant, but in another lot he claimed downstream.)* This would have placed his family near the river that was so important to them for travel and communication. Also, building here required less timber cutting to clear the land for building and for planting crops.

Typical early shelters consisted of cabins built of squared logs. All the rudimentary furniture and farm implements were carved by hand out of the surrounding forest. The Roy House on display at The Acadian Village in Van Buren today (Photo13-3) provides an excellent example of how these early homes were built and the description following Photo 13-3 gives us more information about these homes. The first home for François and Marie-Luce was probably similar to this.

Photo 13-3: The Roy House, moved to the Acadian Village in Van Buren from a location near Hamlin, Maine, is an example of a 19th century log home built using pièce-sur-pièce construction with "stacked and pegged" joinery at the corner joints. American Folklife Center photograph by David Whitman, 1991. From acim.umfk.maine.edu/acadian_houses.html

A more complete description of the early pioneer houses is given in Van Buren Maine History (by Martine A. Pelletier and Monica Dionne Ferretti, St John Valley Publishing Co, Inc, Madawaska ME, 1979, page 26):

> The first action of the pioneer in Madawaska was to erect a temporary shelter for his family. Little more than a leanto or shed, it served as living quarters while he cleared the land for immediate planting. He needed grain to survive. But before winter set in he had built a home of round or squared logs (about 18 x 25 ft) and 1½ stories high. The logs were cut and notched at the corners and chinked with any available material- clay, stones, moss, buckwheat kernels or horsehair. The ground floor was of rough board of hewn spruce, the upper floor – straight poles. The height of the room was generally 7 feet. Windows were small, few in number, and curtainless. A large stone fireplace built at the center of the house furnished light, warmth and ventilation. In front of it was cut a trap door which opened into a root cellar and on its hearth were a variety cooking pots and water containers.

Chairs (usually 3 or 4) were built to fit the need, the one used for peeling potatoes, for instance, was small and low. The height of the seat was usually determined by the size of the person using it although hearth chairs were given high
backs and low seats for comfort. The seat was of solid wood, interwoven deer-
skin, cowhide, elm bark or straw. Milk in containers (or bowls), eating utensils
(carved out of wood) and an occasional rare piece of china usually occupied a
wall shelf.

Wooden bedsteads were placed at the corners of the room and surrounded by
curtains. Trundle beds and rude cradles were used for the younger children as
were a kind of wooden pallet which folded up against the wall during the day. A
loom, skeining and spinning wheels, reel or winder, were often kept in the gar-
ret. There were no stairs, a ladder being used instead. A kitchen table and sometimes a chest at the foot of a bed completed the furnishings. Everything, including farm implements, was carved out of the surrounding forest by the man of the
house. The axe, drawknife, auger and grinding stone were his only tools, but his
skill was great and there are many talented craftsmen among his descendants in
the St. John Valley.

Later François and Marie-Luce's grandson Benoni (Belonie) [9i] {1521}, son of François-Xavier
Violette [2e] {280}, moved the original log house from down near the river to high ground just above
where the dam and grist mill were located. Benoni and his wife, Suzanne Theriault {1523}, lived in
that house at the new location. Later, their son Ambroise [40g] {1530} enlarged the house after he
inherited it by building a two-story house around the original log house. That house still stands today
house (see Photo 13-4) and is currently (2014) owned and lived in by Ann Deveau Violette [673]
{5312} (570), widow of Valerien Violette [320b] {4214} (569). Valerian was the son of Rene Violette
[123m] {2671}, son of Ambroise [40g] {1530} and Marie Madore Violette {2278}. The current Violette Brook is pictured in Photo 13-5; the dam upstream has been removed.

Photo 13-4: The Violette House today (June 2008)

Photo13- 5: Violette Brook, near where François built his dam and grist mill

Early industry: François builds a grist mill

A critical food component in all times is the flour used to make bread and other similar foodstuffs. Early pioneers would quickly plant grain crops to grow the sources of this flour, though sometimes native grains would already be growing in an area that they could use at the start. But just having the grain was not enough – it had to be milled (ground) into a fine flour to make it useful for bread-making.

François must have been enterprising, for he built a grist mill early on to grind grains for the settlers in the area. The lot he claimed lay along Picquanositac Brook, which he could use for water power. By building a dam across the stream the water on the upstream side of the dam would be at a much higher elevation than downstream and that drop was used to turn water wheels, which were mounted on shafts. The power developed by this system was used through systems of gears or belts-and-pulleys to operate all types of early machinery; in this case the grinding stones. He built the dam about 0.6 miles (1 km) upstream along the brook from its mouth (or 0.3 miles, or 0.5 km "as the crow flies") once he had cleared some land around that area. This would have put the dam and the grist mill away from flooding along the St John but still close enough for easy access.

The grist mill is gone, having been taken out of service and dismantled in the 1950s. However, an excellent example of what the grist mill may have looked like is part of the Acadian Village. Through a gift from Alderic O. [478c] {4680} (1916-2013) and Alice B. {5967} Violette (1917-2013) (VFA #100 and 101), similar mill equipment was purchased in the area and moved into a new building constructed to house it. The Violette Industrial Building, as it is called, has descriptive material and displays of early mills and industry. See photos 13-6 and 13-7.

Photo 13-7: Part of the equipment associated with the grist mill on exhibit. This is where the flour would be discharged into containers for the customers.

Photo 13-6: Alderic Violette [478c] {4680} at entrance to Violette Industrial Building (June 2008)

A town forms

Towns form where people come to do business, for a town is where the businesses and governmental functions are concentrated. The presence of a grist mill drew people from all around the area as they brought their harvested grain to be milled and came to pick up or purchase flour. So it was inevitable that a village should develop where François operated his mill. The name of the brook from which the mill got its power was changed from Picquanositac to Violette Brook, after the man who first harnessed its power for his use. And the town that slowly grew also came to be called Violette Brook. However when Maine became a state in 1842 the town's name was changed to Van Buren, in honor of the young nation's eighth President.

A pioneer passes

François died in 1824 at age 79, 34 years after he pioneered in the upper St John River valley. His wife, Marie-Luce [2]{759}, who pioneered the area with him, died around 1800 – just ten years after moving to that area. François was to marry again: first to Marie-Rose Cormier [3] {290} in July 1803 (she died in November 1811), and then to Genevieve Tardif [4] {296} in January 1814 (she died in May 1864). We will learn more of these other wives and of some of the children in Chapter 14.

Appendix 13-A

Petition for Land in Madawaska Settlement

This is a copy of the petition made in 1789 by François and others living in the French Village along the Hammond River in southern New Brunswick. They wanted to leave the lands they had settled on twenty or more years ago and relocate to the upper St John River valley, above the Great Falls and below the Madawaska Settlement made a few years earlier. See the transcription that follows the exhibit.

Petition of Francois Violette (1745-1824) and his brothers-in-law for land on the St. John River, 1789

To His Excellency thomas Carleton Esq Governor in and Over the provence of New Brunswick and its teretories theirunto Belonging Vise the merit of the Same &c. &c. &c.

and his Majestys Honourabel Cousel

The Memorile of Joseph Sear *(Ed Note: Cyr)* Humlby Shewith that he and Oliver tebed *(Ed Note: Thibodeau)* and Joseph tareyo *(Ed Note: Theriault?)* and fracis Violet *(Ed Note: François Violet)* Wishes to Settel ? the grat falls in the River St. John and Madewasasean in the Vakent Lands and Wishes that Youl give the Lands for them Selves and fameleys Such of them as is Abel to settle and giv us the Islands in frunt of the lands Wee Shall Settel in the River and Shall Rest as in Duty bound shall Ever pray

Qeensboroug the   Joseph Sear

26 August 1789   Oliver tebedo

                    Joseph tareyo

                    francis Violet

Appendix 13-B

Petition by François in December 1789

Following is a copy of the four pages of the petition made December 21, 1789 by François and others living in the French Village along the Hammond River in southern New Brunswick. This is the second petition made by Tibodo (Oliver Thibodeau), Tarrio (Joseph Theriault), and Violet (François Violet); Joseph Sear had joined them in the earlier petition in August 1789 but his name does not appear here. We do not know why Sear did not join in this petition nor do we know why this second petition was necessary. But we see in Appendix 13-D that Joseph Sear/Cire/Cyr did receive a grant in the same 1794 Soucy Concession where the others got theirs. See the transcription to the right of each page of the exhibit.

To His Excellcy Thomas Carleton Esq

Lieutenant Governor of His Majestys Province of New Brunswick &c. &c. &c.

The Petition of Olover Tibodo Sen[r], Joseph Tarrio Sen[r], & Francis Violet Sen[r]

Humby Sheweth

That your Petitioners are descended from the early Settlers of Acadia at the time it was under the dominion of France and have been educated in the Roman Catholic persuasion.

That they are at present Inhabitants of a place called the French Village on the little Kennebecasis (Ed Note: also called the Hammond River) where they possess small Lotts of Two Hundred Acres each.

That your petitioners are incumbered with large Families for whose settlement in Life they look forward with much anxiety and it is their earnest wish to see them settled around them on Lands of their own which they cannot expect in the part of the Country where they now devile *(sic)*.

That your Petitioners are informed that Government offer encouragement in Lands to such Persons as shall settle high up the River St. John

Which your petittioners are desirous of doing not only in order to obtain such Lands for their Families but as they may have the ? of a Priest in the performance of the rites and ceremonies of their Religion and the superintendence of their Children's Education.

That having always Remeaned themselves since the cession of Acadia to great Britain as faithful peaceable and industrious Subjects & Settlers

Your petitioners humbly pray that Lands proportioned to the Numbers of their Familes may be granted to them & their Children (a list whereof is annexed) at a place called the Madawasca, between the Seven Islands of the River de Vert on the River St John

And Your Petitioners as in duty bound shall every pray &

The Mark of Oliver Tibodo Senr

The Mark of Francis Violet

The Mark of Joseph Tarrio Junior for his Father Jospeh Tarrio Senior

Witnesseth E Hardy

Oliver Tibodo's Family consist of

Oliver Tibodo Senr
His Wife & Sons named
Oliver   Aged 23 years
Gregory   21
Tearman   20
Paul   19
Toussant   15
Francis   9
George   8
Baptiste   6
And three (Daughters   Total 13

Joseph Terrio's himself + Wife & 6 sons

Joseph   21
Gerard   19
William   15
Francis   14
Simon   12
Lawrence   8
Four daughters Total 12

Francis Violet himself + Wife + 7 Sons

Augustine 17 *(Augustin)*
Francis   15 *(François-Xavier)*
Charles   14
D'Aubique 12 *(Dominique, he was actually 6)*
Lewis   10 *(Louis)*
William   9 *(Benoni, 4)*
Alexander   3 mo *(Alexandre)*
Four Daughters Total 3

In the whole 38

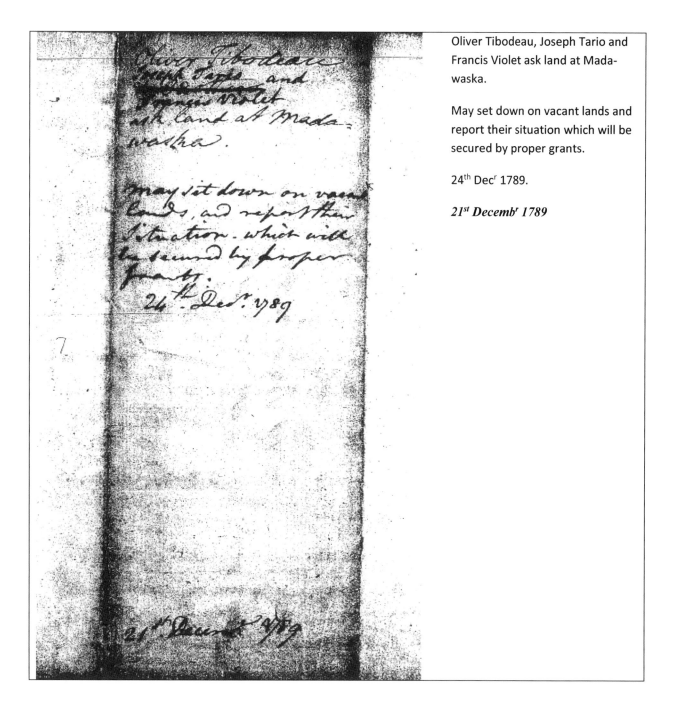

Oliver Tibodeau, Joseph Tario and Francis Violet ask land at Madawaska.

May set down on vacant lands and report their situation which will be secured by proper grants.

24th Decr 1789.

21st Decemb^r 1789

Appendix 13-C

How we arrived at the boat size for transporting the family up the St John River

We don't know exactly what type or size of boats François and his family used to make the move from the Hammond River area to the upper St John River area. To try to get an estimate of how large those boats might have been we have made some assumptions and followed those through with some calculations as shown below. Remember that the assumptions are pure speculation!

Two strong people can carry a combined total of 160-200 pounds (73-91 kg) if it is carefully balanced and four people twice that (320-400 pounds; 145-181 kg). That would include the weight of the canoe/pirogue and its contents. Assuming the average weight of the adults and older children to be 150 lbs (68 kg) and of the smaller children to be 50 lbs (22.7 kg), two larger people would add another 300 lbs (136 kg) the "people load" could be split up among the boats so that the total of people and cargo was probably in the range 400-800 lbs (181-363kg). This would require a displacement (the amount of water displaced by the loaded boat) of 6.4 to 12.8 cubic feet (0.18 to 0.36 m³). If we assume a draft (the depth the loaded boat settles into the water) of 6-8 inches (15-20 cm) then it would take a boat with an area at waterline of about 12-25 square feet (1.12-2.32 square m). If we assume that the boats had a beam (the width at the widest point) of around 2'-6" (76.2 cm), the length would have to be no more than 10-20 feet (3-6 m) long. This size canoe or pirogue would be easy to build and handle.

Appendix 13-D

Property Description of Lands in Soucy Concession

The information in this Appendix provides the property description of the lands that François and the others were granted in the Soucy Concession, so-called because the first name listed was Soucy. The grants were actually registered in August 1794, though we believe that the grants were authorized or made in December 1789.

The material here was taken verbatim from the web site The Upper St. John River Valley at www.upperstjohn.com in the section Land Grants and Surveys.

Land Grants: August 1794

On August 2, 1794, the British authorities in New Brunswick granted nine tracts of land and three small islands, containing 5,253 acres, within "the county of York, on the River Saint John, between the Great Falls of that river and the entrance of the River Verte [Green River]," to twenty-seven people, mostly of Acadian descent.

Below is a list of persons receiving grants, the lot number and/or tract number, in some cases the number of acres, and other information. In exchange for these grants, the grantees promised to "yield and pay" unto King George III, his heirs, successors, or to his Receiver-General, 2 shillings for every 100 acres, starting ten years from the date of the grant. The grant was also made conditional upon the grantees improving the land, clearing it and either planting on it or grazing cattle upon it, or building a home on it. *(Ed Note: For the text of the conditions of the grant Appendix 13-E.)*

The land is divided into nine tracts on both sides of the St. John, between Grand Falls and the Green River:

The first tract is on the north bank, twelve miles above Grand Falls, across from the mouth of a stream then called the Nisouguantique; *(Ed Note: Picquanositac Brook, or Violette Brook today.)*

the second tract is on the north bank, upstream from the first tract (15 miles from Grand Falls), a bit less than ¼ mile above the mouth of the Grand River;

the third tract is on the south bank, across the river from the second tract;

the fourth tract is also on the south bank, opposite the middle of the island called "La Grande Isle";

the fifth tract, on the north bank, just above the Green River and bordering on a lot granted in 1790;

the sixth tract, on the south bank, begins across from the mouth of the Green River on the bounds of the 1790 grant;

the seventh tract, on the north bank, is lot number 9 in the second division of the 1790 grant;

the eighth tract, on the south bank, is lot number 10 in the first division of the 1790 grant;

the ninth tract, on the south bank, is lot 14 in the first division of the 1790 grant.

Also granted were three islands, now called "Les Trois Isles," a bit upstream from Keegan, Maine.

Following the list of grantees is the detailed description of these tracts from the grant document.

First name	Last Name	Lot#	Tract#	Acres, Other information
Joseph, junior	Souci		1	200
Aaron	Cire		2	200
Augustin	Violette	1	3	
Francis	Violette	2	3	
Joseph	Cire	3	3	
Fierement	Cire	4	3	
Joseph, junior	Cire	5	3	
François	Cormier	1	4	
Baptiste	Cormier	2	4	
Alexis	Cormier	3	4	
Pierre	Cormier	4	4	
Louis	Le Blond	5	4	
Gregoire	Tibideau	6	4	
Fierement	Tibideau	1	5	
Oliver, junior	Tibideau	2	5	
Jean	Tibideau	3	5	
Joseph, junior	Terrio	4	5	
Joseph	Terrio	5	5	
Baptiste	Tibideau	6	5	
Oliver	Tibideau	7	5	
Germain	Souci		6	200
Louison	Willet		7	lot #9, 2nd division, in 1790 grant to Muzeroll and others
Baptiste	Sherrit		8	lot #10, 1st division, in 1790 grant to Muzeroll and others
Joseph	Micheau		9	lot #14, 1st division, in 1790 grant to Muzeroll and others
Aaron	Cire			}
Augustin	Violette			}
Francis	Violette			}
Joseph	Cire			} the three islands
Fierement	Cire			}
Joseph, junior	Cire			}

(Ed Note: Souci could also be Soucy or Soucie; Cire could also be Sear or Cyr; Tibideau could also be Thibodeau; Terrio could also be Terriault; Willet could also be Ouellette; and Micheau could also be Michaud. Muzeroll from the table or Mazeroll from the text below is also Mazerolle.)

The source of this information is: "Appendix No.37, Grant to Joseph Souci and twenty-six others. Dated 2nd August 1794." in First Statement on the part of Great Britain, according to the Provisions of The Convention Concluded Between Great Britain and the United States, on the 29th September, 1827 for Regulating the Reference to Arbitration of the Disputed Points of Boundary under the Fifth Article of the Treaty of Ghent (1829), pp.260-265.

The Grants can be found in the Provincial Grantbook, Volume B, page 421, Grant number 292. Much of this information is available in the on-line searchable database of land grants maintained by the Provincial Archives of New Brunswick at http://www.lib.unb.ca/gddm/data/panb /panbweb.html

The material here was also taken verbatim from the web site The Upper St. John River Valley at www.upperstjohn.com in the section Land Grants and Surveys.

Description of the nine tracts included in this grant:

The first tract (being a lot of two hundred acres) beginning on the north-easterly bank or shore of the said River Saint John, about twelve miles above the Great Falls aforesaid, and nearly opposite the mouth or discharge of the stream or rivulet, commonly called Nisouguantique, thence running north sixty degrees east by the magnet, one hundred and forty-eight chains, four poles each; thence north thirty degrees west, fifteen chains; thence south sixty degrees west, until it meets the said northeasterly bank or shore of the said River Saint John; thence following the several courses of the said bank or shore, down stream, to the bounds first mentioned.

The second tract being a lot of two hundred acres beginning on the north-easterly bank or shore of the River St. John aforesaid, about 15 chains above the mouth or entrance of Grande Rivière which discharges into the River St.John, about 15 miles above the Great Falls. Thence running north sixty degrees east by the magnet, one hundred and fifty chains, of four poles each; thence north thirty degrees west, fifteen chains; thence south sixty degrees west, unitl it meets the said north-easterly bank or shore of the River St.John; thence following the several courses of the said bank or shore down stream to the first-mentioned bounds of this second tract.

The third tract beginning at a cedar post, on or near the south-westerly bank or shore of the River Saint John aforesaid, nearly opposite to the second tract above described; thence running south sixty degrees west by the magnet, one hundred and forty-eight chains, of four poles each; thence north thirty degrees west, seventy-five chains, or to meet the upper or north-western line of lot number five in this tract; thence south sixty degrees east, along the said line of lot number five, until it meets the south-westerly bank or shore of the River Saint John aforesaid; thence along the said bank or shore, following the several courses thereof, down stream, until it meets the first-mentioned bounds of this third tract, or a line running north sixty degrees east therefrom, containing in the whole thereof one thousand and twenty-five acres, more or less, with the usual allowance of ten per cent for roads and waste, and being divided into five lots, or plantations, numbered from number one to number five, both inclusive, whose respective numbers, fronts, marks, contents and division lines are expressed and described on the plan hereunto annexed

The fourth tract beginning at a cedar post, placed on or near the south-westerly bank or shore of the River Saint John, nearly opposite to the middle of the island, commonly called Grand Isle, and about six miles and one half mile below the mouth of the River Verte above described; thence running south sixty degrees west by the magnet, one hundred and forty-eight chains, of four poles each; thence north thirty degrees west, ninety chains, or until it meets the upper or north-westerly line of the lot number six in this tract; thence north sixty degrees east along the said line of lot number six, until it meets the said southwesterly bank or shore of the River Saint John; thence along the said bank or shore following the several courses thereof, down stream, until it meets the first-mentioned bounds of this fourth tract, or a line running north sixty degrees east therefrom, containing in the whole thereof one thousand two hundred and sixty acres, more or less, with the usual allowance of ten per cent for roads and waste, and being divided into six lots or plantations, numbered from number one to number six, both inclusive, whose respective numbers, marks, fronts, or breadths, contents in acres and division lines, are expressed and described on the plan hereunto annexed.

The fifth tract, beginning on the north-easterly bank or shore of the River Saint John aforesaid, at a marked white maple tree, standing on or near the said bank or shore, a few chains above the mouth of the River Verte before mentioned, being the lower bounds of the lot number one, granted to Etienne Tibideau, in the second tract or division of the grant to Joseph Mazeroll and others; thence running north forty-five degrees east, by the magnet, along the lower or south-easterly line of the said lot number one, one hundred and sixty-nine chains, or four poles each; thence south forty-five degrees east, one hundred and five chains, or until it meets the lower or south-easterly line of the lot number one in this fifth tract; thence along the said line of lot number one, south forty-five degrees west, until it meets the aforesaid north-easterly bank or shore of the River Saint John; thence along the said bank or shore, following the several courses thereof up stream, until it meets the first-mentioned bounds of this fifth tract, or a line running south forty-five degrees west therefrom, containing in the whole thereof one thousand six hundred and five acres, more or less, with the usual allowance of ten per cent. for roads and waste, and being divided into seven lots or plantations, numbered from number one to number seven, both inclusive, whose respective numbers, marks, fronts, contents, and division lines, are expressed and described on the plan hereunto annexed.

The sixth tract, being a lot of two hundred acres, beginning on the south-westerly bank or shore of the said River Saint John, nearly opposite the mouth of the River Verte aforesaid, at a marked birch treee, standing on or near the said bank or shore, being the lower bounds of the lot number one, granted to Joseph Ma-zeroll in the first tract or division of the aforesaid grant to him and others; thence running south forty-five degrees west, by the magnet, along the lower line of the said Mazeroll's lot number one, one hundred and forty-five chains, of four poles each; thence south forty-five degrees east, fifteen chains; thence north forty-five degrees east, until it meets the said south-westerly bank or shore of the River Saint John; thence along the said bank or shore, following the several courses thereof up stream, until it meets the first-mentioned bounds of this sixth tract, or a line running north forty-five degrees east therefrom.

The seventh tract, being the lot number nine, as described in the second tract of division of the aforesaid grant to the said Mazeroll and others, beginning at a stake placed on or near the north-easterly bank or shore of the said River Saint John, at the upper bounds of lot number eight, granted to Paul Cere in the grant aforesaid; thence along the upper or north-westerly line of the said lot number eight, north forty-five degrees east, by the magnet, one hundred and forty-five chains, of four poles each; or to meet the line bounding the said second tract or division of the said grant in that district to the rear or north-easterly; thence along the said rear line north forty-five degrees west, eighteen chains and twenty-five links, or to meet the lower line of lot number ten, in the said second division of the said grant; thence along the said line of lot number ten south forty-five degrees west, until it meets the said north-easterly bank or shore of the River Saint John; thence along the said bank or shore, following the several courses thereof down stream, until it meets the first-mentioned bounds of this seventh tract, or a line running south forty-five degrees west therefrom, contain-ing in the whole thereof two hundred and forty-seven acres more or less, with the aforesaid usual allowance.

The eighth tract, being the lot number ten as described in the first tract or divi-sion of the said grant to Mazeroll and others, beginning at a marked hackmatack tree, standing on or near the said south-westerly bank or shore of the River Saint John, at the upper bounds of the lot number nine, granted to Accarie Ailliot in the first division of the said grant; thence along the upper or north-westerly line of the said lot number nine, south forty-five degrees west, by the magnet, one hundred and forty-three chains, of four poles each, or to meet the line bounding the said first tract or division of the said grant in that district, to the rear or south-westerly; thence along the said rear line north forty-five degrees west, twenty chains, or to meet a tract of four poles wide reserved for a road, between the lots number ten and eleven in the said first division of the said grant; thence along the said reserved road north forty-five degrees east, until it meets the aforesaid south-westerly bank or shore of the River Saint John; thence following the several courses of the said bank or shore down stream, until it meets the first described bounds of this eighth tract, or a line running north forty-five degrees east therefrom, contraining in the whole thereof two hundred and fifty-six acres, more or less, with the aforesaid usual allowance.

The ninth tract, being lot number fourteen in the said first division of the said grant, beginning at a marked dry maple tree, standing on or near the said south-westerly bank or shore of the River Saint John, being the upper bounds of lot number thirteen, granted to Joseph Cere, junior, in the said first division of the said grant to the said Mazeroll and others; thence running along the upper line of the said lot number thirteen south forty-five degrees west, by the magnet, one hundred and forty-five chains, of four poles each, or to meet the aforesaid rear line of the said first division of the said grant in that district; thence along the said rear line north forty-five degrees west, fourteen chains and fifty links, or to meet the lower line of lot number fifteen, granted to John Martin, in the said first division of the grant aforesaid; thence along the said lower line of lot number fifteen, north forty-five degrees east, until it meets the aforesaid south-westerly bank or shore of the River Saint John; thence following the several courses of the said bank or shore down stream, until it meets the first-mentioned bounds of this ninth tract, or a line running north forty-five degrees east therefrom, containing in the whole thereof two hundred and twenty-four acres, more or less, wtih the said allowance of ten percent for roads and waste.

The three islands are situate in the said River Saint John, nearly in front of the third tract herein described, being bounded by the waters of the said River Saint John, containing altogether thirty-six acres, more or less.

[...]

The letter of grant is dated 2nd August 1794. The Grant was registered as number 292, on 16th August 1794.

CHAPTER 14 – THREE FAMILIES IN THE VALLEY

Time Span: 1789-1848

We know that François married three times and had families with all three wives. This was not uncommon in the days where childbearing was often a route to early death for women. Altogether he had 23 children and over 150 grandchildren, and his first grandchild was born before his fifteenth child was born! But were the circumstances for each of the three families – born over a 48-year period from 1770 to 1818– the same? Evidence shows that the first family was probably better off than the subsequent two. Part of that can be explained by where the individuals settled and what it took to develop their land, and part by the opportunities that changed as the population grew.

A description of the Upper St John River Valley

In the immediate area around Van Buren ME/St Leonard NB the water surface elevation of the St John River is 420-430 feet (128-131 meters) above sea level, so from the area they left along the Hammond River in lower New Brunswick they gained some 400 feet (122 m) in elevation. The lower ends of the lands François and Marie Luce settled along the Hammond River were about 25 feet (7.6 m) above sea level along the river and around 250 feet (76 m) in the upper parts. And the land forms and general appearance and features were very similar.

In the Upper St John, land elevations at distances from the river follow roughly the pattern in the table below. Though these relationships continue through that area, there are some minor variations in some localities. Where the Grand River joins the St John the lower zone extends further back from the rivers and the higher ground is further away.

Table 14-1: Land elevations at various distances from river

US side					Distance	Canadian side				
1.0 mi	¾	½	¼	⅛	< from >	⅛	¼	½	¾	1.0 mi
1.6 km	1.3	0.8	0.4	0.2	River	0.2	0.4	0.8	1.2	1.6 km m
665 ft	655	560	505	490	420 ft	435	455	505	560	620 ft
203 m	200	171	154	149	128 m	133	139	154	171	189 m

These topographic features were important to the earliest settlers, for the lower intervales or bottomlands along the rivers had a much higher value – especially immediately after settlement – than higher lands further from the river. There were no roads, so all communication and travel took place along the river systems and having river access was important. Further, these bottomlands were less forested and the soil more fertile from flooding over the millennia. Farms could more easily get started in the intervals without having to clear trees and stumps to open up the land.

Remember that these early settlers were not wealthy, and probably only had the resources they brought with them. There were no markets from which to buy food and no catalogs from which to order furnishings and appliances. They could travel downriver again to the cities or towns to purchase items they might need, but that cost a lot in terms of time and expense, and probably cash that they did not have. We think that François may have had as much as £100 from the sale of his lands along the Hammond, but we don't know if they had been paid right away.

The advantages of being first

Those who came first could choose lands that were more advantageous. Three specific attributes would mean a distinct advantage to the claimant:

- Lands along the river were in the fertile intervale zone, where fewer trees needed to be cleared to plant crops and build farms, and where the soil was richer from eons of buildup.
- Lands having a stream passing through meant opportunities to use the stream's hydraulic power for industry and manufacturing.
- Lands on large islands in the St John River had few, if any, trees and had excellent forage for livestock which could be maintained with little or no effort.

And François had the best opportunity being one of the original settlers. On the north side of the river he chose a very advantageous site through which the Grand River flows and the land was near its outlet. The Grand River is a tributary to the St John. And on the south side he later chose a site through which the Picquanositac flows. While the Grand River is fairly flat and has little fall in that area, the Picquanositac has more fall and had the potential for developing water powered mill sites. Picquanositac was the local Native American name for the stream which was later renamed Violette Brook. Choosing these locations meant these settlers had to be pioneers but once, for they could quickly settle and plant and establish themselves without having to do as much clearing. Those who came later had to settle for rear lots or lots in the second or third tiers of lots back from the St John River, and those with the less advantageous lots had to clear land into the second, third, and fourth generations of descent.

Being able to raise crops quickly and easily meant they were also able to grow more than they consumed, which allowed them to sell the excess and thus gain funds for other purposes. The holders of prime land were thus able to evolve from subsistence farming to business roles which allowed education opportunity for successive generations, who then could cultivate political fervor and strength.

How the land was divided originally – Soucy Concession

So here these families found themselves in this yet-unsettled land and on their own resources to establish land ownerships and farms and homesteads. See Maps 12-6 and 12-7 in Chapter 12 to see how their lands were laid out downriver, and Maps 13-3 and 13-4 in Chapter 13 (repeated here as Maps 14-2 and 14-3 below) showed the pattern in their new lands along the Upper St John. Quoting from Chapter 13:

> "As we noted earlier in this chapter the grantees were responsible for selecting and laying out their own lots, but we believe that the rules for lot dimensions were set in the terms of the concession. The lots were to be 200 acres in area (81

ha) with the usual front of 60 rods (990 ft, 302 m). This would make the lots 8,800 feet (1.67 miles, 2,682 m) deep."

Under the original Soucy Concession there were nine tracts of land granted along with three small islands. The total grant was 5,235 acres (2,119 hectares) in area. Several of the tracts were subdivided into lots, and there were 27 people awarded a grant. The stretch of the St John River included in the Soucy Concession runs from First Island, a short distance above Grand Falls, upstream to Seventh Island, near Lille ME, a distance of 20-25 miles (32-40 km). That distance in rods[1] is 6,400-8,000. Tracts 1 through 6 are shown in their approximate locations on Map 1 on the next page; Tracts 7 through 9 were re-grants of three lots in the earlier Mazerolle Concession, and were further upriver.

The description of those nine tracts and of the islands was contained in **Appendix 13-D** of Chapter 13, and that also showed the names of the grantees and what they were granted. Map 14-1 shows the approximate location and arrangement of those grants. From **Appendix 13-D**, we see that both François and his eldest son Augustin were given grants of land in Tract 3 and that both were also part of the grantees of the three islands (along with several Cyrs – listed as Cire). Augustin was granted Lot 1 of Tract 3, and François Lot 2 of Tract 3, so their original grants were adjacent to each other. Joseph Cyr had Lot 3; Phirmin Cyr, Madeleine Violet's future husband, had Lot 4; and Joseph Cyr, Jr, Lot 5. Tract 3 is described as having an area of 1,025 acres (415 ha), including a 10% allowance for roads and "waste", and the property lines running back from the river are said to be around 148 chains (of four poles each).

The conditions to receive title under the grant were as follows:

- Payment of 2 shillings per 100 acres (40.5 ha) annually, (about one day's wages) due September 29th.
- Erect one good dwelling to be at least 20 feet by 15 feet (6.1 m by 4.6 m) within 3 years.
- Clear or drain 3 acres (1.2 ha) for every 50 acres (20.2 ha) of plantable land.
- Have 3 head of cattle for every 50 acres (20.2 ha).

---

[1] The rod (also pole) was a common surveying unit of the time and represents a distance of 16 ½ feet (~5 m). Two rods or poles make up a chain, so there are 160 chains in a mile. Actually, there are two definitions of the chain as a surveyor's measurement: the earlier chain, called Rathbone's chain, was two rods but a later chain unit, called the Gunter's chain, was four rods so there are 80 Gunter's chains per mile. You have to be careful to know which chain definition was in use when reading maps using these measurements. Fortunately, the descriptions used in the Soucy Concession make reference to "chains of four poles each".

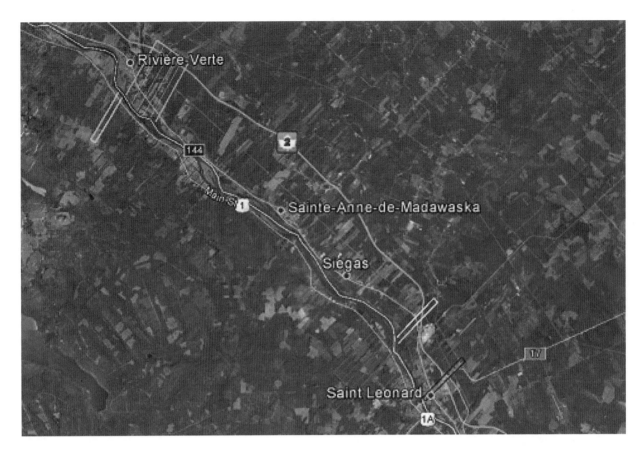

Map 14-1: Approximate layout of tracts and lots in the Soucy Concession. Tract 1: blue; Tract 2: cyan; Tract 3 and lots: violet; Tract 4 and lots: red; Tract 5 and lots: orange; Tract 6: green.

We know from the names in the grants which parcels (Tract and Lot) each individual was granted. And we know that around 1791 those individuals had settled on and subsequently improved those lands to meet the terms of the grant by 1794. We also know that Augustin and François had taken Tract 3, Lots 1 and 2 respectively. From Map 14-1 we see that those lots were on the south side (now the US side) and about opposite where Grand River enters the St John River. But as Map 14-1 shows, the lots granted in the Soucy Concession were spaced out, with Tracts 1 and 2 being single lot grants, Tracts 3, 4, and 5 having five lots each, and Tract 6 being a single lot grant as well. So that left a considerable amount of land between those tracts to be further claimed and settled.

Copies of portions of the original map of the Soucy Concession are shown in Maps 14-2a and 14-2b below. Map 14-2a shows the five lots in Tract 3 on the south bank, where François Sr and Augustin received grants, and Map 14-2b shows the Tract 1 parcel on the north bank granted to Aaron Cere (Cyr). Map 14-2b also contains a comment about the grant to François Jr in 1826 of a parcel just downstream from Cere's. That comment indicates the parcel size as 300 acres (121.4 hectares) but does not show the boundaries. The overlap in Maps 14-2a and14- 2b are from how the archived maps were copied from the original.

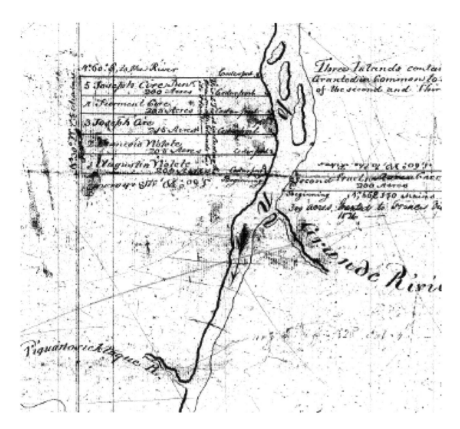

Map 14-2a: Soucy Concession Tract 3 and lots

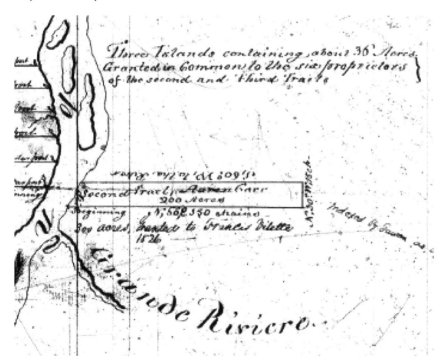

Map 14-2b: Soucy Concession Tract 1 and later Francis Violette grant

We have no record of grants being made by the British after 1794, so any claiming of lands after that time must have been done by individuals marking out and "staking their claim" to new parcels. It appears from later maps that those claimants subsequent to the 1794 grants followed the same pattern of lot layouts, with relatively narrow frontages and very deep side lot lines.

It was not long after 1794 when the dispute became heated between the US and Great Britain over territory and borders between the two countries. The 1783 Treaty of Paris defined much of the border between the United States and British North America. The US was greatly interested in expanding its domain westward over the continent as we know from acquisitions such as the Louisiana Purchase (1803). And in 1804 the Lewis & Clark expedition was authorized by the US government to search for a route to the Pacific Ocean, and it was not long after that other land acquisitions were made in the west. Defining a boundary for most of the eastern states was easy, since one border was obviously the Atlantic Ocean. The northeastern border proved to be more difficult; for both Great Britain and the US wanted the valuable timber resources represented by the forests in northern Massachusetts (remember that all of what is now Maine was at that time part of Massachusetts until Maine statehood in 1820). The St John River played the important role of being the transportation corridor for harvested timber (or timber products) to get to the markets along the coast. Both Massachusetts and New Brunswick granted timber rights in the north woods, and conflicts constantly arose. So settlement of the boundary question became increasingly important.

One step was made when the State of Maine was created in 1820 by carving out the northern part of Massachusetts. But the residents in the St John Valley and the Madawaska Territory remained in limbo as to their citizenship during those years. That did not stop them from claiming more lands and it did not stop new settlers from coming in and acquiring land.

It would not be until 1831 that any census would be made and that was commissioned by the new State of Maine. They engaged John G. Deane and Edward Kavanagh to survey the Madawaska Settlement. Both men were members of the Maine Legislature, and Kavanagh in 1831 became a member of the U. S. House of Representatives for Maine. Both Maine and New Brunswick were being cautious and had agreed that until a boundary had been agreed upon neither would undertake any acts of aggression in the disputed zone.

The Deane & Kavanagh survey put in writing the state of the settlement and its development up to that date. The report covered the area from the St. Francis River (near present day Madawaska) to Grand Falls on both sides of the St John River, and their listings show that by 1831 most of the land along both banks of the river had been settled and claimed. Maps 14-3a and 14-3b (upstream and downstream) show the result of that survey, taken from a map drawn by Maurice Michaud in 1964. Michaud's map attempts to show the relative property locations and labels them with the names provided by the Deane & Kavanagh survey. Remember that Deane and Kavanagh made their survey *37 years* after the Soucy Concession grants were formalized in 1794, and about *42 years* after those settlers first claimed their lands. Much had changed over those years, and not only were there many new names that appeared on lots, but many or most of those original settlers had claimed additional lands. Many of the original settlers had since died, and now not only had the children of the original settlers claimed lands but so also had children of those children – grandchildren of the original settlers.

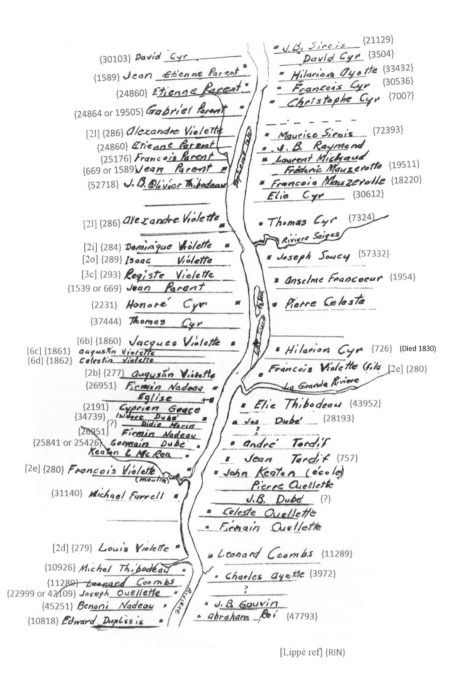

Map 14-3a: Upstream property owners in Soucy Concession, circa 1831. From Van Buren Maine History, Martine A. Pelletier and Monica Dionne Ferretti, 1979. Notations show Lippé references [Blue] and Genealogical Database references {Red}. See below.

Map 14-3b: Downstream property owners Soucy Concession, circa 1831. From Van Buren Maine History, Martine A. Pelletier and Monica Dionne Ferretti, 1979. Notations show Lippé references [Blue] and Genealogical Database references {Red}. See below.

(Ed Note: The Deane & Kavanagh Survey notes can be found as reported by Kathy Brock starting at http://archiver.rootsweb.ancestry.com/th/read/ACADIAN-CAJUN/1998-09/0904819103. There are seventeen parts but the links to all are found at the bottom of this first part. This seems to contain the actual report prepared by Deane & Kavanagh.

The survey notes have been transformed into tabular form by C. Gagnon and can be found at http://www.upperstjohn.com/aroostook/deane-kavsouth.htm for the south bank, and http://www.upper-stjohn.com/aroostook/deane-kavnorth.htm for the north bank. Those tables are ©2000-2008 C. Gagnon.)

We show on Maps 14-3a and 14-3b where the Violette family was located in the Deane & Kavanagh survey. They are indicated on the maps by their reference number in **The Descendants of François Violet,** by Rita Violette Lippé, 1984, in square brackets [ ], and their Record Identification Number (RIN) reference in the **Genealogical Database** built and maintained by Rod Violette in curly brackets { }. Rita is the founder of the Violette Family Association, and Rod is the Genealogist for the Association. You can see those named in the following sections in descendant tables showing the children and grandchildren of François in **Appendix 14-C**; their RINs are shown there.

- The two locations on Map 14-3a with the name François [2e] {280} refer to François, son of François [1] {6} and Marie Luce [2] {759}.
- The Alexandre [2l] {286} refers to the son of François and Marie Luce. His lot nearly opposite the Siegas River shows a house, while the one further upstream does not and only has "possessory clearing". Alexandre was the last of the children born along the Hammond.
- The Augustin at [2b] {277} on the south bank opposite the Grand River refers to the son of François and Marie Luce and is his original grant. He was one of the pioneers of the area.
- The Augustin [6c] {1861} and Celestin at [6b] {1862} refer to the sons of Augustin and Elizabeth and are probably on the lot their grandfather François was originally granted.
- The Jacques Violette at [6b] {1860} is the son of Augustin and Elizabeth. This was probably Lot 3 of the original grant and was acquired from his parents.
- The Dominique [2i] {284}, Isaac [2o] {289}, and Alexandre [2l] {286} refer to sons of François and Marie Luce.
- The Augustin [2b] {277} at the two locations on Map14-3b could either be the son of François and Marie Luce, or Augustin son of Augustin and Elizabeth. No house was shown on those two lots, and Deane & Kavanagh reported only possessory clearing on the north bank lot and some clearing on the south bank lot.
- The lands marked {43952} on Map 14-3a were originally owned by Charles [2j] {24}, son of François and Marie Luce, but upon his death around 1817 became the property of his wife, Theotiste {25}. Theotiste then married Eloi Thibodeau {43952} whose name appears on the map.
- The Cyprian Grace at {2191} was the husband of Venerande Violette [15d] {302}, daughter of Charles [2j] {24} and Theotiste {25} Violette.

François' second marriage, to Marie Rose Cormier in 1803, produced five children between 1803 and 1810. All of these children could have been property owners or married to property owners by 1831 except the fourth child who died at age two.

François' third marriage, to Genevieve Tardif in 1814, produced three children between 1814 and 1818. These likely were not property owners or married to property owners by 1831 since they would have been 13-17 years old.

The original Violette lands granted to François and Augustin, his son, are where the village of Keegan is located today. Keegan is part of Van Buren. These are the lots in Map 14-3a having the names Jacques Violette [6b] {1860}, Augustin [6c] {1861}, Celestin [6d] {1862}, and Augustin [2b] {277}, the latter being his original grant. Jacques, Augustin, and Celestin were the sons of the original Augustin.

The added parcel François claimed that contains Violette Brook became the property of his son François [2e] {280} by 1831. This was where the original François [1] {6} built his grist mill. That and the parcel owned by Michael Farrell {31140} constitute where most of the town of Van Buren is today.

Appendix 14-A contains excerpts from the Deane & Kavanagh report and shows roughly how the lots were spread out along the river. An excerpt from the original 1794 Soucy Concession Grants naming the grantees and what they were granted was included in **Appendix 13-B**, and the conditions applying to those grants and the earlier grants was included in **Appendix 13-C**, both from Chapter 13.

Interim land acquisitions

Comparing Maps 14-3a and 14-3b with Map 14-1, we can see how our ancestors spread out across and along the river. The Deane & Kavanagh report reveals the existence since about 1791 of a grist mill owned and operated by François Violet (1744-1824) on Violette Brook, formerly known as Picquanositac, and flowing into the St John River on the south side. The mill was reconstructed in 1824 and was in almost continuous use until the 1950's. The community that grew around the mill was called Violette Brook but in 1842 the name was changed to Van Buren, in honor of the eighth U. S. President. This tract of land was claimed by François soon after his original grant and it had been passed on to his son, François, and then to his grandson Beloni.

We also see a parcel of land on the north side (the subsequent New Brunswick side) around the mouth of the Grand River that François also claimed soon after his first settlement. This land also passed on to his son François, who still held it and lived on it in 1831.

The original families spread out

The first petition (**Appendix 13-A**) had the names of Joseph Cyr, Olivier Thibodeau, Joseph Terriault, and François Violet while the second (**Appendix 13-B**) had only Thibodeau, Terriault, and Violet. The wives of Cyr, Terriault, and Violet were all sisters of Thibodeau: Marguerite Blanche, Marie-Madeleine, and Marie-Luce, respectively. All four families lived in the Kennebecasis-Hammond River-French Village area (see Chapter 12). But yet we find the names of Cyr, Thibodeau, and Violet on Map 14-1 but *not* Terriault; the Terriaults apparently settled further upriver in the Grand Isle area, which is between the Mazerolle Concession grants and the Soucy Concession grants (downriver from the Green River and upriver from Seventh Island in Map 1), and the Cyrs may have settled in the Soucy Concession area. We find the name Hilarion Cyr in Map 3a on the lot just upstream from that of Francois Violet (fils) on the St Leonard side and we find the name Elie Thibodeau on the lot just downstream from the Violette lot. Hilarion is the son of Joseph Cyr and would have been around 18 years old in 1790. We do not know if he settled that lot on his own or inherited that lot from his father, Joseph Cyr, who died in 1803. Elie Thibodeau may be Eloi Thibodeau, who married the widow of Charles Armand Henri Violet, François's son, who died in 1808. If so, that land may have been settled by Charles at the start.

Marguerite Blanche Thibodeau, wife of Joseph Sear (Cyr), would become famously known during a famine in the Madawaska area in 1797 as *Tante Blanche* (Aunt Blanche) for helping many in that time of need. Wearing snowshoes, she brought extra clothing and provisions to people suffering from hunger and cold, while the men from the community attempted to hunt for food. Tante Blanche "was venerated with great respect and devotion by all the colonists. She cured the sick, found lost articles, reconciled enemies. Her reprimands to delinquents and drunkards were more feared than those of the bishop." (From "Tante Blanche was heroine of Colonists' black famine", www.acadian.org /blanche.html) Tante Blanche was awarded a singular honor – her remains are buried inside the church at St Basile.

Land ownership expands by the time of statehood

When comparing the original Soucy Concession lots (Map 14-1) with the land holdings found by Deane & Kavanagh (Maps 14-3a and 14-3b) you can see that not only did the original grantees acquire more land, but many others came to settle in the area.

The next glimpse we can get of land ownership comes when the international boundary was established and the ability to establish land rights was settled on New Brunswick and the new state of Maine (Maine was formed from part of the original Massachusetts). The boundary was agreed upon in 1842, and by 1845 Maine/Massachusetts, and 1848 for New Brunswick, the governments were able to record the settlers' claims by issuing them grants for the lands they held at that time. A similar process took place on the New Brunswick side. Maps 14-4a through 14-4d (upstream to downstream) show the ownerships and lot arrangements as established by the grants in 1845/8. These maps are limited to the land in the Van Buren Plantation map on the US side and the St Leonard map (NB Map 44) on the British North American side. (***Ed Note: Notice that we are careful to not use the term Canada or Canadian because that entity did not come into being until 1867***)

What started as 23 lot owners in 1794 had expanded (in the Van Buren area) to many more ownerships by 1831 as additional lands were claimed. By 1845/8 what lands had been unclaimed in 1831 were now claimed and many of the original lots had been subdivided to provide land for subsequent generations. (We use the term "ownerships" to denote owned lots instead of simply where they lived because some people owned more than one lot). And since for the most part the ownerships in 1831 were contiguous, that meant that many of the 1831 lots had been split by 1845/8. Probably most of those lots splits came about to accommodate children of the original owners. This lot splitting is especially evident in what was originally Lots 1 through 5 of Soucy Concession Tract 3, granted to Augustin Violet, Francois Violet, Joseph Cyr, Firmin Cyr, and Joseph Cyr Jr, respectively. What was five lots in 1790 had become about twenty lots by 1845/8, but most of them are owned by either Violets or Cyrs – the original grantee families.

As used otherwise in this chapter, the info in Maps 14-4a through 14-4d in square brackets [ ] is the reference number in ***The Descendants of François Violet,*** by Rita Violette Lippé, 1984, and their Record Identification Number (RIN) reference in the ***Genealogical Database*** built and maintained by Rod Violette in curly brackets { }.

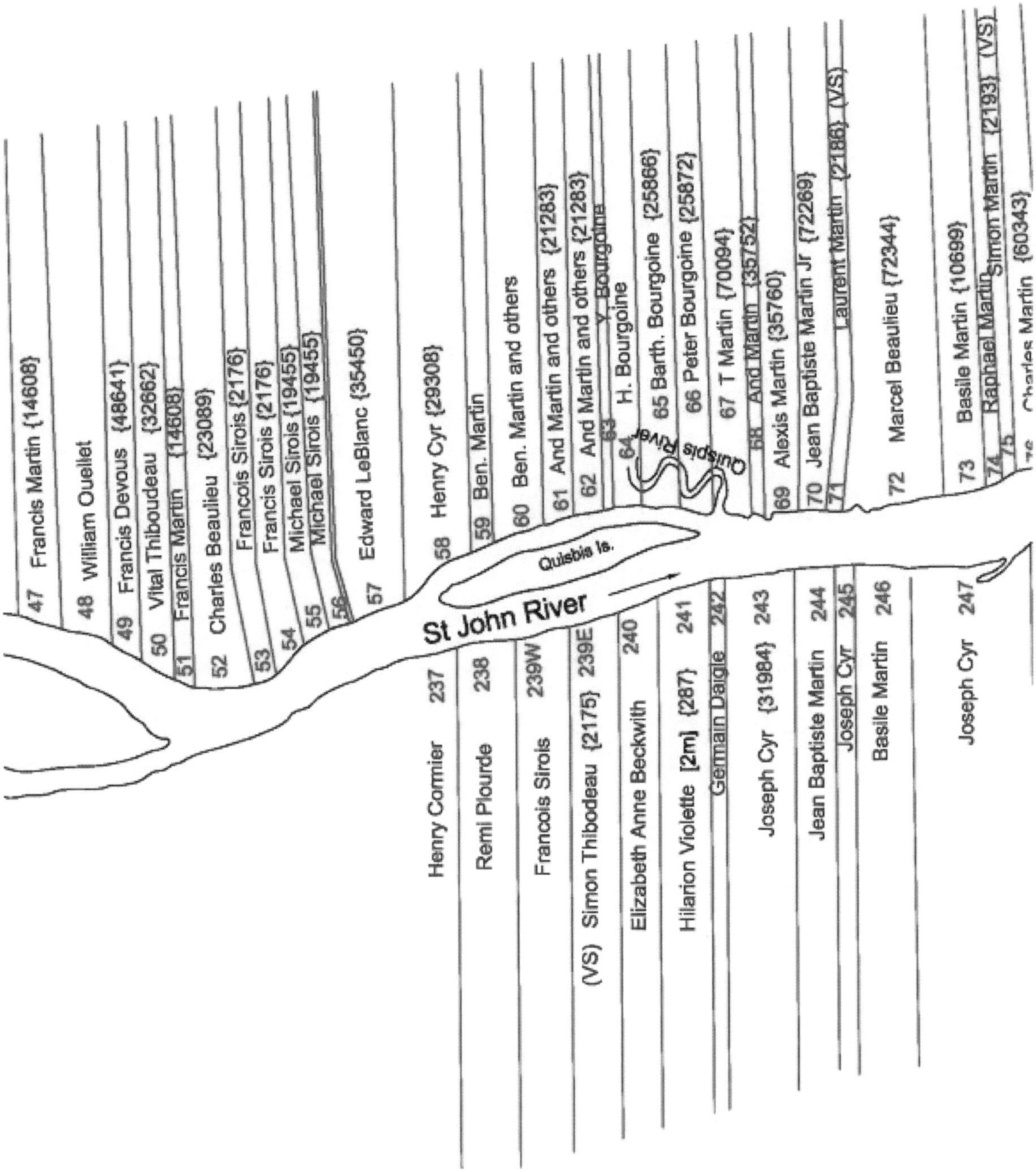

Map 14-4a: Land ownership in 1845/8 – part 1

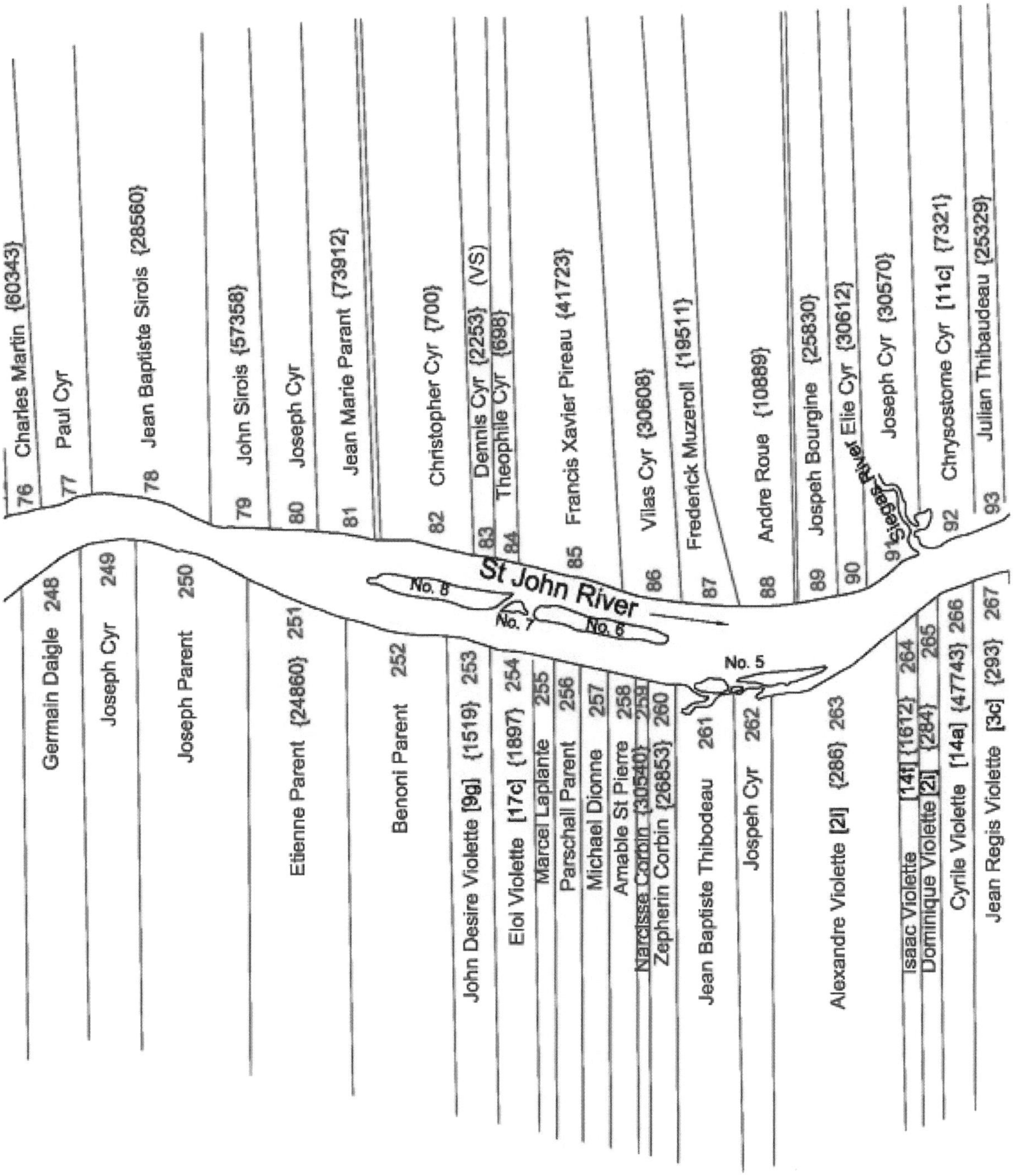

Map 14-4b: Land ownership in 1845/8 – part 2

76 Charles Martin {60343}
77 Paul Cyr
78 Jean Baptiste Sirois {28560}
79 John Sirois {57358}
80 Joseph Cyr
81 Jean Marie Parant {73912}
82 Christopher Cyr {700}
83 Dennis Cyr {2253} (VS)
84 Theophile Cyr {698}
85 Francis Xavier Pireau {41723}
86 Vilas Cyr {30608}
87 Frederick Muzeroll {19511}
88 Andre Roue {10889}
89 Jospeh Bourgine {25830}
90 River Elie Cyr {30612}
91 Siegas
92 Chrysostome Cyr [11c] {7321}
93 Julian Thibaudeau {25329}

St John River

No. 8
No. 7 No. 6
No. 5

248 Germain Daigle
249 Joseph Cyr
250 Joseph Parent
251 Etienne Parent {24860}
252 Benoni Parent
253 John Desire Violette [9g] {1519}
254 Eloi Violette [17c] {1897}
255 Marcel Laplante
256 Parschall Parent
257 Michael Dionne
258 Amable St Pierre
259 Nardisse Corbin {30540}
260 Zepherin Corbin {26853}
261 Jean Baptiste Thibodeau
262 Jospeh Cyr
263 Alexandre Violette [2l] {286}
264 Isaac Violette [14f] {1612}
265 Dominique Violette [2l] {284}
266 Cyrile Violette [14a] {47743}
267 Jean Regis Violette [3c] {293}

209

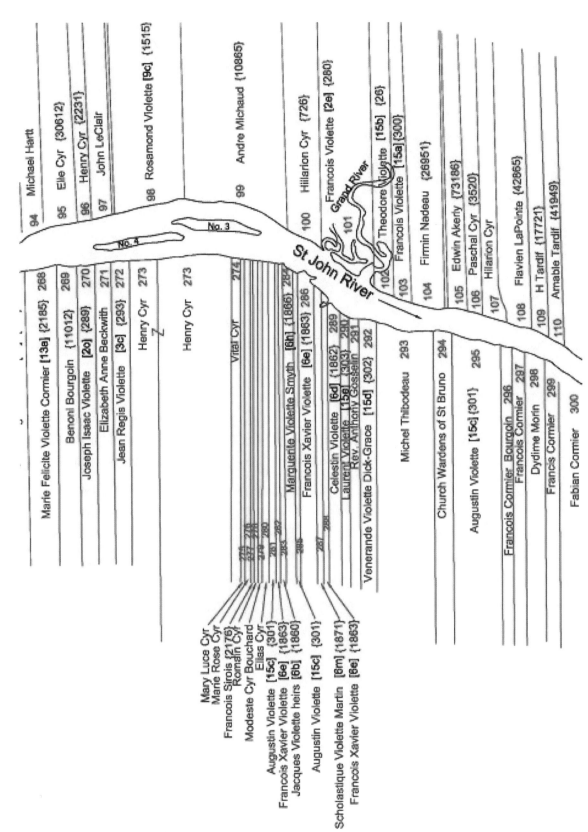

Map 14-4c: Land ownership in 1845/8 – part 3

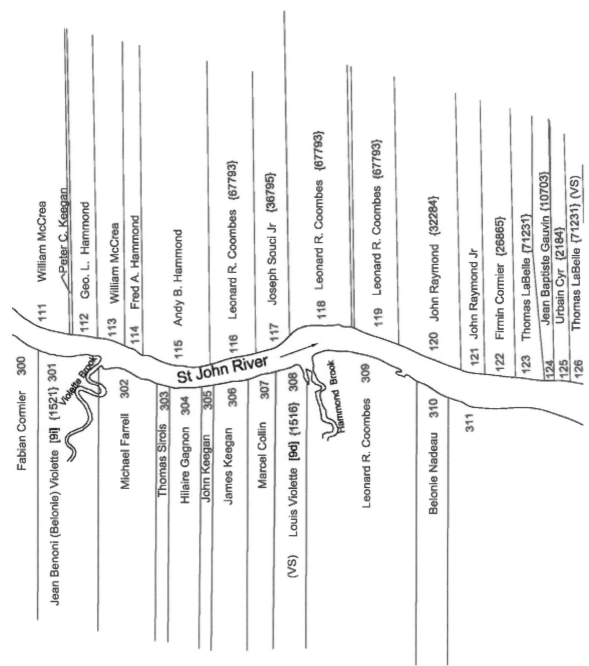

Map 14-4d: Land ownership in 1845/8 – part 4

Who settled where?

When the family moved in 1790 or 1791 the children ranged in age from 6 months (Marie-Anne) to 20 years (Marguerite). By the time the Deane & Kavanagh survey was done in 1831 the Violette sons shown with holdings there were considerably older: Augustin – 60, François Jr – 57, Louis – 52, Dominique – 48, Alexandre – 42, and Isaac – 35. François Sr had died in 1824, seven years before, at age 79, and those children's mother, Marie Luce, died around 1800 at age 50. Isaac was born in 1796, or six years after they arrived in the area. Charles died around 1817 at age 42 and Benoni in 1812 at age 27, before the records in Maps 14-2 and 14-3 were made. In keeping with the practice of the times, the female children would not have filed claims on their own, but in conjunction with their husbands.

When the international boundary was set and Maine and New Brunswick were able to finally recognize the settlers land holdings by issuing deeds, another fourteen years had passed and there were many more changes in land ownership and the generations were moving along. By 1845 – 55 years after François I and Augustin received the first grants under the Soucy Concession – many of the lots that existed in 1831 had been subdivided to accommodate the third generation, and a fourth generation had already been born and needing land to live on. François and Marie Luce's first great-grand-child (Suzanne Hebert {24960} daughter of Marguerite Cyr {7307} [5a], and granddaughter of Marguerite Violet Cyr, was born in 1816 and would have been 29 years old in 1845.

Where did they start their homes?

We don't know how the family was distributed on the land when they first arrived in the Upper St John Valley. Did the older children claim lots and develop them right at the start, or did their claims come after the parent's lots were developed? Referring to the list in **Appendix 13-B** we see that Oliver Thibodeau, Sr, had a son Oliver Thibodeau, Jr, who was 23 at the time and sons Gregory, Fearman, and Paul were 21, 20, and 19; Joseph Theriault had sons Joseph (21) and Gerard (19); and François' oldest son, Augustin, was 17. Map 14-3b shows one lot with François' name on it in 1831; one lot with the name J. B. Oliver Thibodeaux on it (this could have been Jean-Baptiste, the oldest brother, but we think it was Oliver, the son of Jean-Baptiste); but no lots with a Theriault. For the next generation, there are several lots under Augustin's and Alexandre's names, and one each under Dominique, Benjamin, and Louis. One lot shows the name Michal Thibodeau; we think this refers to Michael Thibodeau, great-grandson of Jean-Baptiste Thibodeau {787}, who was Marie-Luce's brother. There are lots with the names Elie and Michel Thibodeau but our genealogical database does not have either name at this time. Obviously from Maps 14-3a and 14-3b many more families came to the area between 1789 and 1831; perhaps some of these came as separate petitions back in 1789-90.

One unexpected discovery from studying the maps is that what became an important land holding for François and his family was not their original granted property. That is the 300-acre (121.4 hectare) lot numbered 301 in Map 14-4d – the lot through which Violette Brook runs. This lot became important to the wealth of the family because the stream provided a source of water power that François used to operate a grist mill. This business was so important to the growing community that it must have been successful for François. And being able to establish a successful commercial business meant that he did not need to rely on subsistence farming for his family's livelihood. This passed on to his son and then grandson. The lots in the Soucy Concession granted to Augustin and François were about 1,000 to 1,300 feet (305-396 meters) upstream. We understand that the grantees were responsible for selecting and staking out their own lots in the Soucy Concession. Had they reconnoitered the area before and established their requested property as a result, or had they relied on some general description to define their lots? There was no question that François quickly claimed what was to be Lot 301, for Deane & Kavanagh reported that he had acquired the land and built the grist mill in 1791. That was about a year after they arrived. There is no record of any official grants between those of the Soucy Concession and those in 1845 in the area, so we are not sure how those owners shown on Maps 14-3a and 14-3b came to own any lots beyond the original lots granted in the Soucy Concession.

Between 1831 and 1845 the families grew, and more and more land was needed. By the time the international boundary was established, and Maine and New Brunswick created deeds for the lands owned at that time, most of the lots described by Deane & Kavanagh in 1831 had been divided into smaller lots as shown in Maps 14-4a through 14-4d. Some of the more affluent acquired more than one lot though they only lived on one. This may have provided them with additional land for their children, or some may have simply held the land as an investment. After all, it must have become very clear by 1845 that the area was going to grow and that desirable land would be limited.

For the rest of this chapter we will look at a number of the early individuals in turn and describe as best we can from information available where they lived and how they fared. In each case we will show by their name their life span and their reference numbers in *The Descendants of François Violet* and in the *Genealogical Database,* as referenced earlier. You can see those named in the following sections in descendant table showing the children and grandchildren of François in **Appendix 14-C**; their RINs are shown there. *(Ed Note: in the following we abbreviate Upper St John River as USJR for brevity.)*

The community names Van Buren and St Leonard were not in use until sometime after 1845 and the general community spanning both sides of the St John River associated with the Soucy Concession was called Grand River in those early days. The maps shown in Maps 14-4a through 14-4d cover the general Grand River area. Grand River is the term used in the following to describe that area.

An earlier start at Hammond River

François was prepared for a running start when he settled the Upper St. John River Valley with a handful of other Acadian pioneers in 1791. The following is a recap of events reported in Chapter 13.

Though the Lower St. John River Valley had originally been settled by the French around 1635, it later came under British control and settlement was expanded primarily by two groups: English-speaking settlers who migrated from the British Isles and French-speaking settlers who migrated from Acadia when driven out by the British starting in 1755. Among the British settlers were William Hazen, James White, and James Simonds, who operated a merchant trader outlet in the city of St John, at the mouth of the river of the same name. We find a 1782 account for François Violette with that firm, showing he was there at that time. Further, James White wrote a letter in 1782 to the Lt. Governor of Nova Scotia (which included New Brunswick territory at that time) stating that the "*French of Kennebecasis had driven forty sticks down Vie Kennebecasis to the St. John market and had sixty more ready to drive in the next season*". By sticks he meant tall pine or ton timber which served as masts for the clipper ships of the day. This is how the French-speaking Acadians like François Violet, then being subjects of the British-held colony of Nova Scotia, earned store credit at merchant trader sites like Hazen and White. These traders marketed the timber driven down river to St. John.

From the commercial relationships he had already formed, François Violet in 1791 was able to secure a 100 pound note from St John merchant Henry Darling, who also held title to Darling Island at the mouth of Hammond River on the Kennebecasis River. Though we can't know it with assurance, it is likely that a loan of this size gave François sufficient capital to construct the first grist mill when he settled upriver on Violette Brook. Such mill operators ground their neighbors' wheat for a share of the crop, and were thus able to acquire amounts of flour beyond their family needs, and so could move their enterprise into merchant trading positions.

How did François come to be a miller?

From what we know about François' activities on his holdings along the Hammond River, he engaged in agriculture and farming and did some logging. But nowhere do we see any reference to him operating a grist mill, or mill of any type, during their more than 20 years on those lands. While the need for a grist mill in the pioneer country of the Upper St John River is obvious, why was François the one to build it, aside from his probable availability of funds to start the operation? A little digression is in order.

François petitioned for those USJR lands along with Joseph Cyr, Joseph Theriault and Olivier Thibodeau. Let's look at some relations:

- François Violette was married to Marie Luce Thibodeau, daughter and tenth child of Jean Baptiste and Marie LeBlanc Thibodeau.
- Joseph Cyr was married to Marguerite Blanche Thibodeau, daughter and sixth child of Jean Baptiste and Marie LeBlanc Thibodeau.
- Joseph Theriault was married to Madeleine Thibodeau, daughter and ninth child of Jean Baptiste and Marie LeBlanc Thibodeau.
- Olivier Thibodeau was son and third child of Jean Baptiste and Marie LeBlanc Thibodeau.

Jean Baptiste Thibodeau's parents were Jean-Pierre and Marguerite Hebert Thibodeau, and his Thibodeau grandparents were Pierre and Jeanne Theriot Thibodeau. This Pierre Thibodeau had been born in Poitou, France, about 1631 and immigrated to Acadia around 1651. He was the founder of Chipoudy (now Hopewell in New Brunswick) in 1698 and in 1699 he was awarded the title of Seigneur de Chipoudy. Pierre was the lumber agent for the government and shows up in census records from 1671 through 1701; he died in 1704 at age 73. But more importantly to our story, Pierre owned and operated grist mills and lumber saw mills at Pre Ronde (about 10km up the Annapolis River, also called Dauphin River) and at Chipoudy.

Béatrice Craig found that the Thibodeaux formed a milling clan (*Backwoods Consumers and Homespun Capitalists, Béatrice Craig, University of Toronto Press, Scholarly Publishing Division, 2009, pp. 106-107*) and she also found that during the Grand Derangement, a Thibodeau can be found owning a grist mill in Montmagny, Quebec, a city along the St Lawrence River.

So milling was closely associated with the Thibodeau family, though we don't know if the generation we are interested in or the prior generation was actively involved in milling. We do know that the parents of the Thibodeau children listed above must have moved to the new area since Jean-Baptiste's death is listed at St Basile NB, which was the parish for the region (his wife, Marie LeBlanc, died before 1765, and before they all moved to the USJR). The Thibodeau grandfather, Jean-Pierre Thibodeau died in 1746 in Grand Pre NS, and the grandmother, Marguerite Hebert Thibodeau, died sometime before 1727. So it is possible that the milling knowledge and skills came to the USJR area with Jean-Baptiste and through the Thibodeau family got passed on to François Violet. Being a miller was a valuable occupation for the pioneering Violette family, regardless how the skills and knowledge came to them.

François in 1793 took on the role of road commissioner in the Madawaska settlement when it was still but a civil parish of York County, New Brunswick. He filed with the Provincial authority his petitions for license to occupy lands and received his land titles from that government, yet the grist mill he developed circa 1791 ended up being located on the American side of the St. John River.

We think that François lived his life on the lot he settled in 1791 on the south side of the USJR and where the grist mill was built.

The Families

François Violet (I) 1744-1824 [1a] {6}

François Sr received a grant of land in the Soucy Concession but also claimed two very valuable plots of land after the original settlement. One, now on the US side, included the Picquanositac stream – since renamed Violette Brook – which provided for siting a grist mill. The other, now on the Canadian side, included La Grande Rivière (Grand River) – which provided added water access and fertile farmlands. The latter still contains the remnants of the Violette farm in St. Léonard, New Brunswick today (2013). These lower, flatter, lands meant you could plant a crop without driving the oxen uphill. His lot in the Concession is further upstream, around where Keegan ME is now located.

All these lots had substantial stands of timber in their rear parts, away from the lower intervale lands. This timber could be cut to sell as well as to provide a source of building materials for the farms themselves.

Marie Luce Thibodeau Violet, 1750-1800 [1a I] {759}

Marie Luce pioneered the area with her husband and lived there until she died about nine years later. She bore twelve children during their time at Hammond River and another three in the USJR area. She was born in the Lower St John River area in 1750.

Marguerite Genevieve Violet Cyr, 1770-1802 [2a] {276}

Marguerite was the first child of François and Marie Luce, and was 20 years old when they moved to the USJR area. She married Jean-Baptiste Cyr {1852} in 1793, two years later, and we think they lived upstream from the Grand River area. Jean-Baptiste was the son of Jean-Baptiste Cyr {1853} and Marie Judith Guerette-Dumont {737}. Marguerite had six children prior to her death in 1802. Both her marriage and death are recorded at St Basile and they lived in the St David, Madawaska, area and near the St Basile church. Her sister Madeleine Violet Cyr lived nearby.

Augustin Violet, 1771-1849 [2b] {277}

Augustin, the oldest son of François and Marie Luce, received one of the Soucy Concession grants but also acquired several other properties in his lifetime. His marriage was recorded at St Basile at age 28 and his death at age 77. He married Elizabeth Cyr {1855} and they had 15 children. Elizabeth was the daughter of Lt Jacques Cyr {1856} and Elisabeth Ursule Belanger Cyr {1857}. She was born in Port Joli QC in 1780 and was married at age 20.

Augustin's first lot was Lot 1 of Tract 3 in the Soucy Concession, and he is shown as an owner in 1831 by Deane & Kavanagh. He also received deeds for Lots 261, 265, and 295 in 1845; the first two are in the area of his original grant.

Marie Genevieve Violet Cyr, 1774-1853 [2c] {278}

Born at Kennebecasis, Marie Genevieve came north with the family at age 17 and was married the next year to Antoine Cyr {1876}, son of Jean-Baptiste Cyr dit Croc {722} and Marguerite Cormier Cyr {723}. They had nine children between 1793 and 1814. We see Anthony Cere (Antoine Cyr) on the 1790 grant list in the Mazerolle Concession upriver, so we believe that she moved to that area.

François Violet (II), 1774-1856 [2e] {280}

François was one of the more illustrious of the children of François and Marie Luce since he stayed in the Van Buren/St Leonard area and made quite a name for himself. He was six years old when he arrived at USJR and married Marguerite Fournier {1512} in 1803, at age 18. She was the daughter of Jean-Baptiste Fournier {1593} and Felicite Martin dit Barnabe Fournier {1594}. Marguerite's family also came upriver to the Mazerolle area but she was born downriver. She and François were married when both were 18 and lived in the Van Buren area. They had ten children between 1804 and 1821; the first seven or eight births were registered at St Basile, the ninth at Van Buren, and the tenth back at St Basile.

Francois was deeded Lots 101 and 103 on the New Brunswick side. Lot 101 was an important lot because the Grand River passes through it.

Charles Amand Henri Violet, 1775-1817 [2j] {24}

Charles was born at Kennebecasis around 1775 and came north with his family at age 16. He married Theotiste Tardif {25} at age 33 (she was 17). They had six children between 1808 and 1817, and he died around 1817. Theotiste was the daughter of Jean-Baptiste Tardif {757} and Marie-Anne

Dube Tardif {756}, who settled in the Mazerolle Concession area. After Charles' death, Theotiste married Eloi Thibodeau {43952} and they had eleven children between 1818 and 1837, all of which births were registered at St Basile.

We see Eloi Thibodeau's name on Map 3a (the 1831 Deane & Kavanagh survey map) across the Grand River from the parcel owned originally by François I but subsequently by François II. François I probably also claimed the parcel that has Thibodeau's name on it, but it was subsequently owned by Charles. Apparently Eloi sought to dispossess Theotiste's children with Charles from the "Violette lands". So Uncle François, their neighbor across the Grand River, petitioned the New Brunswick government to restrain Thibodeau from selling what François held to be his nephew's rightful inheritance. François, then a captain of the militia may well have had sufficient influence with the British authorities in New Brunswick to win that battle. Theotiste's eldest son François Xavier would have been 16 at the time of this affair, so still a minor. Thus François II took up the case in favor of his five nephews and one niece. This was (and is) a valuable piece of farmland; there is still farming on part of that land and another part is an RV campground (as of 2014).

Louis Violet, 1779-? [2d] {279}

Louis was about twelve years old when the family came upriver. We have no further information about him.

Marie Anne Josephte Violet Mercure, 1780-? [2f] {281}

Marie Anne was born in the Kennebecasis area and came north at age eleven. She married Louis Michel Mercure {714}, son of Louis Mercure {10667} and Madeleine Thibodeau Mercure {10668} recorded at St Basile. Louis received a grant in the Mazerolle Concession. We have records of one child, born in 1804, and Marie Anne must have died soon after because we know that Louis married Victoire Levasseur Mercure {19445} in 1807 and they had three more children.

Madeleine Violet Cyr, 1781-1853 [2g] {282}

Madeleine came upriver at age ten and married Firmin Chrysostome Eupheminin Cyr {1883}, son of Capt François Cyr {3757} and Marie-Anne Guilbeau Cyr {1885} in 1804. The Cyr family came from Ecopaq, where Firmin was born, to the USJR area. Firmin and Madeleine had fifteen children between 1805 and 1831, all registered at St Basile. Madeleine died in 1853 at age 72. There was a Fereman Cere Sr and Fereman Cere Jr shown in the 1790 grants, and a Fierement Cire in the 1794 grants. The "Cere Sr" is probably Firmin Germaine Cyr {3758}, son of Jean-Baptiste Cyr {722} and Marguerite Cormier Cyr {723}, while the "Cere Jr" was probably Firmin Chrysostome Eupheminin Cyr, who later married Madeleine and who claimed grants both in 1790 and 1794.

They lived in the St David, Madawaska, area and near the St Basile church. Her sister Marguerite Genevieve Violet Cyr lived nearby.

Dominique Violet, 1783-1850, [2i] {284}

A youngster of eight when the family moved upriver, Dominique married Angelique Fournier {1602} in 1808 and they had three children between 1809 and 1812, when Angelique died. Angelique was the daughter of Jean-Baptiste Fournier {1593} and Felicite Martin Fournier {1594}, also the parents of François II's wife Marguerite. Dominique then married Rosalie Michaud {1606} in 1813 and they had another fourteen children between 1815 and 1830. Rosalie was the daughter of Alexandre Michaud {1889} and Marie Euphrosine Tardif Michaud {1890}, who were from Kamouraska Quebec.

Dominique acquired lands just upstream from where François and Augustin first settled and was still on those lands in 1831 and 1845.

Benoni Benjamin Violet, 1785-1812 [2k] {285}

Benoni came upriver at age six and was married in 1810 to Marie Perpetue Josette Fournier {1891}, daughter of the same Jean-Baptiste Fournier {1593} and Felicite Martin Fournier {1594} who were parents of the wives of François II and Dominique. Benoni and Marie had two children, in 1811 and 1812, and Benoni died in 1812.

Marie Venerande Violet Fournier, 1787-1812 [2h] {283}

Marie came upriver at age four and later married Jean-Baptiste Fournier {1886} in 1808 at St Basile. Jean-Baptiste was a son of the same Jean-Baptiste Fournier {1593} and Felicite Martin Fournier {1594} parents of the wives of François II, Dominique, and Benoni.

The Fourniers received a land grant in the Madawaska/St David area so they don't show up on our maps.

Alexandre Violet, 1789-1856 [2l] {286}

Alexandre was about two when he got to USJR. He married Josette Pelletier {1894} in 1813, recorded at St Basile. She was the daughter of Nicolas Pelletier {754} and Genevieve Duplessis-Sirois {755} from the Kamouraska Quebec area. They had five children between 1815 and 1824. Alexandre married Marie Anne Mazerolle {2228} in 1824, daughter of Louis François Mazerolle {1908} and Marie Anne Tardif {1909} and they had six children between 1825 and 1833. Josette died in 1882, so perhaps she and Alexandre were divorced. Marie Anne also died in 1882.

Alexandre is shown as owner of Lot 263, upstream from his father's lots and across from Island No. 6.

Pierre Hilarion Violet, 1792-1871 [2m] {287}

Pierre Hilarion was the first child born to François and Marie Luce in their new lands, in 1792. He married Madeleine Consigny-SansFaçon {1910} in 1818, daughter of Louis SansFaçon {1911} and Madeleine Thibodeau {1912}. Madeleine Violet had been married to Pierre Levasseur {41684} in 1803 and they had one child, but Pierre Levasseur died in 1816. Pierre Hilarion had no children that we know of. Pierre and Magdeleine apparently did not live in the Grand River area.

Elizabeth Violet, 1794-1811 [2n] {288}

Elizabeth was born in Van Buren and died there in 1811 at age 17.

Joseph Isaac Violet, 1796-1850 [2o] {289}

Isaac was born at Van Buren and was married in 1818 to Victoire Thibodeau {1913}, daughter of Jean-Baptiste Thibodeau {1933} and Marie Anne Cormier Thibodeau {1934}. They had nineteen children between 1818 and 1844 and lived in the Van Buren area. Isaac died in 1850 and Victoire married Louis Desaultes dit LaPointe {53575} in 1851. We have no record of children from that marriage.

Isaac and Victoire's family is interesting in that this is the first that started leaving the USJR area. Daughter Louise married Louis Violette {1516}, son of François Violet II {280} and Marguerite Fournier Violet {1512} and they moved to Wisconsin. Louis had been previously married to Suzanne Thibodeau {2034}, daughter of Joseph Thibodeau {2037} and Marie-Josephte Cote Thibodeau {15929}. Jean Rosimond Violette {1917}, Marie Anne Nancy Violette {1918}, William François Julien Violette {1922}, Damase Thomas Violette {1925}, Marie Anne Violette {1927}, François Violette {1928}, and Demerise Violette {1932} all died in Old Town ME.

Upon the death of Marie Luce around 1800, François I married Marie Rose Cormier in 1803.

Marie Rose Cormier Violet, 1765-1811 [1a II] {290}

Marie Rose's birth was registered at St Basile in 1765, the daughter of Jean-Baptiste Cormier {1848} and Marie-Madeleine Landry Cormier {1849}. She was first married to Germain Soucy {16482}, who died in 1802 at Grande Isle. Germaine was among the first settlers and he received land under the same 1794 grants (see Chapter 13) as François [1a] {6} and Augustin [2b] {277}. Marie Rose had five children from her first marriage and another five with François.

Joseph Violette, 1803-? [3a] {291}

Joseph was the first of the children born to François and Marie Rose. He was married to Julie LeClerc {1936} dit Francoeur in 1842. She was the daughter of Anselme LeClerc dit Francoeur {1954} and Marie Luce Parent LeClerc {1955} from the St Lawrence River area in Quebec. The couple had four children born between 1843 and 1858. We don't know the dates of death for either.

We find this couple in St Leonard in the census of 1871.

Marie Victoire Violette Pelletier, 1804-1845 [3b] {292}

Victoire married Benoni Pelletier {2174} in 1825. He was the son of Nicholas Pelletier {754} and Genevieve Duplessis-Sirois {755}, who were also the parents of Alexandre Violette's wife Josette. They had eleven children between 1825 and 1843, and Victoire died in 1845 on their homestead in what is now St John Plantation and was buried in Frenchville ME. Benoni married Leocadie Nadeau {53576} in 1846 and they had four children.

Jean Regis (Richard) Violette, 1806-? [3c] {293}

Richard married Modeste E. Michaud {1941} in 1831 and they had eleven children between 1831 and 1851. She was the daughter of François Michaud {1956} and Angelique LePage Michaud {1957}. Richard received a land grant in the Fort Kent area, and we see that many of their children were reported married and died in the Frenchville area.

(male) Violette, 1807-1809 [3d] {1935}

This male child, whose name we do not know, died in 1809 at age nineteen months.

Jean Felix Violette, 1810-? [3e] {295}

We have little information about Jean Felix except his birth in 1810.

Upon the death of Marie Rose, François married Genevieve Tardif in 1814.

Genevieve Tardif Violet, 1782-1864 [1a III] {296}

We do not know where Genevieve was born but she was the daughter of Jean-Baptiste Tardif {757} and Marie-Anne Dube {756}. They were from the Kamouraska and Rivière Ouelle areas of Quebec, so Genevieve may have been born in the former. Her father died at St Basile at age 93 and her mother at St Basile at age 99. This was the first marriage for Genevieve; she was born only nine years before François moved his family to the Upper St John. Genevieve had three children with François, but we do not know if she remarried after his death. She lived another 40 years and died in Quebec; she probably did not remarry.

Luc Violette, 1814-1887 [4a] {297}

Luc married Arthemise Pelletier {1958} in 1848 and they had ten children between 1849 and 1873. She was the daughter of Charles Pelletier {1969} and Josette Landry Pelletier {1970}, born in 1833. They were married in Frenchville ME and most of their children were married in nearby Fort Kent, though one child was married further south in Patten ME. Luc died in January 1887, and Arthemise in January 1905, both in Fort Kent.

Elisabeth Violette, 1816-? [4b] {298}

We only know about Elisabeth's birth in 1816.

Francois Violette, 1818-1882 [4c] {299}

Francois was born in Van Buren and died in Madawaska. That's the only information we have about him.

Appendix 14-A

How the Lots Were Laid Out

The pattern of lot shape and layout in the Upper St John River area changed over time from the first grants to the modern era. The first grants in what was called the Madawaska Territory were made by the British Government through the Governor of New Brunswick

But it became important by 1846 to have specific descriptions made of the claimed lands, because in 1842 the Webster-Ashburton Treaty established finally the border between the United States and British North America to be the St John River (remember, there was no "Canada" until 1867). At that time matters had to be regularized, and so the river lots were surveyed in 1846 by John S. Webber and all the other lots were surveyed in 1860 by John Gardner. And, in 1845 deeds were given and registered conveying the lands on the US side of the river from Maine and Massachusetts to the land owners at the time. When they first settled the area was claimed by both British North America and Massachusetts, and what is now Maine was part of Massachusetts. With the Treaty in 1842, Maine became a state.

Now that each of those areas had come under some organized government - which had the capability of recording land ownership, title, and deeds - having detailed surveys were important for those surveys could then be used in future transactions. The 1846 surveys documented the claims made prior to that time and recorded them in actual measurements. The lots documented then were the ones laid out following the pattern described earlier, so these are the long, skinny lots we see on maps still today.

But after 1791 as the families grew, and as more people moved into the area, the demand for land meant that additional lots had to be created. Gradually, any spaces between the original claims filled in but there was still not enough land, so additional "rear" lots were created that roughly followed the same pattern as the riverfront lots. The long dimension of the rear lots kept roughly the same compass bearing as the front lots. These rear lots were not as deep as the original lots.

There is an anomaly in how those original lots were apparently laid out however. As described above, a 200-acre (81 ha) lot having a 60-rod (302 m) frontage would have a depth of 533 rods (2681 m). If we look at the map showing the surveys of 1846 we see a number of lots containing roughly 300 acres (121 ha), not 200, and with frontages of roughly 80 rods (402 m), not 20, and depths of 400-700 rods (2012-3520 m). So these are approximately 50% larger in area than the Concession basis. Was this due to splitting and acquisition of neighboring lots, or was it due to expansion of claims laterally? There is no evidence of what happened in that 40 years between 1791 and 1831.

An Arbitration Agreement was made in 1827 between the United States and Great Britain where it was agreed that neither side would take unilateral action in the disputed territory along the St John River. As a result, there were no land grants issued from 1827 to 1845, the crucial period of the settling-in of François' children. We therefore have to rely on records before 1827 and after 1845 to deduce what happened to our families back then.

Township and Range Mapping

Around 1820, when Ohio was added to the growing United States, the US government developed a system of surveying and mapping public lands prior to their being claimed or sold. This system was based on townships containing 36 sections, where each section was approximately six miles square, and is known as the Public Land Survey System (PLSS). The Townships were arranged in rectangular grid pattern, and their numbering started from meridians and baselines. The Township designations run north and south in tiers. Each north-south tier is called a Range, and the Ranges are numbered east and west from the starting point in each area. Originally proposed by Thomas Jefferson, the PLSS began shortly after the Revolutionary War and was further implemented with the Land Ordinance of 1785 and the Northwest Ordinance of 1787.

These public lands surveys were started after those original settlements in the Upper St John River valley but before the national boundaries were set, and in that region both Massachusetts and Maine had claims to the area, though Maine was not a state yet. Surveying was done to establish the Principal Meridians in what was to become Maine, with the result that townships were established as shown in Map 14-A-1 below. This is a cropped area of a much larger map produced by George W. Coffin, Land Agent for the Commonwealth of Massachusetts and published in 1835. In the center of each township is shown either the letter "C" (for Commonwealth of Massachusetts) or "M" (for Maine). In other than the six townships on the right in Map 14-A-1 you will see a notation near the top of the township such as N°16, N°15, and so on; those are the Township numbers and they progress from south to north in this area. Above the top row of townships you will see notations such as 5th R, 4th R, 3rd R, 2nd R, and 1st Range; these are the range numbers and progress from east to west in this area. The townships to the east of the 3rd Range have instead of a N° designation a letter designation; thus you will see G, H, I, and K in the 2nd Range, and D, E, and F in the 1st Range. Notice that there is a township between Township D and Township E; that was set aside as a Grant for the Town of Plymouth.

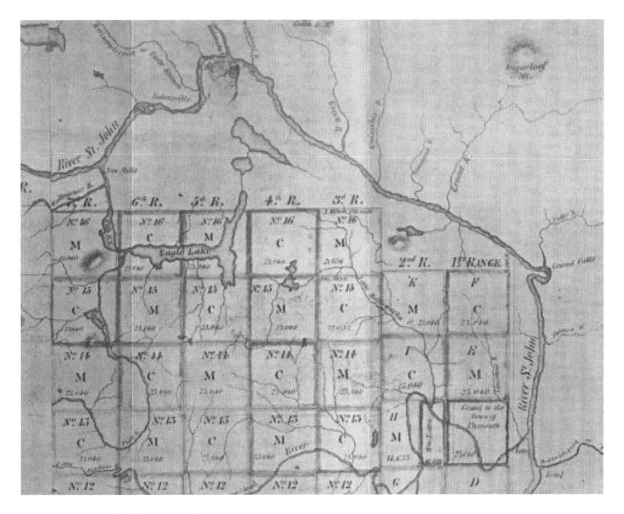

Map 14-A-1: Part of Coffin map, 1835

But north and east of the township-and-range pattern there was no such subdivision of the land because those were not public lands at that time. These lands had been settled previously. The lake you see in Map 14-A-1 just above Township K in the 2nd Range is Violette Lake, and the stream running from it to the St John River is Violette Brook. Notice the Grand River entering the St John just upstream from the mouth of Violette Brook. This will help place you on the map and the lands we are discussing here are in that area.

Mapping in 1877

Our first precise look at the result of 85 years or so of growth and development is shown in a map published in 1877 by Roe & Colby, of Philadelphia PA.

Map 14-A-2 shows a section of that map centered along the river on Van Buren. The dashed line you see running horizontally near the bottom of Map 14-A-2 is the top line of Township K, and the dashed line running vertically at the right in Map 14-A-3 is the east line of the 1st Range.

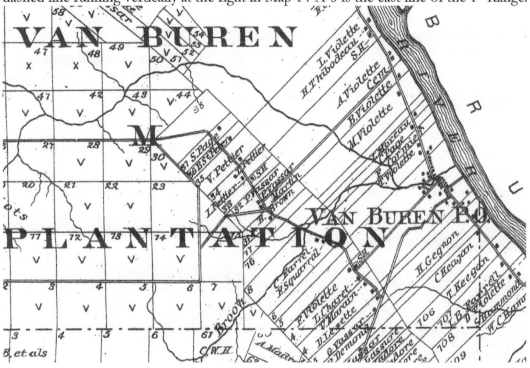

Map 14-A-2: Portion of Roe & Colby map from 1877 showing lots in Van Buren ME area.

The names on Roe & Colby's map are those living there at the time. That map does not show measurements but does show lot numbers. Map 14-A-3 on the next page shows a larger portion of the Roe & Colby 1877 map. In Map 14-A-3 you can see the township-and-range pattern as well, with some additions. The dashed line near the bottom in Map 14-A-3 represents the tops of Townships K and F that we saw in Map 14-A-2, but note that Townships L, M, and G have been added. Township L is designated as Cyr Plantation, Township M as Van Buren Plantation, and Township G as Hamblin Plantation. These townships follow the pattern as the rest except for their naming. "Plantation" in Maine refers to an organized form of municipal self-government similar to but with less power than a town or a city. Plantations cannot, however, make local ordinances. This type of municipality usually includes the word Plantation as part of its full name, as in Van Buren Plantation or Cyr Plantation. The Plantation was the early form of organization and, as the population grew, the Plantation could become a town or city. This happened in the Van Buren Plantation but not the Cyr Plantation or

Hamblin Plantation. The plantation concept is unique to Maine and is not used in any other part of the country.

Maps 14-4a through 14-4d in the text of this chapter cover an area extending from north of the limits in Map 14-A-3 to the just below the large lot shown roughly opposite the letter "N" in "Brunswick" and below Van Buren. You can still see some of the same family names on this 1877 map as were there on the 1845 maps in Maps 14-4a through 14-4d, but a lot of ownerships have changed.

Map 14-A-3 Larger portion of Roe & Colby 1877 map.

You can see the arrangement of lots in the Van Buren area on Maps 14-A-2 and 14-A-3. Notice the original lots arranged along the river, and then a series of lots behind them further away from the river. These would have the original settlers and the first generation following. And there is a series of lots aligned along the road leading away from Van Buren (toward Caribou) which would have been settled in the early 1800s after that road was built. And the smaller squares to the west of those tiers of lots are the individual 180-acre lots that were originally established.

Appendix 14-B

Deane & Kavanagh Survey

Table 14-B-1 shows an extract from the Deane & Kavanagh 1831 survey covering the portion of the south bank of the Upper St John River that lies within the 1794 Soucy Concession grants area, and Table 14-B-2 shows a similar extract covering the north bank. The source of the base material these tables were drawn from were http://www.upperstjohn.com/aroostook/deane-kavsouth.htm for Table 14-B-1, and http://www.upperstjohn.com/aroostook/deane-kavnorth.htm for Table 14-B-2.

Table 14-B-1: Excerpt from Deane & Kavanagh 1831 survey, south bank (going downstream)

Name of owner or occupant	Date bought or settled	Amount of land claimed	Previous owners and dates of settlement or purchase in chronological order, most recent to earliest	Remarks
(173 lots)	---	---	---	---
Augustin **Violette**		40 rods front	- Olivier Thibedeau - François Cormier, "who is dead" but had deed from British	from Acadia; house and 50 acres cleared
(14 lots)	---	---	---	---
Larion **Violette**		35 rods front 75 rods front	- Simon Thibedeau - Pierre Vasseur, late husband of his wife	from Madawaska; Pierre Vasseur left one son, Jean, who is 18 yrs. old; house, barn, 50 acres cleared
(8 lots)	---	---	---	---
Alexandre **Violette**	1819	30 rods front		from Madawaska
Alexandre **Violette**		60 rods front	- Germain Pelletier, 1819, sold by his father Nicholas to Violette	paid $20; says 10 acres cleared "but we could not see much clearing"
(4 lots)	---	---	---	---
Alexandre **Violette**		60 rods front	- Justin Pelletier, "12 or 13 years before"	12 acres chopped down, some cleared
Alexandre **Violette**	1810	90 rods front		lives on lot; built on it 18 years ago; 50 acres cleared
Dominique **Violette**	1819	60 rods front	- Joseph Mercure	from Madawaska
Dominique **Violette**	1805	60 rods front		house, barn, 70 acres cleared

Table 14-B-1: Excerpt from Deane & Kavanagh 1831 survey, south bank (going downstream) (cont'd)

Name of owner or occupant	Date bought or settled	Amount of land claimed	Previous owners and dates of settlement or purchase in chronological order, most recent to earliest	Remarks
Jean Baptiste **Violette**		60 rods front	- Benoni Violette, his father, 1806	from Madawaska; his mother and father are dead, he's the only surviving child; lives on lot they occupied; house, barn, 18 acres cleared
Isaac **Violette**	1826	60 rods front		from Madawaska; 25 acres cleared
Richard **Violette**	1827	60 rods front		from Madawaska; lives up the river; 6 acres cleared
(4 lots)	----	----	----	----
Jacques **Violette**		120 rods front	- Augustin Violette - François Violette (who is dead)	from Madawaska; house, barn, 10 acres cleared
Augustin **Violette**		10 rods front	- Joseph Violette (his father)	no buildings
Celeste **Violette**		10 rods front	- Joseph Violette (his father)	10 acres cleared, no buildings
Augustin **Violette**		90 rods front	- inherited from his father	lives on North bank near the church; barn and 30 acres cleared
(8 lots)	----	----	----	----
François **Violette**	1801		- François Violette (his father), 1791	from Acadia; his father built a mill on lot, on Violet Brook, but is long since worn out; began to improve lot 4 years ago, house, barn, grist-mill; moved onto lot 3 years ago; Also claims lot on N. bank on both sides of mouth of Grand river, deed from British May 16, 1826, 90 rods front, 300 acres, two of his sons have a house and live on the lot
(4 lots)	----	----	----	----
Louis **Violette**	"a few years ago"	60 rods front		from Madawaska; son of Fran'cois Violette; new house, barn, 10-20 acres cleared; lot adjoins small stream coming from south; Louis was said to be at work on our Military road near the forks of the Madawumkeag
(16 lots)	----	----	----	----
Augustin **Violette**	1826 or 1827	60 rods front		from Madawaska; cut down some, but none is cleared

Table 14-B-2: Excerpt from Deane & Kavanagh 1831 survey, north bank (going upstream)

Name of owner or occupant	Date bought or settled	Amount of land claimed	Previous owners and dates of settlement or purchase in chronological order (most recent to earliest)	Remarks
(24 lots below)				
Augustin **Violette**		50 rods front		from Madawaska; possessory clearing of 4-5 acres
(25 lots below)				
François **Violette**	16 May 1826		-deeded to him by the British	land on **both sides of the Grand River**; deed of a gift; 300 acres, two of his sons occupy it; house, barn, extensive clearings
An old grant	2 Aug 1794	5,253 acres; nine tracts divided into 24 lots	- deed	*"one of the lots in the 1st large grant deeded to Aaron **Cyr** (Larion Cyr); grantees in the deed are: Joseph **Souci** Jr., Augustin **Violette**, François **Violette**, Joseph **Cyr**, Phirmain **Cyr**, Joseph **Cyr** Jr., François **Cormier**, Aaron **Cyr**, Jean Baptiste **Cormier**, Alexis **Cormier**, Pierre **Cormier**, Louis **LeBlond**, Gregoire **Thibedeau**, Phirmain **Thibedeau**, Joseph **Terrieau**, Olivier **Thibedeau**, Jr., Joseph **Terriault** Jr., Jean **Thibedeau**, Baptiste **Thibedeau**, Olivier **Thibedeau**, Germain **Souci**, Baptiste **Charet**, Louis **Ouellette**, Joseph **Michaud**"*
(16 lots above)				

The British Grant of 1794

Information on the grantees of 1794 and the possessors of the lots in 1831, provided by George Thibedeau to Deane and Kavanagh during their 1831 survey of the Madawaska Settlements.

Table 14-B-3: Original grantees and later owners

Original 1794 Grantee	Location and amount of land	Owner in 1831	Remarks	Lot in 1845/8
Joseph Souci, Jr.	North bank 3 miles below Grande River	Leonard Coombs	Coombs' family has been there one year; he came the year before	
Aaron or Larion Cyr	45 rods above the Grande River, North Bank; 60 rods front	Mr. Needham, a merchant in Fredericton	took it up for debt; old house, barn, not now occupied; 50 acres cleared	
Augustin Violette	South bank, opposite to the mouth of the Grande River	Jacques Violette, his son		
François Violette *(deceased by 1831)*		Augustin Violette, his son		
Joseph Cyr	South bank	Thomas Cyr	lives on North bank	
Phirmain Cyr *(deceased by 1831)*	South bank	Henri Cyr, his son		
Joseph Cyr, Jr.		Henri Cyr		
François Cormier *(deceased by 1831)*	South bank, opposite to the Grand Isle	His son		
Jean Baptiste Cormier *(deceased by 1831)*	South bank	- part occupied by Benjamin Thibedeau - part by Henri Souci - part by one other		
Alexis Cormier *(deceased by 1831)*	South bank	Julien Thibedeau *(occupies lot)*		
Pierre Cormier	South Bank	*(now occupied by himself)*		
Louis LeBlond *(moved to Canada)*	South Bank	Jean Baptiste Vasseur *(occupies lot)*		

Table 14-B-3: Original grantees and later owners (cont'd)

Original 1794 Grantee	Location and amount of land	Owner in 1831	Remarks	Lot in 1845/8
Gregoire Thibedeau	South Bank	J. B. Vasseur *(occupies lot)*		
Phirmain Thibedeau	North Bank	*(occupies lot)*		
Olivier Thibedeau	North Bank	Phirmain Thibedeau *(occupies lot)*		
Jean Thibedeau	North Bank	- 1/2 Phirmain Thibedeau - 1/2 Henri Vasseur		
Joseph Terrieau, Jr., now Sr.	North Bank	*(occupies lot)*		
Joseph Terrieau (deceased by 1831)	50 rods front	Laurent Terrieau (his son)		
Baptiste Thibedeau	North Bank	- 20 rods front occupied by Phirmain Ducette - 40 rods front occupied by Baptiste Olivier Thibedeau		
Olivier Thibedeau	North bank and on both sides of the Green River	- 50 rods front by George Thibedeau - 10 rods front by Phirmain Ducette		
Olivier Thibedeau, Jr. (drowned 1830)	North Bank	Phirmain Thibedeau		
Jean Thibedeau	North Bank	- 1/2 occupied by Phirmain Thibedeau - 1/2 occupied by Henri Vasseur		
Germain Souci (deceased by 1831)	South Bank, nearly opposite to the mouth of Green River	- 1/2 occupied by his son, Jean Baptiste Souci - 1/2 occupied by Louis Thibedeau	Louis Thibedeau lives on North bank, first house above Green River	
Louis Ouellette		Joseph Cyr		
Baptiste Charette ('has gone to Canada' by 1831)		Joseph Aiotte		
Joseph Michaud (deceased by 1831)		- 1/2 occupied by his son - 1/2 occupied by Bonaventure Lisotte, son of Pierre		

This information is from "Report by Messrs. Deane and Kavanagh," edited by W.O. Raymond, in *Collections of the New Brunswick Historical Society* (St.John, N.B.) number 9 (1914), pp.435-437. ***Ed Note: The 1845/8 Lot number info was added by the Editors of the current work.***

Appendix 14-C

The First Three Generations of Violettes in the Upper St John River Valley

Table 14-C-1 lists all known information about the members of the first three generations of Violettes living in the Upper St John River Valley from 1790 on. The table also shows information about the spouses of the Violettes.

Name refers to the person's name. **Gen.** identifies which generation the person is from. **RIN** is the Record Index Number in our genealogical database. **Lippé** refers to the identifier in Rita Violette Lippé's *Descendants of François Violet*. **Parent RIN** gives the RIN for the parent of the person. **Child #** shows the sequence of marriage for the person's family and birth order from that marriage. **Birth Year**, **Death Year**, and **Spouse name** are self-explanatory. **Spouse RIN** has the same meaning as the other RINs. **Mar Seq** refers to the sequence of this marriage for the person in **Name**. **Spouse Parent RIN** has the same meaning as the other RINs.

As an example of the Child #, Genevieve Violet, RIN 278, is the 3rd child of the first marriage for RIN 6, François Violet; Jean Regis Violet is the 3rd child of the second marriage for RIN 6; and Elizabeth is the 3rd child of the third marriage for RIN 6. You will see in the spouse section for RIN 6 that Marie-Luce Thibodeau is Mar Seq 1, Marie Rose Cormier is Mar Seq 2, and Genevieve Tardif is Mar Seq 3.

The double horizontal lines separate the generations.

The last name is spelled Violet for those born before 1800 and Violette for those born in 1800 or after. This is consistent with how the names appear in official records.

Table 14-C-2: First Three Generations of Violettes in Upper St John Valley

Name	Gen.	RIN	Lippe	Parent RIN	Child #	Birth Year	Death Year	Spouse name	Spouse RIN	Mar Seq	Spouse parent RIN
GENERATION 1											
Francois Violet	1	6	1	3			1744	1824	Marie-Luce Thibodeau	759	1	787
"								Marie Rose Cormier	290	2	1848
"								Genevieve Tardif	296	3	757
GENERATION 2											
Marguerite Violet	2	276	2a	6	1-1	1770	1802	Jean-Baptiste Cyr	1852	1	1853
Augustin	2	277	2b	6	1-2	1772	1849	Elizabeth Cyr	1855	1	1856
"								Marie Boutin	1858	2	1874
Genevieve	2	278	2c	6	1-3	1774	1853	Antoine Cyr	1876	1	722
Francois Violet	2	280	2e	6	1-4	1774	1856	Marguerite Fournier	1512	1	1593
Charles Amand Henri Violet	2	24	2j	6	1-5	1775	<1818	Theotiste Tardif	25	1	757
Louis Violet	2	279	2d	6	1-6	1779	?				
Marie Anne Josephte Violet	2	281	2f	6	1-7	1780	<1807	Louis Michel Mercure	714	1	10667
Madeleine Violet	2	282	2g	6	1-8	1781	1853	Firmin Chrysostome Eupheminin Cyr	1883	1	3757
Dominique Violet	2	284	2i	6	1-9	1783	1850	Angelique Fournier	1602	1	1593
"								Rosalie Michaud	1606	2	1889
Benoni Benjamin Violet	2	285	2k	6	1-10	1785	1812	Marie Perpetue Josette Fournier	1891	1	1593
Marie Venerande Violet	2	283	2h	6	1-11	1787	1812	Jean-Baptiste Fournier	1886	1	1593

Name	Gen.	RIN	Lippe	Parent RIN	Child #	Birth Year	Death Year	Spouse name	Spouse RIN	Mar Seq	Spouse parent RIN
Alexandre Violet	2	286	2l	6	1-12	1789	1856	Josette Pelletier	1894	1	754
"								Marie Anne Mazerolle	2228	2	1908
Pierre Hilarion Violet	2	287	2m	6	1-13	1792	1871	Magdeleine Consigny-SansFacon	1910	1	1911
Elizabeth Violet	2	288	2n	6	1-14	1794	1811	-			
Joseph Isaac Violet	2	289	2o	6	1-15	1796	1850	Victoire Thibodeau	1913	1	1933
Joseph Violette	2	291	3a	6	2-1	1803	?	Julie LeClerc dit Francoeur	1936	1	1954
Marie Victoire Violette	2	292	3b	6	2-2	1804	1845	Benoni Pelletier	2174	1	754
Jean Regis Violette	2	293	3c	6	2-3	1806	1879	Modeste E. Michaud	1941	1	1956
male Violet	2	1935	3d	6	2-4	1807	1809	-			
Jean Felix Violette	2	295	3e	6	2-5	1810	?	-			
Luc Violette	2	297	4a	6	3-1	1814	1887	Arthemise Pelletier	1958	1	1969
Elisabeth Violette	2	298	4b	6	3-2	1816	?	-			
Francois Violette	2	299	4c	6	3-3	1818	1882	-			
GENERATION 3											
Marie Marguerite Cyr	3	7307	5a	276	1-1	1794	1866	Joseph Hebert	14599	1	25026
Jean-Baptiste Cyr	3	57227		276	1-2	1794	?	-			
Augustin Cyr	3	7309	5c	276	1-3	1796	1881	Marie Rose Michaud	57327	1	31865
Marie Luce Louise Cyr	3	7308	5b	276	1-4	1798	1870	Chrysostome Thomas Martin	31781	1	20685
Regis Cyr	3	7310	5d	276	1-5	1802	?	Euphrosine Martin	14602	1	16641
Salomon Cyr	3	7311	5e	276	1-6	1801	1874	Marie Olive Nadeau	14603	1	32081
Marie Claire Violet	3	1859	6a	277	1-1	1799	1838	Simon Thibodeau	2175	1	10669
"								Francois Sirois	2176	1	10671
Jacob Jacques Violet	3	1860	6b	277	1-2	1802	1838	Angelique Godin	62875	1	22822
Augustin Maxime Violette	3	1861	6c	277	1-3	1804	?	Victoire Consigny-SansFacon	2177	1	10673
Celestin Violette	3	1862	6d	277	1-4	1805	1846	Marguerite Martin	1981	1	1990
Francois Xavier Violette	3	1863	6e	277	1-5	1807	1873	Appoline (Pauline) Martin	1992	1	2007
Antoine Violette	3	1864	6f	277	1-6	1808	1825	-			
Marie Angele Violette	3	1865	6g	277	1-7	1810	1868	Honore Mercure	2178	1	10675
Marguerite Violette	3	1866	6h	277	1-8	1812	1876	James Smyth	2179	1	10677
Marie Violette	3	36985	6i	277	1-9	1813	1835	Jean Desire Pelletier	2180	1	754
Philippe Violette	3	1868	6j	277	1-10	1815	1886	Judith Martin	2008	1	2012
Catherine Violette	3	1869	6k	277	1-11	1815	?	-			
Salome Violette	3	1870	6l	277	1-12	1817	1877	Jean Baptiste Beaulieu	2181	1	10679
Scholastique Violette	3	1871	6m	277	1-13	1819	1876	Francois Regis dit Isaie Martin	2182	1	10681
Eulalie Violette	3	1872	6n	277	1-14	1821	1889	Luc Albert	2183	1	2244
Severe Violette	3	1873	6o	277	1-15	1823	1823	-			
Marie Reine Violette	3	31609		277	2-1	1831	?	-			
Marie Salome Cyr	3	7312	7a	278	1-1	1793	1818	Alexandre Bourgoin	14604	1	20471
Rose Cyr	3	35690	7b	278	1-2	1795	1873	Benoni Martin	43070	1	18887
Victoire Elizabeth Cyr	3	7318	7c	278	1-3	1798	1862	Firmin Vital Cyr	14606	1	22739

Name	Gen.	RIN	Lippe	Parent RIN	Child #	Birth Year	Death Year	Spouse name	Spouse RIN	Mar Seq	Spouse parent RIN
Marguerite Cyr	3	57581		278	1-4	1802	1809	-			
Marie Louise Cyr	3	7314	7d	278	1-5	1804	?	Marcel dit Laliberte Collin	14607	1	28766
Marie Luce Justine Cyr	3	7315	7e	278	1-6	1806	?	Francois Martin	14608	1	16641
Scholastique Cyr	3	7316	7f	278	1-7	1809	1863	Louis St Amand	14609	1	43095
Marguerite Cyr	3	7317	7g	278	1-8	1812	1837	Amable Thibodeau	14610	1	36092
Jean Jeremie Cyr	3	43014		278	1-9	1814	?	-			
Angelique Radegonde Violette	3	1513	9a	280	1-1	1804	1809	-			
Marie Luce Violette	3	1514	9b	280	1-2	1805	1809	-			
Rosimond Violette	3	1515	9c	280	1-3	1806	1888	Nancy Marie Anne Rose Cyr	2014	1	2029
"								Nathalie Anastasie Violette	7261	2	300
Louis Violette	3	1516	9d	280	1-4	1807	1880	Suzanne Thibodeau	2034	1	2037
"								Louise Violette	2039	2	289
Marie Violette	3	1517	9e	280	1-5	1809	1823	-			
Modeste Violette	3	1518	9f	280	1-6	1811	1845	Urbain Cyr	2184	1	30602
Jean Desire Violette	3	1519	9g	280	1-7	1812	1901	Elisabeth Cormier	2051	1	2065
Marie Luce Violette	3	1520	9h	280	1-8	1814	?	-			
Jean Benoni Violette	3	1521	9i	280	1-9	1817	1879	Suzanne Theriault	1523	1	1591
Marguerite Violette	3	1522	9j	280	1-10	1821	1827	-			
Francois Xavier Violette	3	300	15a	24	1-1	1808	1901	Sophie Parent	2118	1	669
Theodore Violette	3	26	15b	24	1-2	1810	1864	Marie Louise Parent	27	1	669
Augustin Violette	3	301	15c	24	1-3	1811	1894	Marie Rose Michaud	622	1	1956
"								Marie Nathalie Thibodeau	1112	2	2137
Venerande Violette	3	302	15d	24	1-4	1813	1879	Cyprien Dick-Grace	2191	1	10693
Laurent Violette	3	303	15e	24	1-5	1815	1878	Elizabeth Louise Cyr	1056	1	726
Francois Violette	3	304	15f	24	1-6	1817	?	-			
Louis Michel Adrien Mercure	3	716	10a	281	1-1	1804	1876	Marie Venerande Pelletier	717	1	754
Marie Luce Cyr	3	7320	11b	282	1-1	1805	1869	Augustin Daigle	14612	1	23888
Chrysostome Cyr	3	7321	11c	282	1-2	1806	1885	Anastasie Cyr	14613	1	3504
Celeste Cyr	3	7325	11g	282	1-3	1807	?	Hilaire Cyr	14618	1	22739
Barbe Cyr	3	7319	11a	282	1-4	1809	1870	Francois Daigle	14611	1	23888
Thomas Didyme Cyr	3	7324	11f	282	1-5	1811	1877	Eleonore Daigle	14617	1	26031
Elisabeth Cyr	3	24951		282	1-6	1812	1871	Regis Bonhomme Daigle	24950	1	23888
Romain Cyr	3	1108	11d	282	1-7	1814	1878	Marie Cyr	14615	1	22739
Theodore Cyr	3	7323	11e	282	1-8	1816	1890	Clarisse Landry	7323	1	31480
Hubert Cyr	3	57050		282	1-9	1818	1820	-			
Zephirin Cyr	3	7326	11h	282	1-10	1820	1859	Modeste Daigle	14619	1	26031
Mathilde Cyr	3	10799		282	1-11	1821	1869	Marcel Thibodeau	10798	1	10695
Francois Cyr	3	7328	11j	282	1-12	1824	1872	Salome Daigle	14621	1	26031
Marie Leocadie Cyr	3	57051		282	1-13	1826	1830	-			
Ositee Cyr	3	14647	11i	282	1-14	1830	1851	Michel Cyr	10078	1	10887
Flavie Cyr	3	7329	11k	282	1-15	1831	?	Hippolyte Cyr	14622	1	26050
Marie Felicite Violette	3	1603	13a	284	1-1	1809	1870	Cyprien Cormier	2185	1	2065
Sophie Violette	3	1604	13b	284	1-2	1811	1811	-			

Name	Gen.	RIN	Lippe	Parent RIN	Child #	Birth Year	Death Year	Spouse name	Spouse RIN	Mar Seq	Spouse parent RIN
Francois Regis Violette	3	1605	13c	284	1-3	1812	1812	-			
Marie Louise Violette	3	1608	14b	284	2-1	1815	1816	-			
Marie Emilie Violette	3	1609	14c	284	2-2	1815	1838				
Regis Violette	3	1610	14d	284	2-3	1816	?	Marguerite Cormier	2082	1	2065
"								Marie Louise (Lisette) Martin	2090	2	2096
"								Artemise Sirois	2098	3	2099
Elizabeth Violette	3	1611	14e	284	2-4	1818	?	Laurent Martin	2186	1	1990
Isaac Violette	3	1612	14f	284	2-5	1820	1887	Julie Michaud	2101	1	2112
Cyrille Violette	3	47743	14a	284	2-6	1821	1894	Flavie Lizotte	2067	1	2080
Benoni Violette	3	1614	14h	284	2-7	1823	1823	-			
Antoine (Anthony) Violette	3	1615	14i	284	2-8	1824	1903	Christine Thidodeau	1620	1	2114
Marguerite Violette	3	1616	14j	284	2-9	1827	1879	Regis Thibodeau	2187	1	2114
Marie Athalie (Nathalie) Violette	3	1617	14k	284	2-10	1830	?	Francois Xavier (le Gros) Violette	2188	1	
Laurent Violette	3	1619	14m	284	2-11	1837	?	-			
Sylvain Violette	3	1618	14l	284	2-12		?	Emilie Paradis	2116	1	2134
Jean Baptiste Violette	3	1892	16a	285	1-1	1811	?	Julienne Thibodeau	2138	1	10695
Jean Benjamin Violette	3	1893	16b	285	1-2	1812	1812	-			
Isaac Fournier	3	57399		283	1-1	1808	1810	-			
Sophie Fournier	3	7330	12a	283	1-2	1810	?	Jean-Baptiste Bourgoin	7685	1	20471
Basile Fournier	3	57400		283	1-3	1811	?	-			
Suzanne Violette	3	1895	17a	286	1-1	1815	1848	Anselme Grivois	2173	1	10697
Jean Desire Violette	3	1896	17b	286	1-2	1816	1891	Marie Grivois Guidry	2168	1	10697
Eloi Violette	3	1897	17c	286	1-3	1818	1890	Celeste Martin	2192	1	10699
Salome Violette	3	1898	17d	286	1-4	1820	1899	Simon Martin	2193	1	10699
Sophie Violette	3	1899	17e	286	1-5	1824	1901	Joseph Levasseur	2194	1	10701
Alexandre Alexis Violette	3	1903	18a	286	2-1	1825	?	Sophie Gauvin	2195	1	10703
Jean Baptiste Violette	3	1904	18b	286	2-2	1827	1916	Dorimine Hermine Berube	2196	1	10705
female Violette	3	31610		286	2-3	1828	1828	-			
Angelique Violette	3	1905	18c	286	2-4	1829	1868	Frederick Soucy	2197	1	10707
Charlotte Violette	3	1906	18d	286	2-5	1831	1926	Severe Violette	1976	1	1860
Benoni (William) Violette	3	1907	18e	286	2-6	1833	1905	-			
Marie Basilisse Violette	3	1914	19a	289	1-1	1818	1900	Sifroid Lepage	2199	1	10709
Marie Luce Violette	3	1915	19b	289	1-2	1820	?	Louis (Chamberlain) Chamberland	2200	1	10711
Louise Violette	3	2039	19c	289	1-3	1821	1870	Louis Violette	1516	1	280
Jean Rosimond Violette	3	1917	19d	289	1-4	1822	<1900	Marie-Anne Thibodeau	2202	1	2114
"								Arthemise Parent	2203	2	10713
Marie Anne Nancy Violette	3	1918	19e	289	1-5	1823	1900	Joseph Michaud	2201	1	10715
Henriette Violette	3	1919	19f	289	1-6	1825	1825	-			
Martine Violette	3	1920	19g	289	1-7	1826	?	-			
Suzanne Violette	3	1921	19h	289	1-8	1828	1898	Amable Roy dit DesJardins	1265	1	43516
Francois Julien Violette	3	1922	19i	289	1-9	1829	?	Emerise Vaillancourt Viencourt	6940	1	59252
Sophie Violette	3	1923	19j	289	1-10	1831	1832	-			

Name	Gen.	RIN	Lippe	Parent RIN	Child #	Birth Year	Death Year	Spouse name	Spouse RIN	Mar Seq	Spouse parent RIN
Bruno Violette	3	1924	19k	289	1-11	1832	1846	-			
Damase Thomas Violette	3	1925	19l	289	1-12	1833	1893	Jeanne (Jane) Lemieux-Betters	45148	1	?
"								Caroline Simon	2205	2	?
"								Adeline Guy	2206	3	45140
Joseph Violette	3	1926	19m	289	1-13	1835	1836	-			
Marie Anne Violette	3	1927	19n	289	1-14	1837	1900	Damian Leblanc	2207	1	10719
"								George Perron	37775	2	48467
Francois Frank Violette	3	1928	19o	289	1-15	1839	1920	Marie Angeline (Desanges) Letourneau	2208	1	69507
Clarissa Clara Violette	3	1929	19p	289	1-16	1840	?	Joesph Lizotte	2209	1	10723
Vitaline Violette	3	1930	19q	289	1-17	1841	1916	-			
Henriette Violette	3	1931	19r	289	1-18	1843	1843	-			
Demerise Violette	3	1932	19s	289	1-19	1844	1902	-			
Marie Violette	3	1937	20a	291	1-1	1843	1908	Francis Francois Michaud	2210	1	11295
Louis Violette	3	1938	20b	291	1-2	1847	1847	-			
Joseph Violette	3	1939	20c	291	1-3	1850	?	-			
Belonie Violette	3	1940	20d	291	1-4	1858	?	-			
Marie Natalie Pelletier	3	38709		292	1-1	1825	1826	-			
Cyrille Pelletier	3	7331	21a	292	1-2	1827	1901	Berthe Ozithee Nadeau	14624	1	29171
Ozithee Pelletier	3	7332	21b	292	1-3	1828	1898	Agapit Nadeau	14626	1	45251
Elie Pelletier	3	38707		292	1-4	1830	1831	-			
Jean Baptiste Pelletier	3	7333	21c	292	1-5	1832	?	Helene Deschenes	14627	1	47735
"								Edith Milliard Basque	14628	2	69551
Benoni Pelletier	3	38708		292	1-6	1833	1854	-			
Isaie Pelletier	3	7338	21h	292	1-7	1834	1900	Elizabeth Nadeau	14632	1	43714
Antoine Benoni Pelletier	3	38710		292	1-8	1836	1836	-			
Denis Pelletier	3	7335	21e	292	1-9	1841	1908	Philomene Gendreau	14630	1	18216
Vitaline Pelletier	3	43030		292	1-10	1842	1826	-			
Raymond Pelletier	3	7339	21i	292	1-11	1843	?	Genevieve Ouellette	14633	1	43665
Flavie Pelletier	3	7334	21d	292	2-1	1851	?	Olivier Harvey	14629	1	57417
Theodore Pelletier	3	7337	21g	292	2-2	1855	1929	Julie Gendreau	14631	1	
Simon Pelletier	3	7336		292	2-3	1857	?	-			
Elisabeth Pelletierr	3	57420		292	2-4	?	1915	Pierre Gendreau	57421	1	
Francois Violette	3	1942	22a	293	1-1	1831	1831	-			
Simon Violette	3	1943	22b	293	1-2	1832	1906	Zoe Thiboutout	2211	1	10727
Obeline Violette	3	1944	22c	293	1-3	1834	<1859	Georges Boutot-Thiboutot	2212	1	62876
Angelique Violette	3	1945	22d	293	1-4	1836	~1859	Joseph Franck	2213	1	10729
Raymond Violette	3	1946	22e	293	1-5	1838	1844	-			
Eleonore Violette	3	1947	22f	293	1-6	1840	1913	Pierre Peter Lafrance	2214	1	10731
Marguerite Catherine Violette	3	1948	22g	293	1-7	1842	1863	Joseph Franck	2213	1	10729
Sophie Violette	3	1950	22i	293	1-9	1844	1848	-			
Elizabeth Violette	3	1951	22j	293	1-10	1849	?	-			
Flavie Violette	3	1952	22k	293	1-11	1851	?	-			
Thomas Violette	3	1953	22l	293	1-12	1851	?	-			

Name	Gen.	RIN	Lippe	Parent RIN	Child #	Birth Year	Death Year	Spouse name	Spouse RIN	Mar Seq	Spouse parent RIN
Thaddee Violette	3	1960	23b	297	1-1	1849	1919	Elizabeth (Lizzie) Hafford	2218	1	10739
Luc Violette	3	1961	23c	297	1-2	1851	1852	-			
Simon Luc Violette	3	1959	23a	297	1-3	1853	1925	Edith Langlais	2215	1	10733
"								Marie LaFerriere	2216	2	10735
"								Edith Sophie Francoeur LeClerc	2217	3	10737
Isaie Violette	3	1962	23d	297	1-4	1854	1856	-			
Frederic Violette	3	1963	23e	297	1-5	1857	?	Olive Langlois	2219	1	10741
Henri Albani Violette	3	1964	23f	297	1-6	1859	1916	-			
Josephine Violette	3	1965	23g	297	1-7	1862	?	Baptiste Theriault	2220	1	10743
Francis (Frank) Violette	3	1966	23h	297	1-8	1864	?	Alice Michaud	2221	1	10745
William Violette	3	1967	23i	297	1-9	1866	1904	-			
Andrew Violette	3	1968	23j	297	1-10	1873	1908	-			

Appendix 14-D

Owners of Lots on Maine Side of River in 1845

The tables in this appendix record information about the owners who were given deeds by Maine and Massachusetts in 1845 and New Brunswick in 1848. We show the RIN number for those who are contained in Rod Violette's genealogical database and the reference numbers from Rita Violette Lippé's 1984 book. Table 14-D-1 shows the owners of lots in the original Van Buren Plantation (on the Maine side of the river), and Table 14-D-2 shows the owners of lots on the New Brunswick side in the same area.

Table 14-D-1: Owners of lots on Maine side of river in 1845

Lot #	Owner	RIN	Rita Ref	Spouse	RIN	Rita Ref	Gen
231	Francois Deschenes			Marie-Anne Cormier			
232	Anselme Guedry-Grivois	2173		Suzanne Violette	1895	17a	3
233	Romain Guedry-Grivois			Marie Comeau			
234	Jean Baptiste Violette	1892	16a	Julienne Thibodeau	2138		3
235	Vital Thibodeau						
236	Damien Cormier			Victoire Theriault			
237	Henry Cormier						
238	Remi Plourde			Marguerite Thibodeau			
239W	Francois Sirois			Florence Lizotte			
239E	Simon Thibodeau	2175		Claire Violette	1859	6a	
240	Elizabeth Anne Beckwith						
241	Hilarion Violette	287	2m	Magdeleine Consigny-SansFacon	1910		2
242	Germain Daigle			Celeste Mercure			
243	Joseph Cyr	31984					
244	Jean-Baptiste Martin						
245	Joseph Cyr						
246	Basile Martin			Archange Thibodeau			
247	Joseph Cyr						
248	Germain Daigle			Celeste Mercure			
249	Joseph Cyr			Euphemie LaRochelle ?			
250	Joseph Parent			Marie Lucy Parent			
251	Etienne Parent	24860		Charlotte Ouellette			
252	Benoni Parent			Adelaide-Edith Sirois (Benoni a Gabriel)			
253	John Desire Violette	1519	9g	Elisabeth Cormier	2051		3
254	Eloi Violette	1897	17c	Celeste Martin	2192		3
255	Marcel Laplante			Marie Laplante a Etienne			
256	Parschall Parent			Modeste Sansfacon			
257	Michael Dionne						
258	Amable St Pierre			Henriette Dupont			
259	Narcissse Corbin	30540		Marie Anne Parent a Etienne			
260	Zepherin Corbin	26853		Leocade Theriault			
261	Jean Baptiste Thibodeau			Marie Anne Tardif			
262	Joseph Cyr						
263	Alexandre Violette	286	2l	Marie Anne Mazerolle	2228		2
264	Isaac Violette	1612	14f	Julie Michaud	2101		3
265	Dominique Violette	284	2i	Rosalie Michaud	1606		2
266	Cyrile Violette	47743	14a	Flavie Lizotte	1902, 2067		3

Lot #	Owner	RIN	Rita Ref	Spouse	RIN	Rita Ref	Gen
267	Jean Regis Violette	293	3c	Modeste E. Michaud ?	1941		2
268	Cyprien Cormier	2185		Marie Felicite Violette	1603	13a	3
269	Benoni Bourgoyn	11012		Salome Cyr			
270	Joseph Isaac Violet	289	2o	Victoire Thibodeau	1913		2
271	Elizabeth Anne Beckwith						
272	Jean Regis Violette	293	3c	Modeste E. Michaud	1941		2
273	Henry Cyr			Anastasie Bourgin ?			
274	Vital Cyr						
275	Mary Luce Cyr			Eloi Thibodeau			
276	Marie Rose Cyr			Jean Frederic Cote			
277	Francois Sirois	2176		Florence Lizotte	36847		
278	Romain Cyr			Louise Michaud			
279	Modeste Cyr Bouchard			Luc Bouchard			
280	Elias (Elie) Cyr			Suzanne Cyr			
281	Augustin Violette	301	15c	Victoire Consigny-Sansfacon ?			2
282	Francois Xavier Violette	1863	6e	Appoline (Pauline) Martin	1992		3
283	Jacques Violette heirs	1860	6b	Angelique Godin	62875		3
284	James Smyth	2179		Marguerite Violette	1866	6h	3
285	Augustin Violette	301	15c	(Marguerite Violette)	1112		2
286	Francois Xavier Violette	1863	6e	Appoline (Pauline) Martin	1992		3
287	Scholastique Violette Martin	1871	6m	Francois Regis dit Isaie Martin	2182		3
288	Francois Xavier Violette	1863	6e	Appoline (Pauline) Martin	1992		3
289	Celestin Violette	1862	6d	Marguerite Martin	1981		3
290	Laurent Violette	303	15e	Elizabeth Louise Cyr	1056		3
291	Rev. Anthony Gosselin						
292	Cyprien Dick-Grace	2191		Venerande Violette	302	15d	3
293	Michel Thibodeau			Julie Cormier			
294	Church Wardens of St Bruno						
295	Augustin Violette	301	15c	Marie Nathalie Thibodeau	1112		2
296	Francoise Cormier Bourgoin			Moise Bourgoin			
297	Francois Cormier			Charlotte Fournier or Emerance Langlais			
298	Dydime Morin			Nathalie Marquis			
299	Francois Cormier			Emerance Langlais			
300	Fabian Cormier			Emelie Langlais			
301	Jean Benoni (Belonie) Violette	1521	9i	Suzanne Theriault	1523		3
302	Michael Farrell			Julie Dubay			
303	Thomas Sirois			Marie-Luce Martin			
304	Hilaire Gagnon			Eleonore Levasseur			
305	John Keegan			Mary Mullen			
306	James Keegan			Marie Luce Parent			
307	Marcel Collin			Louise Cyr			
308	Louis Violette	1516	9d	Louise Violette	2039	19c	3
309	Leonard R. Coombes			Ann			
310	Belonie Nadeau			Marie Moreau			

Owners of Lots on New Brunswick Side of River in 1848

Table 14-D-2: Owners of lots on New Brunswick side of river in 1848

Lot #	Owner	RIN	Rita Ref	Spouse	RIN	Rita Ref	Gen
47	Francis Martin	14608		Marie Luce Cyr	7315		
48	William Ouellet						
49	Francis Devous	48641		Euphemie Dumont	24956		
50	Vital Thiboudeau	32662		Eleonore Morin	32663		
51	Francis Martin	14608		Marie Luce Cyr	7315		
52	Charles Beaulieu	23089		Francoise Mercure	23088		
53	Francois Sirois	2176		Florence Lizotte	36847		
54	Francois Sirois	2176		Florence Lizotte	36847		
55	Michael Sirois	19455		Henriette Theriault	32461		
56	Michael Sirois	19455		Henriette Theriault	32461		
57	Edward LeBlanc	35450		Rose Cyr	35451		
58	Henri Cyr	29308					
59	Ben. Martin						
60	Ben. Martin & others						
61	Andre Martin & others	21283		Judith Bourgoin	21284		
62	Andre Martin & others	21283		Judith Bourgoin	21284		
63	Y. Bourgoine						
64	Hilaire Bourgoine			Susan Thibodeau			
65	Barthelemy Bourgoine	25866		Ursule Thibodeau	25867		
66	Peter Bourgoine	25872		Eleonore Theriault	61233		
67	Crysostome (Thomas) Martin	70094		Locade Lebel	42199		
68	Andre Martin	35752		Mathilde Cyr	35753		
69	Alexis Martin	35760		Charlotte Michaud	35761		
70	Jean Baptiste Martin Jr	72269					
71	Laurent Martin	2186		Elizabeth Violette	1611	14e	3
72	Marcel Beaulieu	72334		Marguerite Chasse	72335		
73	Basile Martin	10699		Archange Thibodeau	10700		
74	Raphael Martin						
75	Simon Martin	2193		Salome Violette	1898	17d	3
76	Charles Martin	60343		Marguerite Chasse	47040		
77	Paul Cyr						
78	Jean Baptiste Sirois	28560		Angele Paradis	28561		
79	John Sirois	57358		Clementine Nadeau	57359		
80	Joseph Cyr						
81	Jean Marie Parant	73912		Angele Cyr	3517		
82	Christopher Cyr	700		Euphrosine Levasseur	701		
83	Dennis Cyr	2253		Eleonore Violette	2016	35b	3
84	Theophile Cyr	698		Judith Lizotte	699		
85	Francis Xavier Perrault	41723		Angelique Sirois	41724		
86	Vilas Cyr	30608		Marie Louise Lizotte	30609		
87	Frederic Mazerolle	19511		Modeste Lizotte	19510		

Lot #	Owner	RIN	Rita Ref	Spouse	RIN	Rita Ref	Gen
88	Andre Roue	10889		Louise Cyr	10890		
89	Joseph Bourgoin	25830		Suzanne Thibodeau	70167		
90	Elie Cyr	30612		Suzanne Cyr	30613		
91	Joseph Cyr	30570		Angele Cote	30571		
92	Chrysostome Cyr	7321	11c	Anastasie Cyr	14613		
93	Juliennne Thibodeau	25329		Lambert Tardif	25328		
94	Michael Hartt						
95	Elie Cyr	30612		Suzanne Cyr	30613		
96	Honore Cyr	2231		Anastasie Bourgoin	2232		
97	John Leclair						
98	Rosimond Violette	1515	9c	Nancy Marie Anne Rose Cyr	2014		
99	Andre Michaud	10865		Julienne Cyr	3514		
100	Hilarion Cyr	726		Charlotte Tardif	727		
101	Francois Violette	280	2e	Marguerite Fournier	1512		
102	Theodore Violette	26	15b	Marie Louise Parent	27		
103	Francois Xavier Violette	300	15a	Sophie Parent	2118		
104	Firmin Nadeau	26951		Marie Rose Cyr	3508		
105	Edwin Akerly	73186		Mary Coombs	73187		
106	Pascal Cyr	3520		Victoire Beaulieu	30171		
107	Hilaire Cyr			Celeste Cyr			
108	Flavien LaPointe	42865					
109	Henri Tardif	17721		Theotiste Michaud	58675		
110	Amable Tardif	41949		Henriette Ruest	41950		
111	William McCrea						
112	George L. Hammond						
113	William McCrea						
114	Fred A. Hammond						
115	Andrew B. Hammond			Gloriana Coombs			
116	Leonard R. Coombes	67793		Ann Long	67794		
117	Joseph Souci Jr	36795		Marguerite Genevieve Cyr	36049		
118	Leonard R. Coombes	67793		Ann Long	67794		
119	Leonard R. Coombes	67793		Ann Long	67794		
120	John Raymond	32284		Angelique Vaillancourt	32285		
121	John Raymond Jr						
122	Firmin Cormier	26865		Julie Cyr	26866		
123	Thomas LaBelle	71231					
124	Jean Baptiste Gauvin	10703		Marguerite Michaud	10704		
125	Urbain Cyr	2184		Modeste Violette	1518	9f	3
126	Thomas LaBelle	71231					

CHAPTER 15 – THE NATIONALITY OF OUR ANCESTORS

A question among Violettes and others descended from those first settlers in the Upper St John River valley is "from what nationality are we descended"? We know our ancestors spoke French and lived in areas that are part of Canada today, so our first response might be "French Canadian".

We also know that many of the people who settled in the Upper St John River Valley were called Acadians, but is that a nationality and does it apply to our family?

And then we learned that our family descended from François and Marie-Luce Violet, who lived and married within the British Empire. Does that mean we are descended from the British?

We have to go back and review some history to find our answers, for that whole region was in a state of flux for a century or more as it developed.

The original settlements

Prior to 1497 the whole area from Massachusetts Bay to the mouth of the St Lawrence River was inhabited by native peoples, who had gradually moved into the area from other parts of the continent. 1497 marked the landfall by John Cabot, who then claimed the area for England. Within a short time the area had been visited by fishing and whaling expeditions by the French, the Portuguese, the English, and the Basques, but no group established any communities in this new land at that time. Those seasonal visits continued for another century or so, but by the end of the sixteenth century permanent settlements were being formed by Europeans. The French, for example, opened a trading post at Tadoussac in 1599, and Pierre Dugua tried one on St. Croix Island in 1604. The latter was moved to Port Royal the next year. Samuel de Champlain founded Quebec in 1608. The English tried a settlement at Popham ME around 1607 but this failed. The English then had a settlement at Plymouth MA in 1620, followed by the Massachusetts Bay Colony in 1629. From these various starts, settlements soon sprung up along the Gulf of Maine and up the St Lawrence River, for these were locations readily accessible from the sea. Map 15-1 shows the locations of some of the key pre-1700 settlements. The locations marked with a red box were founded by British interests, those in black by the French.

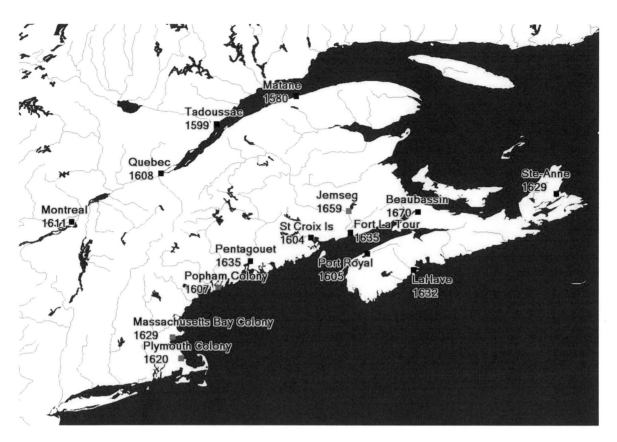

Map 15-1: Settlements prior to 1700

Acadia

The term "Acadia" refers to the region settled by the French that included much of present-day Nova Scotia, Prince Edward Island, New Brunswick, and Maine. The original settlement was at Port Royal (see Map 15-1) but they soon spread to other areas as well. The people who settled Acadia came from many parts of France, so they were not a homogenous group. We described the Acadians, where they came from, and how they lived in Chapter 11.

The first Acadians came in the early 1600s and though they were from France they remained in their lands whether under French or British rule until the mid-1750s, when the British expelled them and dispersed them to many places on the east coast of the continent.

Many Acadians left on their own to avoid an increasingly demanding British rule, and these Acadians dispersed into other nearby parts of the area and away from Acadia. Map 15-2 shows some of the areas where they made their new homes - those places are marked in green. Louisbourg is called out in yellow because that was where our Violet/Violettte ancestors came to this continent. Charles Violet lived there from 1749 through 1758, as we described in Chapters 5 and 9 with additional discussion in Chapters 6, 7, and 8. And it was from there that François moved to the lower St John River area and Hammond River area sometime after his father returned to France; see Chapters 11 and 12.

Map 15-2: Places the Acadians went (green) to avoid British rule

Changing Claims to the Land

Though explorers and fishing crews from several nationalities often visited the area, it was Britain and France who claimed lands for their own. Map 15-3 shows how those two nations roughly divided up the land between them. Remember that there were no formal borders at this time and their claims often overlapped. Again, the red areas show British claims and the white the French claims. The year 1713 marked the end of (the then-current) war between Britain and France; France lost and ceded the portion of Acadia that included the Nova Scotia peninsula to Britain in the Treaty of Utrecht. France kept Île Royale (Cape Breton Island), Île Saint-Jean (Prince Edward Island), and the Îles de la Madeleine (Madeleine Islands), so the French interests did not totally disappear from the North Atlantic community. France also maintained a strong hold of the St Lawrence valley as well. ***The year 1716 marks the birth of our ancestor Charles Violet in Villejésus France.***

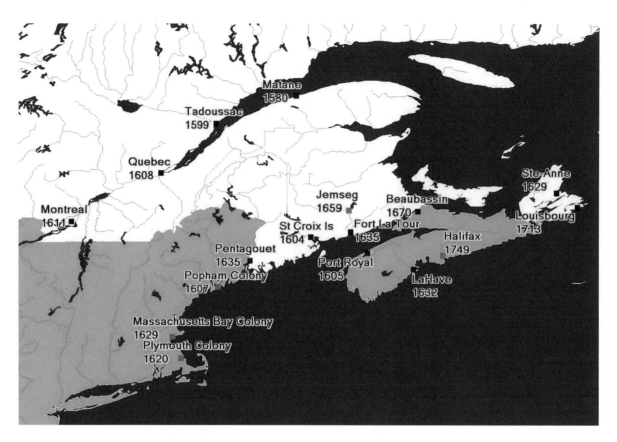

Map 15-3: Rough Division of National Interests after 1713 (British, red; French, white)

War between the two resumed in 1744, however, and lasted until 1763 with a truce between 1748 and 1754. ***1744 also marks the birth of our ancestor François Violet in Saintes, France.*** It was during that truce period 1748-1754 that France wanted to strengthen its holdings in the region and sent thousands of French people to Louisbourg to reconstruct damaged fortifications and rebuild the town. That was how Charles came to Louisbourg, as we described in Chapter 5.

The 1763 Treaty of Paris gave all the holdings in the region to Britain, France having lost the war. In fact, Britain gained possession of all lands east of the Appalachian Mountains as shown in Map 15-4, except France kept Île Royale (Cape Breton Island), Île Saint-Jean (Prince Edward Island), and the Îles de la Madeleine (Madeleine Islands) east of the Nova Scotia peninsula. The defeat by the British of the French in the region in 1758 resulted in those French people returning to France, including Charles but not François. Chapter 9 gave more details.

Map 15-4: Britain Holds Most Lands by the Treaty of 1763

French so far

Up to 1758 we can clearly say that Charles and his son, François, were clearly French nationals. Both were born in France and while Charles returned to France, François stayed on living in what were French lands.

But then François moved

With the British taking over Acadia again, there was a lot of pressure from residents in all parts of British North America to get rid of previous settlers to make room for an increasing number of British subjects. This resulted in the Grand Dérangement in 1755, which removed the Acadians from Acadia but not Île Royale (see Chapter 11). François may have left Louisbourg around the time of the 1758 departure of his father, but we do not know. What we do know is that François ended up in what was called the French Village along the Hammond River in lower New Brunswick; see Chapters 11 and 12. He acquired rights to some land that had been set out under French grants, married Marie-Luce Thibodeau in 1769, and started raising a family.

Problems with British Settlers, Again

But as the British took control over the whole of British North America they gradually did away with the previous French land grants and re-granted the lands to British subjects. Fortunately, two influential Loyalists, Edward Winslow and Ward Chipman, took up the cause of the Acadians and obtained from the government the restoration of some of their property (see Chapter 12). François petitioned Thomas Carleton, Captain General and Lieutenant Governor of the Province of New Brunswick on August 28, 1786 asking that Lots 13 and 14 in the "French Village" on the

Hammond River be granted to him again. In that petition he establishes that he was one of the first settlers in that area and was given rights to the land as laid out by a member of the British Council for Nova Scotia and that later land grants to others had encroached on his parcels. In that petition François acknowledges that he "took the oath of allegiance to his majesty", referring to the King of England. So in taking that oath François at least accepted the fact that he was no longer under French jurisdiction but British. Did that change his nationality? We do not think so, but it probably changed his citizenship to British. And all his children born during his time in the Hammond River area clearly had British North American citizenship.

There may be a parallel between François' family situation and the issues of immigration in the late 20th century and early 21st century in the United States. Marie-Luce Thibodeau's family had fled Acadia, where they had lived for three generations or more, to avoid British persecution. But they moved to a different part of British North America, as did François. There were no immigration rules at that time but they had trouble retaining title to land due to not being British subjects and they certainly did not participate in any other benefits of being British. In effect, they were probably quasi-legal, if not illegal, immigrants. Their children, however, were born in this new country and under British rule and, had the family stayed there, they might have been considered British. And this group of French and Acadians acted differently from the incoming British subjects; they spoke a different language, practiced a different religion, and had different family and social customs. Certainly by the second generation the family would have begun speaking English just as they eventually did in the lands along the Upper St John River where they moved to, and would have become real British subjects.

British North America: Gained then Lost

The settlers in the southern portion of British North America were not only unhappy with the French, but had also become unhappy with the way they were treated by the English government, and especially King George. Settlements all along the Atlantic coast from the Bay of Fundy to Georgia were under British control and from American history we know that this created some very unacceptable conditions for many living in the colonies. This resulted in a Declaration of Independence by thirteen of those colonies – all except those north and east of what is now Maine. The Declaration resulted in military action to rid those thirteen colonies of British influence and occupation, with the final outcome in 1783 of Britain recognizing the colonies' independence. Map 15-5 shows the results of the 1783 Treaty of Paris.

Map 15-5: North America after US Independence; Provinces of Nova Scotia and New Brunswick are shown in different colors though part of British North America. French holdings are shown in dark blue.

The British Empire Loyalists Move In; the Acadians move out

After the establishment of the United States of America there were many citizens of the earlier colonies that did not agree with the revolution and did not want to be US citizens. They remained loyal to Britain, and did not want to remain in the new United States. So, they moved to British holdings in Acadia and British North America. For example, more than 17,000 landed at St John NB and more than 18,000 went to Nova Scotia.

Some of these Loyalists moved to the Hammond River area and the area became much more British-Protestant oriented. The French-speaking people were Roman Catholic and started feeling in the minority. Furthermore, there were no priests living in the region and priests only occasionally visited the area where these families lived. As a result, they did not have regular access to the sacraments and teachings of their religion and felt isolated.

To remedy this, even though they had lived in this area for 20 years or more, François and his brothers-in-law petitioned Thomas Carleton in August 1789 and again on December 24, 1789 to be granted lots along the upper St John River above the Great Falls in the Madawaska region. The term Madawaska at that time referred to the whole undefined area above the Great Falls and included lands on both sides of the St John River.

In the petition François says that he and the other petitioners are descended from the early settlers of Acadia at the time it was under the dominion of France. While it is true that François' parents did move to Acadia, they also seem to have retained their French citizenship and returned to that country within a few years, so technically he was probably not an Acadian. However it certainly was true that his wife, Marie-Luce, was Acadian. On her father's side her great-grandfather moved from France to Acadia prior to 1661 and died in Port Royal, Acadia, in 1704 so her father and his parents were born in Acadia. On her mother's side her great-grandparents Rene Leblanc and Anne Bourgeois were born in Acadia around 1653 and 1661 respectively.

All this was described in more detail in Chapters 12 and 13.

Finally, In Their Own Land

So, the families moved upstream on the St John River and established their own "neighborhood". There were no pressures from people with other beliefs or value systems and they had established land rights and ownership. There were no others living in the area so there was land enough for the parents and for their existing children and those to follow. It must have seemed endless and vast to them. François was 45 and Marie-Luce 39 and they had lived on their previous lands on the Kennebecasis about 20 years, so were probably anxious to get settled again.

In 1789 the region in that northern area was either part of New Brunswick in British North America (remember that Canada as a nation had not yet come to exist – it would not be formed until 1867), or part of Massachusetts in the US (the area now known as Maine was part of the Massachusetts Colony until 1819), or maybe part of Québec in France's Lower Canada. (Lower Canada at that time referred to the area in the lower St Lawrence River – Quebec – while Upper Canada referred to the upper St Lawrence River or present-day southern Ontario) (See Map 15-6) For a period of perhaps 20 years the area was able to grow peaceably and the families were able to get established. Marie-Luce and François' children got married and had children of their own and lived in the same area. They continued with their French-speaking culture and started to build churches in order to entice priests to come serve them. Ecclesiastically they were in the Diocese of Québec, so the priests had a French Canadian background. The white areas in Map 15-6 were French, the red areas British North America, the blue areas US, and the purple area were in dispute among those parties.

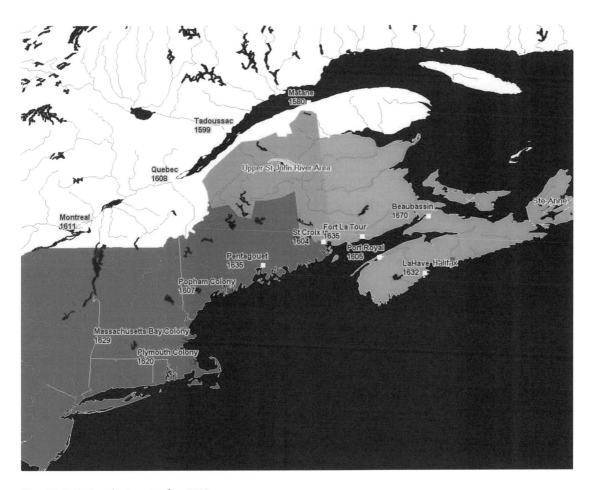

Map 15-6: National Interests after 1783

New Wars Arise – Over Timber

Within a generation or so turmoil began again for those families. The Upper St John River area – generally called Madawaska Territory – had some great farming lands in the intervales along the river bottom but what attracted even more interest was the timber resource. The tremendous growth of British North America and the United States of America, plus the requirements of a growing Europe, created a demand for wood products of all kinds. Shipping still used wind power and ships needed masts, and there were many tall pine trees suitable for making masts. The White Pine was noted for its high strength-to-weight ratio. But, there was an increasing demand for lumber for construction – large items such as beams and posts, as well as sawn lumber such as boards – and there were companies in both the US and New Brunswick ready and willing to cut the Madawaska timber. Having the St John River nearby to carry logs downstream to the market in St John NB gave the area an advantageous position in the market. From St John the timber and lumber was shipped all around the world.

Our ancestors moved to the Upper St John area and mainly established an agricultural economy. Many were only subsistence farmers – raising only what they could consume in their own families – but the productivity of the intervale lands allowed producing crops in excess of what they could consume and they were able to sell their excess crops, creating a market economy. With the timber demands some settlers were able to cut timber for sale, but the high demand needed large companies to mount the campaigns necessary to cut and market timber on a large scale.

The battle over timber rights brought interests from the US and New Brunswick into contention, and at one time there was even the threat of armed conflict. But the issue was finally settled when Maine became a state and the boundary between the US and British North America was decided upon – the Webster-Ashburton Treaty in 1842 established the St John River as the international boundary in the Madawaska Territory.

Our ancestors had lots on both sides of the St John River and freely moved back and forth from one shore to the other. It was all "their" country. They considered all the area as one, but now they were cut in two by an international boundary. Those on the south bank were in the US, while those on the north bank were in New Brunswick.

Conclusion on nationality

So, have we answered the question raised in this chapter's title? What was the nationality of our ancestors?

Perhaps the cleanest way to look at it is by generation:

- François was born in France and his parents remained French, so he was French. Though he lived in Acadia, he was not Acadian. He did pledge allegiance to Britain in order to be able to live in British North America and own land, but there is no evidence that he "became" British.

- Marie-Luce was born in Acadia, of Acadian parents and grandparents, so she was Acadian. Similarly, there is no evidence that she "became" British – we do not even have evidence that she pledged allegiance to Britain, but of course as a woman she would not have been asked to.

- Their children prior to 1789 were born in New Brunswick, in the St John area, and their mother was Acadian so they could be considered Acadian. François was born in France but subsequently came from Acadia, so his children would not be considered French. However, their citizenship was probably British.

- Children born after the move to the Upper St John might be considered Acadians as well, since their mother was Acadian. But the area in which they were born was under British North America – the land grants to their parents were from the British. We could say they were British, but the families kept their French-based culture. One could go by church records, since these were the only records being kept at the time, except that the only church was in St. Basile, on the New Brunswick side of the river. However, as the only church, those records covered those born on both sides of the river.

- Marie-Luce and François' grandchildren were born to families on both sides of the river and only the last three or four were born after the border was established in 1842. So their citizenship was probably determined by that of their parents.

- Their great-grandchildren and those beyond would have either US or New Brunswick/British nationality since the border was officially established in 1842.

- Canada did not come into existence as a nation until much later (Confederation in 1867, autonomous in 1982), so none of those first generations could have been Canadian. In fact, it was probably not until about the fifth generation that any could be called Canadians. It was in the years of François Violet's grandchildren and great-grandchildren that four provinces of British North America entered into Confederation. Rita V. Lippé's Violette Family Genealogy names 108 grandchildren of François I (1744-1824) and Rod Violette's genealogical research has expanded that number to 151. He never lived to see them all. The eldest was born in 1793 when François was forty-nine years old. The youngest was born in 1873, forty-nine years after his death.

References:

Craig, Béatrice and Maxime Dagenais, Lisa Ornstein and Guy Dubay; "The Land In Between", The Upper St John Valley, Prehistory to World War I, Tilbury House, Publishers, Gardiner, ME, 2009

_; "Fortress of Lousibourg", Wikipedia, en.wikipedia.org/wiki/Fortress_of_Louisbourg

_; "Treaty of Paris (1783)", Wikipedia, en.wikipedia.org/wiki/Treaty_of_Paris_(1783)

_; "History of Nova Scotia, Part 1, Ch. 10. Acadia (1654-1684).", www.blupete.com/Hist/NovaScotiaBk1/Part1/Ch10.htm

_; "Parks Canada - History Beneath the Ruins of Beaubassin", www.pc.gc.ca/canada/pn-tfn/itm2-/2009/2009-05-18_e.asp

Violette-Lippé, Rita; "The Descendants of François Violet", Naiman Press, Lawrence, MA, 1984.

Dubay, Guy; various notes from personal research

Violette, Rod; "Francois Violet Life and Times", unpublished monograph

Violette, Rod; "Chronology of Acadia", unpublished monograph

Made in the USA
Lexington, KY
10 August 2014